# ENGLISH
## IN UNITS
## CORE BOOK

JOHN G. FAHY

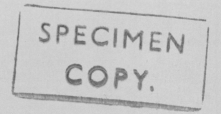

Gill & Macmillan

Published in Ireland by

Gill and Macmillan Ltd,

Goldenbridge,

Dublin 8.

and associated companies throughout the world.

© Selection and editorial matter, John G. Fahy, 1990

© Artwork, Gill and Macmillan, 1990

**Design and Cover:** Design Works, Dublin

**Illustration:** Aidan Dowling

**Photo Research:** Anne-Marie Ehrlich

**Print origination** in Ireland by

The Type Bureau Ltd, Dublin

Printed by Graficas Estella

0 7171 1668 9

# CONTENTS

# UNIT 1
## SCHOOL

## INTRODUCTION

# School

## FIRST TERM

This is an Introductory Unit based mainly on writings about school. It aims to develop your communication skills of LISTENING, SPEAKING, READING and WRITING. Particular attention is paid to LISTENING and SPEAKING.

In this Unit and throughout the book, great emphasis is placed on learning and using new words. So you will need A DICTIONARY. You will also need a WORD COPY, where you can write new words or phrases, together with their meanings. You might like to keep a section at the back for words you usually misspell—the correct version, of course!

# INTRODUCTION EXERCISE

*(for pairs, A and B)*

*You may know some of the pupils in your new class but there are many you will not have met before. Spend five minutes (no more) talking quietly with the boy or girl next to you. Pupil A will then stand up and introduce pupil B to the entire class, beginning 'This is ...' and giving THREE pieces of information which B is willing that the class should know about him/her. B then introduces A in a similar way and so on, right round the class. Each pupil should speak loudly, clearly and slowly so that all can hear.*

*(for groups of four or five)*
*After you have heard this poem 'The New Boy' read aloud, you should read it*
*silently for yourself a number of times and think about it for a few minutes. Now*
*discuss it in your groups.*

## HINTS FOR GROUP DISCUSSION

**A.** Choose a SECRETARY. His or her job is to take very brief notes on the main points expressed and REPORT BACK to the whole class.

**B.** Do you need a CHAIRPERSON for the group?

A chairperson usually sees that everyone gets a chance to speak, that you all keep to the subject and get finished on time. Perhaps you can manage with just a secretary?

(A different person can be secretary or chairperson each time there is a discussion, so everyone should get many turns at this during the year.)

**C.** Do you need to agree on some Basic Rules?

### THE NEW BOY

The door swung inward. I stood and breathed
The new-school atmosphere:
The smell of polish and disinfectant,
And the flavour of my own fear.

I followed into the cloakroom; the walls
Rang to the shattering noise
Of boys who barged and boys who banged:
Boys and still more boys!

A boot flew by me. Its angry owner
Pursued with force and yell;
Somewhere a man snapped orders; somewhere
There clanged a warning bell.

And there I hung with my new schoolmates;
They pushing and shoving me; I
Unknown, unwanted, pinned to the wall;
On the verge of ready-to-cry.

Then, from the doorway, a boy called out:
'Hey, you over there!  You're new!
Don't just stand there propping the wall up!
I'll look after you!'

I turned; I timidly raised my eyes;
He stood and grinned meanwhile;
And my fear died, and my lips answered
Smile for his smile.

He showed me the basins, the rows of pegs:
He hung my cap at the end;
He led me away to my new classroom...
And now that boy's my friend.

*John Walsh*

## SOME QUESTIONS FOR DISCUSSION

*1. What sounds and smells of the new school does the new boy notice at first?*
*2. What are his first feelings?  How do you know?*
*How does he feel at the end of the poem?*
*3. What descriptions in the poem appeal to you?*
*4. Do you think it is a good poem?  Why or why not?*
*5. What did you first notice about your new school or class?*

## REPORT BACK

*1. Remember to speak slowly and clearly so that you can be heard by all.*
*2. Somebody may be appointed to note the main ideas of each group on one or two
questions and put them all together into a clear paragraph or on the blackboard.*

## FOLLOW UP

*Read the poem again silently, think about it and write a paragraph or two about
the boy.*

Read this poem quietly a number of times.  Use your dictionary to find the meanings of any difficult words.  Write them into your Word Copy.

## FIRST DAY AT BOARDING SCHOOL

Like a trapped bird
she hid behind her hair.

Confident buxom girls
crowded the corridors

on their bedroom walls
pictures of pop-stars kissing.

What did they comprehend
of Africa's space and silence?

Like a caged animal
she sniffed the stuffy air,

heard the head's platitudes
resolved never to 'settle down',

pledged herself to wilderness
to bursting through closed doors

behind which they said
she must learn a new language.

*Prunella Power*

## SOME QUESTIONS FOR DISCUSSION

*1. Where does the new girl come from?*
*2. In what ways is she different from the other girls?*
*3. How does she feel about the school and the teachers?*
*4. What description or picture most appeals to you and why?*
*5. Are her difficulties similar to those of any student in a new school  Why or why not?  Discuss the difficulties which face a student in a new school.*

## REPORT BACK

## FOLLOW UP

*Read the poem again silently for yourself and think about it. Then write a little poem or a paragraph about your first day in the new class or school.*

■■■■■■■■■■■■■■■■■■■■■■■■■■■■■■■■■■■■■■■■■■■■■■■■■

# Keeping a Diary

Now is a good time to begin keeping a diary if you do not already do so. You don't need an expensive book, an ordinary copy will do. Just remember to fill in the day and date.

A diary is your own personal private property and best kept at home. You should try to write something every night or at least keep a record of anything unusual or exciting. You could put in descriptions of school events, character sketches (descriptions) of people you meet, jokes, poems you write or short poems you discover and like. You could enter recipes, colourful sayings, football results, even new words and spellings or personal things such as worries, hopes, ambitions, etc.

The style of writing in a diary can be quite informal. As it is written mainly as a record for the writer, some things are just jotted down briefly, without explanation, like a shopping list. Sometimes paragraphs are not developed. You have great freedom to write however you like, in your diary.

Do it well. Someone, a hundred years from now might like to read this!

Apart from your private diary you will be asked, from time to time, to write DIARY-STYLE entries for exercise. You may be asked to read these out in class, so decide what to put in accordingly.

Here is an extract from *The Secret Diary of Adrian Mole aged 13 $^3/_4$,* by Sue Townsend:

**Tuesday January 13th**

My father has gone back to work. Thank God! I don't know how my mother sticks him.

Mr Lucas came in this morning to see if my mother needed any help in the house. He is very kind. Mrs Lucas was next door cleaning the outside windows. The ladder didn't look very safe. I have written to Malcolm Muggeridge, c/o the BBC, asking him what to do about being an intellectual. I hope he writes back soon because I'm getting fed up being one on my own. I have written a poem, and it only took me two minutes. Even the famous poets take longer than that. It is called 'The Tap', but it isn't really about a tap, it's very deep, and about life and stuff like that.

*The Tap, by Adrian Mole*
*The tap drips and keeps me awake,*
*In the morning there will be a lake.*
*For the want of a washer the carpet will spoil,*
*Then for another my father will toil.*
*My father could snuff it while he is at work.*
*Dad, fit a washer don't be a burk!*

I showed it to my mother, but she laughed. She isn't very bright. She still hasn't washed my PE shorts, and it is school tomorrow. She is not like the mothers on television.

**Wednesday, January 14th**

Joined the library. Got *Care of the Skin, Origin of Species,* and a book by a woman my mother is always going on about. It is called *Pride and Prejudice*, by a woman called Jane Austen. I could tell the librarian was impressed. Perhaps she is an intellectual like me. She didn't look at my spot, so perhaps it is getting smaller. About time!

Mr Lucas was in the kitchen drinking coffee with my mother. The room was full of smoke. They were laughing, but when I went in, they stopped.

Mrs Lucas was next door cleaning the drains. She looked as if she was in a bad mood. I think Mr and Mrs Lucas have got an unhappy marriage. Poor Mr Lucas!

None of the teachers at school have noticed that I am an intellectual. They will be sorry when I am famous. There is a new girl in our class. She sits next to me in Geography. She is all right. Her name is Pandora, but she likes being called 'Box'. Don't ask me why. I might fall in love with her. It's time I fell in love, after all I am 13 $\frac{3}{4}$ years old.

**Thursday January 15th**

Pandora has got hair the colour of treacle, and it's long like girls' hair should be. She has quite a good figure. I saw her playing netball and her chest was wobbling. I felt a bit funny. I think this is it! The dog has had its stitches out. It bit the vet, but I expect he's used to it. (The vet I mean; I know the dog is.)

My father found out about the arm on the stereo. I told a lie. I said the dog jumped up and broke it. My father said he'd wait until the dog is completely cured of its operation then kick it. I hope this is a joke.

Mr Lucas was in the kitchen again when I got home from school. My mother is better now, so why he keeps coming round is a mystery to me. Mrs Lucas was planting trees in the dark. I read a bit of *Pride and Prejudice*, but it was very old-fashioned. I think Jane Austen should write something a bit more modern.

The dog has got the same colour eyes as Pandora. I only noticed because my mother cut the dog's hair. It looks worse than ever. Mr Lucas and my mother were laughing at the dog's new haircut which is not very nice, because dogs can't answer back, just like the Royal Family.

I am going to bed early to think about Pandora and do my back-stretching exercises. I haven't grown for two weeks. If this carries on I will be a midget.

I will go to the doctor's on Saturday if the spot is still there. I can't live like this with everybody staring.

### Friday January 16th

Mr Lucas came round and offered to take my mother shopping in the car. They dropped me off at school. I was glad to get out of the car what with all the laughing and cigarette smoke. We saw Mrs Lucas on the way. She was carrying big bags of shopping. My mother waved, but Mrs Lucas couldn't wave back.

It was Geography today so I sat next to Pandora for a whole hour. She looks better every day. I told her about her eyes being the same as the dog's. She asked what kind of dog it was. I told her it was a mongrel.

I lent Pandora my blue felt-tip pen to colour round the British Isles.

I think she appreciates these small attentions.

I started *Origin of Species* today, but it's not as good as the television series. *Care of the Skin* is dead good. I have left it open on the pages about vitamins. I hope my mother takes the hint. I have left it on the kitchen table near the ashtray, so she is bound to see it.

I have made an appointment about the spot. It has turned purple.

## E X E R C I S E S

*1. Write your impressions of your new school or class into your private diary.*
*2. Write a diary-style entry for January 16th, into your school copy, as you imagine Pandora might have written it.*
*\* You might like to read The Diary of Anne Frank, the story of a young Jewish girl in Holland, during World War II.*

# A Story About Communication

The title of this story is taken from an anecdote about a Commanding Officer, in the trenches, in the First World War. He sent a message back down the line to Headquarters but it got very distorted along the way. The original message said: 'Send reinforcements, we are going to advance!'

Read it and use your dictionary to find the meanings of any difficult words.

# Send Three and Fourpence We Are Going to a Dance

*Jan Mark*

Mike and Ruth Dixon got on well enough, but not so well that they wanted to walk home from school together. Ruth would not have minded, but Mike, who was two classes up, preferred to amble along with his friends so that he usually arrived a long while after Ruth did.

Ruth was leaning out of the kitchen window when he came in through a side gate, kicking a brick.

'I've got a message for you,' said Mike. 'From school. Miss Middleton wants you to go and see her tomorrow before assembly, and take a dead frog.'

'What's she want me to take a dead frog for?' said Ruth. 'She's not my teacher. I haven't got a dead frog.'

'How should I know?' Mike let himself in. 'Where's Mum?'

'Round Mrs Todd's. Did she really say a dead frog? I mean, really say it?'

'Derek told me to tell you. It's nothing to do with me.'

Ruth cried easily. She cried now. 'I bet she never. You're pulling my leg.'

'I'm not, and you'd better do it. She said it

was important—Derek said—and you know what a rotten old temper she's got,' said Mike, feelingly.

'But why me? It's not fair.' Ruth leaned her head on the window-sill and wept in earnest. 'Where'm I going to find a dead frog?'

'Well, you can peel them off the road sometimes, when they've been run over. They go all dry and flat, like pressed flowers,' said Mike. He did think it a trifle unreasonable to demand dead frogs from little girls, but Miss Middleton was unreasonable. Everyone knew that. 'You could start a pressed frog collection,' he said.

Ruth sniffed fruitily. 'What do you think Miss'll do if I don't get one?'

'She'll go barmy, that's what,' said Mike. 'She's barmy anyway,' he said. 'Nah, don't start howling again. Look, I'll go down the ponds after tea. I know there's frogs there because I saw the spawn, back at Easter.'

'But those frogs are alive. She wants a dead one.'

'I dunno. Perhaps we could get it put to sleep or something, like Mrs Todd's Tibby was. And don't tell Mum. She doesn't like me down the ponds and she won't let us have frogs indoors. Get an old box with a lid and leave it on the rockery, and I'll put old Froggo in it when I come home. And stop crying!'

After Mike had gone out Ruth found the box that her summer sandals had come in. She poked air holes in the top and furnished it with damp grass and a tin lid full of water. Then she left it on the rockery with a length of darning wool so that Froggo could be fastened down safely until morning. It was only possible to imagine Froggo alive; all tender and green and saying croak-croak. She could not think of him dead and flat and handed over to Miss

Middleton, who definitely must have gone barmy. Perhaps Mike or Derek had been wrong about the dead part. She hoped they had.

She was in the bathroom, getting ready for bed, when Mike came home. He looked round the door and stuck up his thumbs.

'Operation Frog successful. Over and out.'

'Wait. Is he ... alive?'

'Shhh. Mum's in the hall. Yes.'

'What's he like?'

'Sort of frog-shaped. Look, I've got him; OK? I'm going down now.'

'Is he green?'

'No. More like that pork pie that went mouldy on top. Good night!'

Mike had hidden Froggo's dungeon under the front hedge, so all Ruth had to do next morning was scoop it up as she went out of the gate. Mike had left earlier with his friends, so she paused for a moment to introduce herself. She tapped quietly on the lid.

'Hullo?'

There was no answering cry of croak-croak. Perhaps he was dead. Ruth felt a tear coming and raised the lid a fraction at one end. There was a scrabbling noise and at the other end of the box she saw something small and alive, crouching in the grass.

'Poor Froggo', she whispered through the air holes.

'I won't let her kill you, I promise,' and she continued on her way to school feeling brave and desperate, ready to protect Froggo's life at the cost of her own. The school hall was in the middle of the building and classrooms opened off it. Miss Middleton had Class 3 this year, next to the cloakroom. Ruth hung up her blazer, untied the wool from Froggo's box, and went to meet her doom. Miss Middleton was arranging little stones in an aquarium on top of the bookcase, and jerked her head when Ruth knocked, to show that she should come in.

'I got him, Miss,' said Ruth, holding out the shoe box in trembling hands.

'What, dear?' said Miss Middleton, up to her wrists in water-weed.

'Only he's not dead and I won't let you kill him!' Ruth cried, and swept off the lid with a dramatic flourish. Froggo, who must have been waiting for this, sprang out, towards Miss Middleton, landed with a clammy sound on that vulnerable place between the collar bones, and slithered down inside Miss Middleton's blouse.

Miss Middleton taught Nature Study. She was not afraid of little damp creatures, but she was not expecting Froggo. She gave a squawk of alarm and jumped backwards. The aquarium skidded in the opposite direction; took off; shattered against a desk. The contents broke over Ruth's new sandals in a tidal wave, and Lily the goldfish thrashed about in a shallow puddle on the floor. People came running with mops and dustpans. Lily Fish was taken out by the tail to recover in the cloakroom sink. Froggo was arrested while trying to leave Miss Middleton's blouse through the gap between two buttons, and put back in his box with a weight on top in case he made another dash for freedom.

Ruth, crying harder than she had ever done in her life, was sent to stand outside the Headmaster's room, accused of playing stupid practical jokes, and cruelty to frogs.

Sir looked rather as if he had been laughing, but it seemed unlikely, under the circumstances, and Ruth's eyes were so swollen and tear-filled that she couldn't see clearly. He gave her a few minutes to dry out and then said, 'This isn't like you, Ruth. Whatever possessed you to go throwing frogs at poor Miss Middleton? And poor frog, come to that.'

'She told me to bring her a frog,' said Ruth, stanching another tear at the injustice of it all. 'Only she wanted a dead one, and I couldn't find a dead one, and I couldn't kill Froggo. I won't kill him,' she said, remembering her vow on the way to school.

'Miss Middleton says she did not ask you to bring her a frog, or kill her a frog. She thinks you've been very foolish and unkind,' said Sir, 'and I think you are not telling the truth. Now...'

'Mike told me to,' said Ruth.

'Your brother? Oh, come now.'

'He did. He said Miss Middleton wanted me to go to her before assembly with a dead frog and I did, only it wasn't dead and I won't!'

'Ruth! Don't grizzle. No one is going to murder your frog, but we must get this nonsense sorted out.'

Sir opened his door and called to a passerby, 'Tell Michael Dixon that I want to see him at once, in my office.'

Mike arrived, looking wary. He had heard the crash and kept out of the way, but a summons from Sir was not to be ignored.

'Come in, Michael,' said Sir. 'Now, why did you tell your sister that Miss Middleton wanted her to bring a dead frog to school?'

'It wasn't me', said Mike. 'It was a message from Miss Middleton.'

'Miss Middleton told you?'

'No, Derek Bingham told me. She told him to tell me—I suppose,' said Mike, sulkily. He scowled at Ruth. All her fault.

'Then you'd better fetch Derek Bingham here right away. We're going to get to the bottom of this.'

Derek arrived. He too had heard the crash.

'Come in, Derek,' said Sir. 'I understand that you told Michael here some tarradiddle about his sister. You let him think it was a message from Miss Middleton, didn't you?'

'Yes, well...' Derek shuffled. 'Miss Middleton didn't tell me. She told, er, someone, and they told me.'

'Who was this someone?'

Derek turned all noble and stood up straight and pale. 'I can't remember, Sir.'

'Don't let's have any heroics about sneaking, Derek, or I shall get very cross.'

Derek's nobility ebbed rapidly. 'It was Tim Hancock, Sir. He said Miss Middleton wanted Ruth Dixon to bring her a dead dog before assembly.'

'A dead dog?'

'Yes Sir.'

'Didn't you think it a bit strange that Miss Middleton should ask Ruth for a dead dog, Derek?'

'I thought she must have one, Sir.'

'But why should Miss Middleton want it?'

'Well, she does do Nature Study,' said Derek.

'Go and fetch Tim,' said Sir.

Tim had been playing football on the field when the aquarium went down. He came in with an innocent smile which wilted when he saw what was waiting for him.

'Sir?'

'Would you mind repeating the message that you gave Derek yesterday afternoon?'

'I told him Miss Middleton wanted Sue Nixon to bring her a red sock before assembly,' said Tim. 'It was important.'

'Red sock? Sue Nixon?' said Sir. He was beginning to look slightly wild-eyed. 'Who's Sue Nixon? There's no one in this school called Sue Nixon.'

'I don't know any of the girls, Sir,' said Tim.

'Didn't you think a red sock was an odd thing to ask for?'

'I thought she was bats, Sir.'

'Sue Nixon?'

'No Sir. Miss Middleton, Sir,' said truthful Tim.

Sir raised his eyebrows. 'But why did you tell Derek?'

'I couldn't find anyone else, Sir. It was late.'

'But why Derek?'

'I had to tell someone or I'd have got into trouble,' said Tim, virtuously.

'You are in trouble,' said Sir. 'Michael, ask Miss Middleton to step in here for a moment, please.'

Miss Middleton, frog-ridden, looked round the door.

'I'm sorry to bother you again,' said Sir, 'but it seems that Tim thinks you told him that one Sue Nixon was to bring you a red sock before assembly.'

'Tim!' said Miss Middleton, very shocked. 'That's a naughty fib. I never told you any such thing.'

'Oh Sir,' said Tim. 'Miss didn't tell me. It was Pauline Bates done that.'

'Did that. I think I see Pauline out in the hall,' said Sir. 'In the PT class. Yes? Let's have her in.'

Pauline was very small and very frightened. Sir sat her on his knee and told her not to worry. 'All we want to know,' he said, 'is what you said to Tim yesterday. About Sue Nixon and the dead dog.'

'Red sock, Sir,' said Tim.

'Sorry, red sock. Well, Pauline?'

Pauline looked as if she might join Ruth in tears. Ruth had just realized that she was no longer involved, and was crying with relief.

'You said Miss Middleton gave you a message for Sue Nixon. What was it?'

'It wasn't Sue Nixon,' said Pauline, damply. 'It was June Nichols. It wasn't Miss Middleton, it was Miss Wimbledon.'

'There is no Miss Wimbledon,' said Sir. 'June Nichols, yes. I know June, but Miss Wimbledon...?'

'She means Miss Wimpole, Sir,' said Tim. 'The big girls call her Wimbledon, 'cause she plays tennis, Sir, in a little skirt.'

'I thought you didn't know any girls,' said Sir. 'What did Miss Wimpole say to you,

Pauline?'

'She didn't,' said Pauline. 'It was Moira Thatcher. She said to tell June Nichols to come and see Miss Whatsit before assembly and bring her bed socks.'

'Then why tell Tim?'

'I couldn't find June. June's in his class.'

'I begin to see daylight,' said Sir. 'Not much, but it's there. All right, Pauline. Go and get Moira, please.'

Moira had recently had a new brace fitted across her front teeth. It caught the light when she opened her mouth.

'Yeth, Thir?'

'Moira, take it slowly, and tell us what the message was about June Nichols.'

Moira took a deep breath and polished the brace with her tongue.

'Well, Thir, Mith Wimpole thaid to thell June to thee her before athembly with her wed fw-thw-thth-'

'Frock?' said Sir. Moira nodded gratefully. 'So why tell Pauline?'

'Pauline liveth up her thtweet, Thir.'

'No I don't,' said Pauline. 'They moved. They got a council house, up the Ridgeway.'

'All right, Moira,' said Sir. 'Just ask Miss Wimpole if she could thp—spare me a minute of her time, please?'

If Miss Wimpole was surprised to find eight people in Sir's office, she didn't show it. As there was no longer room to get inside, she stood at the doorway and waved. Sir waved back. Mike instantly decided that Sir fancied Miss Wimpole.

'Miss Wimpole, I believe you must be the last link in the chain. Am I right in thinking that you wanted June Nichols to see you before assembly, with her red frock?'

'Why, yes,' said Miss Wimpole. 'She's dancing a solo at the end-of-term concert. I wanted her to practise, but she didn't turn up.'

'Thank you,' said Sir. 'One day, when we

both have a spare hour or two, I'll tell you why she didn't turn up. As for you lot,' he said, turning to the mob round his desk, 'you seem to have been playing Chinese Whispers without knowing it. You also seem to think that the entire staff is off its head. You may be right. I don't know. Red socks, dead dogs, live frogs—we'll put your friend in the school pond, Ruth. Fetch him at break. And now, someone had better find June Nichols and deliver Miss Wimpole's message.'

'Oh, there's no point, Sir. She couldn't have come anyway,' said Ruth. 'She's got chicken-pox. She hasn't been at school for ages.'

# EXERCISES

## A UNDERSTANDING THE STORY

*1. How did Mike usually journey home from school?*

*2. What did he think of Miss Middleton's request?*

*3. Describe Ruth's reactions to the request.*

*4. Can you remember Mike's description of the frog he found?*

*5. How does Miss Middleton see Ruth's action?*

*6. Does Ruth notice anything unusual about Sir when she enters his office? Can you explain it?*

*7. To what does Sir compare the entire episode? Can you explain this?*

## B DISCUSSION

*Discuss this story in your groups (of four or five pupils). Choose a new chairperson and/or secretary. Follow the same rules as before. REPORT BACK after each question or group of questions.*

*1. Do you like or dislike this story? Give your reasons.*

*2. What do you think of each of the characters—Mike Dixon, Ruth Dixon, Miss Middleton and Sir? Base your opinions on actual events or statements in the story. Suggest three words to describe each character.*

*3. What are the different attitudes to living creatures which you find in this story?*

*4. Most good stories are exciting. The point of greatest excitement and tension in a story is called the CLIMAX. Where would you locate the climax of this story? Why? Which words make it more exciting?*

*5. The PLOT is the word used to describe the twists and turns of events in a story. Is this plot too complex? To find out, someone should try to relate it quickly in his/her own words.*

*6. 'THEME' is a word used to describe the key idea behind a story or poem (i.e. what it is about as distinct from what happens (plot)). What does your group think is the theme of this story? Is it mainly about cruelty to creatures or something else? List the themes you find in it.*

*7. From your own experience do you know any story based on something misheard or misunderstood. Choose one from each group for REPORT BACK.*

## FOR PRIVATE STUDY

*Were there words in this story that you normally find difficult to spell? Look again.*

# C SPEAKING AND WRITING CONCISELY

## 1. Telemessages

*a.* You are going to your cousins for the weekend, arriving at the local station at 7 p.m. You want to tell them you are bringing a friend. You will need someone to meet you as you have two heavy cases. However you only have enough money for 10 words. Write out the telemessage.

*b.* Send a telemessage to your sister on holiday in France, notifying her of the sudden death and funeral arrangements of your uncle. Try to be brief but not unfeeling. Rewrite until you are satisfied.

*c.* Send a telemessage of congratulations to your older cousin who is getting married. Try to avoid the usual banal sayings like, 'Congratulations and best wishes'. Rewrite until you are satisfied.

*d.* Work in groups of three - A, B, C, . A briefly writes out a fairly complex story, incident or scene. B then puts that in telemessage form and hands to C. C then interprets the telemessage and checks with A that he or she has understood correctly. Rotate the functions.

## 2. Speaking to an Answering Machine/Tape Recorder

When we speak with someone on the telephone we can ramble on a bit and clarify exactly what we mean if we find that we are being misunderstood. There is no such help from an answering machine.

Using a tape recorder, practise leaving messages as if on an answering machine. Or just work in pairs and speak to each other in turn. Don't write out or prepare your statement. This is an exercise at speaking clearly and logically, under pressure. Try some of the following:

*a.* Your father has sent you to telephone for the vet as he has just found the dog wandering around, bumping into things and foaming at the mouth.

*b.* Ring the doctor, as your two year old brother, whom you are babysitting, has fallen down the stairs.

*c.* Your parents are away for the day. Ring the school, pretending to be ill.

*d.* Your TV set is 'on the blink'. You haven't been able to view 'Neighbours' for the past week. This is your third time ringing the company.

## 3. Giving Directions

*a.* Study the map on the next page. Work in pairs, one of whom is local, the other a stranger. Decide where you are on the map at present. Then answer questions about finding the Post Office, Hotel, Restaurant, etc. Write out the instructions. Do they work? Reverse roles. You might try this exercise without a map, basing it on your knowledge of your own locality or town.

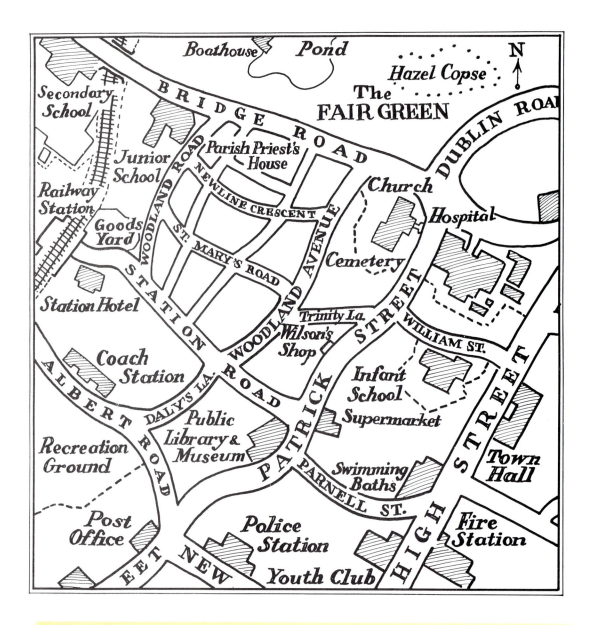

*b. Write out exact and detailed instructions for the performing of simple everyday events such as: putting on a coat; opening a particular window; making a telephone call; making a cup of tea; preparing for a particular class before the teacher walks in; cleaning the board; getting a book from the cupboard etc., etc., Now swap instructions and either mime or act out the exact instruction you receive. Were the directions accurate or did you expect someone to open the cupboard door before he/she had got out of his/her seat?*

Here are two poems with very different views on Nature Study. Read them and use your dictionary to find out the meaning of any new words. Write these into your Word Copy.

## DEATH OF A NATURALIST

All year the flax-dam festered in the heart
Of the townland; green and heavy headed
Flax had rotted there, weighted down by huge sods.
Daily it sweltered in the punishing sun.
Bubbles gargled delicately, bluebottles
Wove a strong gauze of sound around the smell.
There were dragon-flies, spotted butterflies,
But best of all was the warm thick slobber
Of frogspawn that grew like clotted water
In the shade of the banks. Here, every spring
I would fill jampotfuls of the jellied
Specks to range on window-sills at home,
On shelves at school, and wait and watch until
The fattening dots burst into nimble-
Swimming tadpoles. Miss Walls would tell us how
The daddy frog was called a bullfrog
And how he croaked and how the mammy frog
Laid hundreds of little eggs and this was
Frogspawn. You could tell the weather by frogs too
For they were yellow in the sun and brown
In rain.
Then one hot day when fields were rank
With cowdung in the grass the angry frogs
Invaded the flax-dam; I ducked through hedges
To a coarse croaking that I had not heard
Before. The air was thick with a bass chorus.
Right down the dam gross-bellied frogs were cocked
On sods; their loose necks pulsed like sails. Some hopped:
The slap and plop were obscene threats. Some sat
Poised like mud grenades, their blunt heads farting.
I sickened, turned, and ran. The great slime kings
Were gathered there for vengeance and I knew
That if I dipped my hand the spawn would clutch it.

*Seamus Heaney*

## A MEMORY

The waste ground was choked with weeds
They grew above her head
But in the middle of this waste
One flower of golden red.

The little child came every day
To gaze upon this scene
The flower it was the loveliest sight
That she had ever seen.

This flower took root and blossomed
It grew inside her head
And led her on to lovely things
Long after it was dead.

*Alice Taylor*

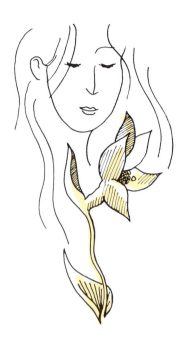

*10. Write a description of the creature you find most frightening or disgusting or beautiful.*

# Correct Writing

## RECOGNITION OF NOUNS, ADJECTIVES, PRONOUNS

**NOUN**

A NOUN is a word that tells us the name of
a)  a person
b)  place
c)  thing
d)  or quality

Example: When *John* went to *Mullingar* in the *boat*, his *happiness* was plain for all to see.

**Nouns**
a)  John
b)  Mullingar
c)  boat
d)  happiness

# E X E R C I S E S

*1. Fill in suitable nouns in the following sentences.*

*The ........... bit the postman.*

*The ............... opens at 9 o' clock.*

*All the ............... watched the ..................... on TV.*

*The ................... gave me tablets for my painful ....................*

*On our first ............. the teacher told us all about our new ................*

*............... went  to ............... for her holidays.*

*On the ................ before the ..................... I was filled with ...................*

*'..................... does not come without hard work', said the teacher.*

*2. Using  the letters of these words, how many nouns can you make from each:*
*COMPLICATION; LITERATURE; ESSENTIAL.*

**3.** *How many nouns can you see, from where you sit?*
*Write them down.*

### 4. GROUP COMPETITION
*Working in groups, how many nouns can you think up beginning with the letter A?*
*STRICT TIME LIMIT. MIS-SPELT WORDS DON'T COUNT.*
*The winning group can choose the next letter.*

> **ADJECTIVE**
> An ADJECTIVE is a word that tells us more about a noun.
> It is a descriptive word used to add colour to a sentence.
>
> Example: the _wily_ cat grabbed the _careless_
> mouse and bit off _his_ tail.

# E X E R C I S E S

**1.** *Think up appropriate adjectives to describe the blackboard; the desk; your school bag; the sound of the 9 o'clock bell; the sound of the last evening bell; the sky outside the window; the teacher; other.*
**2.** *Read 'Death of a Naturalist' again and pick out five adjectives that add particular colour or feeling to the poem. Say what each suggests to you.*

> **PRONOUN**
> A PRONOUN is a word that is used instead of a noun.
> For example: I; you; he; she; it; they; we; each; that; one;
> mine; yours; some. We use pronouns to shorten our communication and to avoid repeating nouns.

# E X E R C I S E

*Try saying the last twelve lines of Seamus Heaney's poem, substituting the original nouns for the pronouns used!*

This is an extract from a printed version of an interview given by Maeve Binchy to RTE. She describes her school days with honesty and humour. Enjoy it.

# A Lethal Striker

At the age of five I went to St Anne's, a lovely little nursery school in Clarinda Park in Dun Laoghaire. It was run by a Mrs Russell, who was one of those wonderful old women with white hair and a straight back that you always saw as somebody's grandmother in old films. She was terribly correct and very kind. There were two other ladies—her nieces, I think—both called Miss Bath. One was fat and one was thin; with typical childish cruelty we called them 'Hot Bath' and 'Cold Bath'. We didn't have a school uniform, but my great excitement was wearing a big bow on my head. The bow was ironed for me every morning and I went off to school looking like a cockatoo! I enjoyed my three years in St Anne's.

My next school was a convent school in Killiney, Co. Dublin, run by the Order of the Holy Child Jesus. These nuns had come to Ireland after the war. It was said that they had come at the invitation of the then Archbishop of Dublin, John Charles McQuaid, because he was terrified that too many middle-class Irish girls were going to convents in England, where they might do that dreadful thing: they might meet someone of a different faith and possibly threaten their own faith and be lost to us forever! I don't know whether all this was true or not, but that is what we always believed.

The nuns were terribly nice and very innocent. They were somewhat like the Somerville and Ross's Irish R.M. coming over here, because they really had no idea what they were about at all. One of them, whom I have met since, used to say that 'one was either sent to the Gold Coast or to Eire on one's missionary duty'. You got the feeling that the Gold Coast might have been a better bargain, because we used to tell them all a pack of lies. They didn't understand the Irish language or its pronunciation; nor did they understand the importance of Irish in the school curriculum. Consequently, the first year that the Leaving Certificate examination was taken in that school I think nearly every student failed Irish. Irish teachers were brought the next year in order to sort that problem out.

All my school reports said that I was bright but lazy: I didn't stir myself enough.I was lucky, in that my mind was quick. I could understand things quickly and then I would spend the rest of the time in a daydream. There were some things I was very poor at—mathematics I didn't understand at all, and I am still practically innumerate—but I was fortunate enough to be at the top of the class.

However, in those days being at the top of the class wasn't nearly as important as being good at games. To have big strong arms and be able to hit the hockey ball miles down the pitch—that was real status. I didn't enjoy games. We all wore green uniforms tied in the middle and we looked like potato sacks of various sizes. I remember standing on the hockey pitch, my legs blue with the cold, hoping that all the action would remain at the far end and that I would not be called on to do anything. I was a real thorn in the flesh for the unfortunate games mistress who had to deal with me: full of sulks, refusing to vault the horse or hit the ball in case I did myself an injury.

But I enjoyed netball. I was very tall, even at the age of fourteen, which led the games mistress to believe that I had great potential on the netball team as a shooter. She figured that I was so tall that even if I just stood there, dreaming of the future and thinking my own thoughts, when the ball came into my hands it would be as easy for me to put it into the net as it was to throw it away. I was a great success. I was in the 1st VII team for netball for two whole years, which was lovely because we went out to other convents on Wednesday afternoons to play netball, and we had tea and buns afterwards. We won all our games and a lot of the other schools protested, saying that I was too old and could not possibly be under fourteen. I was, to use the modern parlance, a lethal striker.

Apart from hockey, the other thing I hated— we all hated it—was being dragged to the beach by the nuns. They would say, 'Come on girls, show some school spirit.' It was very easy for them to say that when they had about nine thousand black petticoats on them and they didn't have to go into the icy sea and show school spirit.

## E X E R C I S E S

*(for group discussion or for individual written or oral work)*

*1. Do you think the writer enjoyed her time at nursery school? What words, sentences or statements in the piece suggest this?*

*2. What did the reports from the convent secondary school say about her? From your reading of the piece do you think these reports were fair to her? Can you find examples to back up what you say?*

*3. Did you enjoy this extract? Why or why not?*

*4. Read the last paragraph again. Write out, in three separate columns, all the nouns, adjectives and pronouns you can find in it.*

*5. Can you fill in the blanks in the exercise below? All the words are used in the extract.*

| | Words used as Nouns |
|---|---|
| A place of incarceration for all from 5 to 18. | _ _ _ O_ _ |
| The gear that goes with it. | _ _ _F_ _ _ |
| Some bird, that Maeve! | C_ _ _ _ _ _ O |
| A way of speaking. | P_ _ _ _ _ _ _ |
| Deadly weapon on the sports field. | _ _ _ _T_R |

| | Words used as Adjectives |
|---|---|
| This word was also used as a noun. | _ _H_ _L |
| Could also suggest envy. | _ _E_ N |
| Causing death. | _ _T_A_ |

26

# Speaking

Do you have any interesting memories of a trip or outing you went on, in primary school?  Prepare to tell it to the class.

## H I N T S

**a.** Get the sequence or order of events clear in your mind so that others can follow you easily.

**b.** Think of a memorable description so that others can visualise or see what you mean.  For example, Maeve says 'We all wore green uniforms tied in the middle and we looked like potato sacks of various sizes'.

# Correct Writing
### RECOGNITION OF VERBS AND ADVERBS

**VERB**

A VERB is an action word.

For example:  The wily cat *grabbed* the careless mouse and <u>bit</u> off his tail.

NOTE that the verb 'to be' is also an action word.  Example:  The girl *is* happy.  His name *was* John.

NOTE also that some verbs are made up of more than one word.  For example: had walked; was leaving; were searching; will go, etc.

## E X E R C I S E S

*1. Fill in the missing verbs. 'Suddenly the classroom door . . . . . . . . . . . . open and into the sudden silence . . . . . . . . . . . . . . Sr Imelda, the English teacher, . . . . a bundle of dog-eared copies.  She . . . . . . . . . . . . . . across the room and . . . . . . it down with a resounding crash on the desk top.  Clouds of chalk . . . . . . . . . . . . in all directions. 'I . . . . . . . . . . . these', she said.  'Even after I . . . . . . . . . . . . three weeks on grammar, . . . . . . . . . . . . .some girls here who . . . . . . . . . . a noun from a verb.'*

27

*2. Prepare to tell the group or class about your favourite sport or pastime (or any sport you like to watch). Pay particular attention to the verbs. Try to get the atmosphere of the sport across by the verbs you use.*

---

**ADVERB**

An ADVERB is a word that tells us more about a) a verb, b) an adjective, c) another adverb.

Examples:

**a)** The teacher called *loudly*.

The pupil snored *blissfully*.

**b)** The teacher was *particularly* kind, after she received the box of chocolates!

The essay was *unexpectedly* good.

She has a *very* deep knowledge of Nature Study.

**c)** The boy walked *very* slowly to school.

She should have finished that project *much* earlier.

*NOTE:* Adverbs often end in '-ly'.

Many adverbs are formed by adding '-ly' to the adjective,

The greyhound was swift.

The greyhound ran *swiftly* over the track.

Adverbs add to the action quality of a sentence.

---

# E X E R C I S E S

*1. Add appropriate adverbs to the following passage and notice the difference:*

*The boy . . . . . . . . . . . . . pushed open the door which creaked . . . . . . . . . . . . .*
*and he then crept . . . . . . . . . . . . . . up the stairs. The moonlight fell . . . . . . . . . . .*
*in patterns on the bannister, creating a strange effect. Nevertheless he moved on*
*up past the first landing, feeling his way by the dusty wall. His heart was thump-*
*ing . . . . . . . . . . . . . . . . against his chest for he was afraid. Yet he pushed on . . .*
*until he came to a great door. He placed his hand . . . . . . . . . . . . . . . on the dusty*
*doorknob and . . . . . . . . . . . . . . turned. With a creak the door swung inwards*
*. . . . . . . . . . . . . . .*

*2. Write a report of a school game or other athletic event, paying particular attention to the verbs and adverbs.*

This extract is taken from James Joyce's novel, 'Portrait of the Artist as a Young Man', in which the main character, Stephen Dedalus, remembers his youth, school days etc. Here, Fr Dolan, who is Prefect of Studies has just come into Fr Arnall's classroom to dole out punishment. Read it, find out the meanings of any difficult words and write them into your Word Copy.

'At your work, all of you!' shouted the prefect of studies. 'We want no lazy idle loafers here, lazy idle little schemers. At your work, I tell you. Father Dolan will be in to see you every day. Father Dolan will be in tomorrow.'

He poked one of the boys in the side with the pandybat, saying: 'You, boy! When will Father Dolan be in again?'

'Tomorrow, sir,' said Tom Furlong's voice.

'Tomorrow and tomorrow and tomorrow,' said the prefect of studies. 'Make up your minds for that. Every day Father Dolan. Write away. You, boy, who are you?'

Stephen's heart jumped suddenly.

'Dedalus, sir.'

'Why are you not writing like the others?'

'I ... my ...'

He could not speak with fright.

'Why is he not writing, Father Arnall?'

'He broke his glasses,' said Father Arnall, 'and I exempted him from work.'

'Broke? What is this I hear? What is this? Your name is?' said the prefect of studies.

'Dedalus, sir.'

'Out here, Dedalus. Lazy little schemer. I see schemer in your face. Where did you break your glasses?'

Stephen stumbled into the middle of the class, blinded by fear and haste.

'Where did you break your glasses?' repeated the prefect of studies.

'The cinderpath, sir.'

'Hoho! The cinderpath!' cried the prefect of studies. 'I know that trick.'

Stephen lifted his eyes in wonder and saw for a moment Father Dolan's whitegrey not young face, his baldy whitegrey head with fluff at the sides of it, the steel rims of his spectacles and his nocoloured eyes looking through the glasses. Why did he say he knew that trick?

'Lazy idle little loafer!' cried the prefect of studies. 'Broke my glasses! An old schoolboy trick! Out with your hand this moment!'

Stephen closed his eyes and held out in the air his trembling hand with the palm upwards. He felt the prefect of studies touch it for a moment at the fingers to straighten it and then the swish of the sleeve of the soutane as the pandybat was lifted to strike. A hot burning stinging tingling blow like the loud crack of a broken stick made his trembling hand crumple together like a leaf in the fire: and at the sound and the pain scalding tears were driven into his eyes. His whole body was shaking with fright, his arm was shaking and his crumpled burning livid hand shook like a loose leaf in the air. A cry sprang to his lips, a prayer to be let off. But though the tears scalded his eyes and his limbs quivered with pain and fright he held back the hot tears and the cry that scalded his throat.

'Other hand!' shouted the prefect of studies.

Stephen drew back his maimed and quivering right arm and held out his left hand. The soutane sleeve swished again as the pandybat was lifted and a loud crashing sound and a fierce maddening tingling burning pain made his hand shrink together with the palms and fingers in a livid quivering mass. The scalding water burst forth from his eyes and, burning with shame and agony and fear, he drew back his shaking arm in terror and burst out into a whine of pain. His body shook with a palsy of fright and in shame and rage he felt the scald-ing cry come from his throat and the scalding tears falling out of his eyes and down his flaming cheeks.

'Kneel down!' cried the prefect of studies.

Stephen knelt down quickly pressing his beaten hands to his sides. To think of them beaten and swollen with pain all in a moment made him feel so sorry for them as if they were not his own but someone else's that he felt sorry for. And as he knelt, calming the last sobs in his throat and feeling the burning tingling pain pressed into his sides, he thought of the hands which he had held out in the air with the palms up and of the firm touch of the prefect of studies when he had steadied the shaking fingers and of the beaten swollen red-dened mass of palm and fingers that shook helplessly in the air.

'Get at your work, all of you,' cried the prefect of studies from the door. 'Father Dolan will be in every day to see if any boy, any lazy idle little loafer wants flogging. Every day. Every day.'

The door closed behind him.

The hushed class continued to copy out the themes. Father Arnall rose from his seat and went among them, helping the boys with gentle words and telling them the mistakes they had made. His voice was very gentle and soft.

## E X E R C I S E S

### *Understanding the Story*

*1. Why is Stephen unable to write?*

*2. What details suggest that Stephen is afraid of Fr Dolan?*

*3. Apart from fright what other emotions or feelings does Stephen have, about the incident?*

*4. Were all the teachers brutal? Explain.*

*5. Read again the paragraph beginning:*

*'Stephen lifted his eyes in wonder...'*

*What adjectives does he use to describe Fr Dolan and what do they suggest about the priest?*

*6. Read again the three sentences:*
*'His whole body was shaking with fright ... the cry that scalded his throat.'*
*Write out each of the verbs in these sentences and say what effect they have on the description.*
*7. Choose a sentence of most memorable description and say why you choose it.*

## DIALOGUE/DISCUSSION

*8. In pairs prepare dramatic readings of the dialogue at the first part of the extract. Perform some of them for the class. Discuss the interpretations.*
*9. Working in pairs, practise and perform the conversation that might have occurred between Fr Arnall and Fr Dolan, later that day. Or rehearse a conversation between Stephen and his mother or father. Or between Stephen and a friend, later that evening.*
*10. Fr Dolan wrongly accuses Stephen of being 'a lazy idle little schemer'. Did you ever suffer an injustice? If so, prepare to describe the incident to the class.*
*11. Can you find out anything else about James Joyce? Report back to the class.*

# Correct Writing

> **THE SENTENCE**
> A sentence is a unit which makes complete sense on its own. It begins with a capital letter and ends with a full stop.

Sentences can be of various lengths. You can have short ones, such as:
*Dogs barked.*
*She fell.*
*He ran.*
You can have simple sentences:
*The girl hit the dog.*
You can have more complex ones:
*The courageous girl who was bringing home the shopping hit the savage dog with the Irish Times and frightened him off.*
We could represent it like this:

| **The girl** | → | **hit** | → | **the dog** |
|---|---|---|---|---|
| NOUN | | VERB | | NOUN |
| Subject | | | | Object |

A sentence must have a VERB or action word. It must also have someone doing the action—a noun or pronoun which is called the SUBJECT of the sentence. It usually has something at the receiving end of the action—a noun called the OBJECT of the sentence. But this is not necessary, as a sentence can make sense without an object, for example, 'Dogs bark.'

**EXTRA INFORMATION**
The statement made about the subject or what follows from the subject in a sentence is called THE PREDICATE.

| *The girl's heart* *SUBJECT* | *was thumping fast* *PREDICATE* |
|---|---|

# E X E R C I S E S

*1. Match the subjects in the left hand column with their correct predicates or endings in the right hand column, to form sentences. All the sentences in (1) and (3) are from A Lethal Striker.*

| SUBJECT | PREDICATE |
|---|---|
| The nuns | wore green uniforms tied in the middle |
| All my school reports | were brought in before the next year |
| Irish teachers | were terribly nice and very innocent |
| We all | said that I was bright but lazy |

*2. Reassemble these phrases into sensible sentences.*
*a. Ruth was leaning/kicking a brick/through the side gate/when he came in/out of the kitchen window.*
*b. which wilted/he came in/when he saw/with an innocent smile/what was waiting for him.*
*c. she stood at the doorway to get inside/as there was no longer room/and waved.*

*3. Put each of these sentences back together again. First see if you can find the VERB and then the SUBJECT of the sentence.*

*a. Anne's age to five I the at went St.*
*b. unfortunate thorn I was real flesh a games in the the of mistress*
*c. poor were I was things at some very there*
*d. duty either one to to the or Gold or Eire coast was sent one's missionary*

## PARAGRAPHS

A paragraph is another bigger unit which makes sense on its own. All the sentences in a paragraph should deal with one main topic or idea.

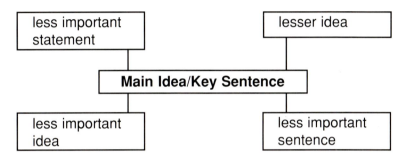

Read this paragraph:

'One evening a farmer's son, a boy called Hogarth, was fishing in a stream that ran down to the sea. It was growing too dark to fish, his hook kept getting caught in weeds and bushes. So he stopped fishing and came up from the stream and stood listening to the owls in the wood further up the valley, and to the sea behind him. Hush, said the sea. And again, Hush. Hush. Hush.'

See how it is constructed:

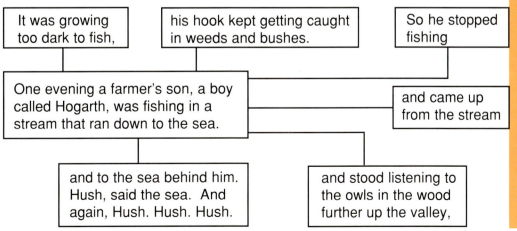

A new paragraph should begin about a third to half-way into a new line. This is called INDENTING. It signals to the reader that:

> **a.** There is a new idea coming up;
> or **b.** That some time has elapsed;
> or **c.** That there is a change of scene;
> or **d.** A change of mood;
> or **e.** New characters are about to be introduced, etc.

PARAGRAPHING IS PACKAGING. Package your thoughts into units. For instance, a story might develop in paragraphs like this.

| | | | |
|---|---|---|---|
| 1 | Set the scene. | 5 | A second attempt —still no luck. |
| 2 | Introduce the characters. | 6 | Introduce new characters. |
| 3 | Pose the problem or dilemma. | 7 | Dramatic solution and happy ending. |
| 4 | Vain attempt to overcome problems. | | |

Indeed a very good story would not be as predictable as this. But it would still keep the ideas separate in distinct paragraphs.

Read this extract:

# The Return of the Iron Man

**Ted Hughes**

**Par 1**

One evening a farmer's son, a boy called Hogarth, was fishing in a stream that ran down to the sea. It was growing too dark to fish, his hook kept getting caught in weeds and bushes. So he stopped fishing and came up from the stream and stood listening to the owls in the wood further up the valley, and to the sea behind him. Hush, said the sea. And again, Hush. Hush. Hush.

This is called a NARRATIVE PARAGRAPH. The events are described in the order in which they happened: a. boy fishing in the evening; b. growing too dark; c. boy stops fishing and listens to the sounds of the night.

**Par 2**

Suddenly he felt a strange feeling. He felt he was being watched. He felt afraid. He turned and looked up the steep field to the top of the high cliff. Behind that skyline was the sheer rocky cliff and the sea. And on that skyline, just above the edge of it, in the dusk, were two green lights. What were two green lights doing at the top of the cliff?

Notice the very dramatic opening. There is a complete change of mood here, from the soft gentle sounds of the sea in the first paragraph, to the boy's sudden fear. This paragraph deals with the single idea of the boy's fear and finding the source of it. It ends in a question, which increases the tension.

Then, as Hogarth watched, a huge dark figure climbed up over the cliff-top. The two lights rose into the sky. They were the giant figure's eyes. A giant black figure, taller than a house, black and towering in the twilight, with green headlamp eyes. The Iron Man! There he stood on the cliff-top, looking inland. Hogarth began to run. He ran and ran. Home. Home. The Iron Man had come back.

**This deals with the very dramatic emergence of the Iron Man. Notice the use of different yet similar words (synonyms) to stress the one idea—huge, giant, towering. The boy flees.**

So he got home at last and gasping for breath he told his dad. An Iron Man! An Iron Man! A giant!

**A new paragraph is needed here because there is a change of scene and time has elapsed.**

His father frowned. His mother grew pale. His little sister began to cry.

**This one deals with the first reactions of his family.**

His father took down his double-barrelled gun. He believed his son. He went out. He locked the door. He got in his car. He drove to the next farm.

**His father's actions are listed—again in narrative order.**

But that farmer laughed. He was a fat, red man, with a fat, red-mouthed laugh. When he stopped laughing, his eyes were red too. An Iron Man? Nonsense, he said.

**The reactions of the farmer are described.**

So Hogarth's father got back in his car. Now it was dark and it had begun to rain. He drove to the next farm.

**His father drives to the next farm.**

That farmer frowned. He believed. Tomorrow, he said, we must see what he is, this iron man. His feet will have left tracks in the earth.

**This paragraph deals with the different reactions of the second farmer. He believes.**

So Hogarth's father again got back into his car. But as he turned the car in the yard, he saw a strange thing in the headlamps. Half a tractor lay there, just half, chopped clean off, the other half missing. He got out of his car and the other farmer came to look too. The tractor had been bitten off—there were big teeth-marks in the steel.

**Here we have a description of the amazing scene in the headlights.**

**NOTICE**

**1.** There is only a single main or key idea in each of the paragraphs.

**2.** All the paragraphs do not begin with the same word or phrase, e.g.

> *One evening*
> *Suddenly*
> *Then*
> *So*
> *His father*
> *His father*
> *But that farmer*
> *So Hogarth's father*
> *That farmer*
> *So Hogarth's father*
> *No explanation.*

Try not to begin all your paragraphs with 'then' or 'next'!

**3.** It is very simply written. Always try to be clear and simple. Yet it has lots of colourful description: the sound of the owls and the hush of the sea ... the sheer rocky cliff ... the two green lights ... the giant black figure, taller than a house ... with green headlamp eyes ... a fat red-mouthed laugh, etc.

# EXERCISES

*Keeping these ideas in mind write three descriptive paragraphs on:*

*1. your new classroom*

*2. new friends*

*3. the view from your window*

*4. Write five imaginative paragraphs on your first day in your new school or class.*

*[You might think of colours, sounds, smells; your feelings, hopes and expecta-tions; ghosts of past students; the thoughts of the classroom itself—indeed any-thing. But USE PARAGRAPHS.]*

*5. Choose any one of the following photographs and write three paragraphs describing exactly what you see.*

*6. Use your imagination! In five paragraphs write a little story, which might be suggested by any one of the photographs.*

*•Working in pairs, and using red biro, correct each other's work, watching for main idea per paragraph.*

*• Your teacher may ask you to read some of your work. Remember LOUDLY, CLEARLY, SLOWLY.*

**SCHOOL IN THE COUNTRY, ONCE UPON A TIME**

Here is an extract from Alice Taylor's book 'To School Through the Fields—an Irish Country Childhood', in which she describes life in a small country school in the 1940s.

# To School Through the Fields

*Alice Taylor*

Going to school and coming back was so enjoyable that it made school itself bearable. My main objection to school was that I had to stay there: it was the first experience to interfere with my freedom and it took me a long time to accept that there was no way out of its trap. I could look out through a window in the back wall of the schoolhouse and see my home away in the distance, with the fields stretching out invitingly and with the Darigle river glinting in the valley. I made many an imaginary journey home through that window: it was not that I wished to be at home so much, but that I wanted to be free to ramble out through the fields. I envied the freedom of the crows on the trees outside the window, coming and going as they pleased.

But school became an accepted pattern and even though it had its black days it had its good ones as well. The black days were mainly in winter when we arrived through the fields with sodden boots and had to sit in the freezing cold with a harsh wind whipping in under the door and up through the floor boards. The school was an old stone building with tall rattling windows and black cobweb-draped rafters, and when the wind howled the whole school groaned and creaked. The floor had large gaping holes through which an occasional rat peeped up to join the educational circle.

The educational process of the day was based on repetition: we repeated everything so often that it had to penetrate into our uninterested minds. A booster, by way of a sharp slap across the fingers with a hazel rod, sharpened our powers of perception. Learning was not optional and the sooner you learnt that fact, the freer from conflict life became. All the same, most of the teachers were as kind as the system allowed them to be, but inspectors breathed down their necks and after them came the

priests to check our religious knowledge. One stern-faced priest peered down at me from his six-foot height when I was in third class and demanded to know: 'What is transubstantiation?'

Education was certainly not child oriented but our way of life compensated for its shortcomings. Sometimes, though unaware of it, we tried to educate our teachers, especially the ones that came from nearby towns to do part-time duty. One of these asked us to write a composition on 'Life on the Farm'. I loved writing compositions and my problem was not how to start but how to finish. I included in my account a description of the sex life of a cow and when I got my copy back from the teacher this section was ringed with a red pencil. A red mark meant an error so I checked every word for spelling in my dictionary but found nothing wrong. I returned to school the following day to ask the teacher what was wrong.

'That sentence should be left out,' she said.

'But why?' I asked.

'It's not suitable,' she answered, giving me a strange look.

On returning home in a very confused state I explained my problem to my mother. She read my composition, smiled and said: 'People from a different background do not always understand'. It took me another couple of years to understand why the teacher did not understand.

Ours was a mixed school and this suited everybody because families and neighbours were not split up but could all go to school together. The boys played football at one side of the yard and girls played hunt and cat and mouse at the other side. At the back of the school the boys' and girls' toilets, which consisted of a timber bench with a circle cut in it to facilitate bottoms of all sizes, were separated by a stone wall. The little toilet building was partly roofed with galvanised but this had grown to a complete roof by years of free-growing ivy.

The school had just two rooms. The master had a room to himself and the second room was shared by the two other teachers: one taught infants and first class at one side of the room, while second and third classes were taught by the second teacher at the other side. It was open plan education and if you got bored at your end you could tune in to the other side, at the risk of a slap across the ear if you were caught out.

We ate our lunch, which consisted of a bottle of milk and two slices of home-made brown bread, sitting on a grassy ditch around the school and we fed the crumbs to the birds. In winter the milk bottles were heated around the fire during classes, often resulting in corks popping from the heat and, if the cork could not pop because it was screwed on we had a mini-explosion and a milk lake.

# EXERCISES

*(for group discussion or for individual written or oral work)*

*1. Re-read the first paragraph. In your opinion is it the first sentence or the second sentence which is the key sentence for the whole paragraph? Explain.*

*2. In paragraph two, the first sentence is the key. But is it slightly misleading? Can you see why?*

*3. What details suggest that the teachers also were under pressure?*

*4. How do you think the writer felt about school? Did she like it, hate it, tolerate it or what? Explain.*

*5. Her mother said, 'People from a different background do not always understand.' Why do you think the teacher did not understand?*

*6. Was school then different, in any way, from school today?*

*7. Can you remember any humorous incidents from your primary schooldays? Think about it and prepare to tell it to the group or class.*

# WRITING

**8.** *Using your dictionary look up any words you didn't understand and write them into your Word Copy.*

**9.** *What do you think school will be like in the year 2050? Write five or six imaginative paragraphs. (Remember: one main/key idea for each paragraph.)*

# MEDIA

**10.** *Using a tape recorder, interview an older person (mother, father, uncle, grandmother, etc.) about his/her schooldays. Play it back to the class. Or interview them and note down what they say.*

# Correct Writing

**PUNCTUATION**

**The Full Stop**
Use a full stop:
**1.** At the end of a sentence.

**2.** To show where letters have been left out or words shortened.
  Use also after initials.
  Reverend Michael Malone, Society of Jesus.  Rev. Michael Malone, S.J.
  Miss Mary Teresa Burke, Editor.  Miss M.T. Burke, Ed.
  It is usual not to punctuate ACRONYMS such as PAYE;
  NATO ( North Atlantic Treaty Organiation);
  RTE (Radio Telefís Éireann); BBC,
  FBI (Federal Bureau of Investigation)etc.

**3.** Use stops in groups of three or four to show that part of a sentence is missing or unfinished.

  **Example:**  With shaking hand she opened the door,
  took one step into the room and...

**The Capital Letter**
  Use a capital letter:
  **1.** To begin a sentence.

  **2.** For people's names and initials:
  President Hillery,
  Josephine McInerney,
  H.H. Munro;
  P.G. Wodehouse;
  Bishop Harty.

**3.** For particular places:
  National Concert Hall;
  Gardiner Street;
  Northern Ireland;
  Co. Cavan.

**4.** For the initials of organisations:
RTE; NATO; FBI.

**5.** For the date:     Friday, the 19th of August.

**6.** For the titles of books, films or plays:

The Merchant of Venice,

The Flight of the Doves,

Neighbours.

**7.** At the beginning of direct speech, even though it is not at the start of a sentence:

The teacher snarled, 'Be quiet, at once!'

**The Exclamation Mark**

Use an exclamation mark to indicate a tone of surprise, shock or humour.  It is used to show extreme feeling of one kind or another.  An exclamation mark might be used with a more sensational headline or statement, as in the example above.

# The Trouble with Donovan Croft

*Bernard Ashley*

Keith Chapman's parents are fostering Donovan Croft.
On the first day of term, Donovan goes to school with Keith.

Small groups of children stood about like strangers in the playground.  There was little of the charging about and booting of balls that went on during most playtimes and before school.  On the first day of the school year everyone was slightly apprehensive.  The new fourth-years, now the senior group and cocks of the walk, showed the most activity, greeting one another with loud shouts and over-enthusiastic thumps on the back.  The rest were very quiet, adjusting to being back in school at all, and taking care of new trousers and frocks.  But the quietest clusters of all, here and there attended by older brothers, sisters and the occasional mum, were the new first-years, last year's top infants who were now very much at the bottom of the pile.  They resembled young deer on the edge of the herd, unsure and frightened but with heads held high.

Every so often a teacher walked through the playground, to be greeted in varying fashions by the different groups.  The new fourth-year children rarely deigned to speak to other than fourth-year teachers, whom they greeted with loud and polite explosions of welcome and wide smiles.  There were two or three new young teachers, ignored by all but the few children who rushed to talk to any adult, and both popular and unpopular teachers who walked through to clamorous attention or to total disregard.  Mr Bryan was mobbed from gate to steps by all but the fourth-years, while Mr Henry might as well have been walking across a beach at midnight.  Mr Roper was already in the building, having been welcomed shortly after eight o'clock by a few shivering individuals whose parents had gone to work early and turned them out at the same time.

44

Class members greeted each other after the six-week break in different ways. Some had seen a lot of their particular friends in the holiday, and there wasn't much new to say. Others, not living so close together, welcomed their classmates with restrained delight, everyone talking and no one listening. Nobody spoke to Shemem Parveen, the brightly-clad Pakistani girl with spiteful fingers, nobody ever did; while Paul Wicks, the football captain who held a place in the District Side even in his third year, was met on all sides by warm disciples. Groups of friends, who played together for different reasons, were reunited. The older 'dinner children' formed a tight band, allowing in a few of the sandwich-bringers as hangers on. Children who went home to dinner made up their own gangs, and those who lived near to one another, or who crossed the road together with the lollipop man, somehow stuck together in the playground. All sorts of reasons brought different children together.

There seemed to be little notice taken of anyone's colour; a good brain, a talented right foot or netball arm were what seemed to matter. The exception were the few Asian children who spoke poor English. They talked together in a fast foreign language by the school steps; the middle of the playground was not for them.

Keith led Donovan in through the Transport Avenue gate. This was Keith's usual gate, and if he ever missed Dave and Tony on the way to school they always met up here. Keith's eyes scanned the crowded playground for his two special friends. They had grown up through the school from the Infants together and they usually sought each other's company. It was an easy friendship, punctuated by thumps and scuffles, snorts and giggles. There were no rules, no special demands were made on one another except their company. It just seemed a natural grouping, like a small pack of dogs hunting together for a reason which none of them understood.

Dave and Tony were there, just inside the gate as usual. Keith saw them wave and heard the familiar shouts—'Wotcher Kee!' from Dave and 'Over here!' from Tony. He grabbed Donovan's arm and tired to steer him over towards them. This was important. He badly wanted them all to get on well together. But as Keith turned round, he became, with Donovan, the focus of considerable attention, and he found his way to Dave and Tony barred by an inquisitive group of children from his year. A new boy in the third year was worth a glance or two.

'Ere, Chapman, who's 'e?'

'Is he new?'

'There's another blackie.'

'Another wog.'

This form of attention was not new to Donovan. He had supposedly swung through the jungle of trees and eaten cat food ever since he first went to infant school with all the other five-year-olds in North London. His reaction now was to stare sullenly ahead with unfocused eyes.

Keith stopped pushing towards Dave and Tony for a moment. He was going to have to say something before he was allowed to get away.

'His name's Donovan. He's living with us. Any objections?'

Nobody objected. Only the older children dared to challenge the strength of the triangle of friendship. Keith and Donovan were now the centre of a little throng. Any friend of Keith's was a friend of theirs, and there was a certain warmth in the circle.

'Hope he's in our class.'

'Ere, mate, are you any good in goal?'

'Is your mum dead?'

The inquiries were necessary to fit Donovan into the order of things, to help them decide their feelings about him. Everyone has a place, and the sooner it is decided and fixed the happier everyone is. Donovan remained silent, so Keith tried to explain.

'His mum' gone back to look after his grandad.'

'Where, Africa?'

'No, Jamaica. But Donovan's living at our house till she gets back. He's like, my foster-brother.'

The words 'foster-brother' carried sufficiently over the gathered heads to reach the ears of Dave and Tony, alert as ears always are to news which might affect the hearers. Neither of the boys spoke, but the beginning of a sneer wrinkled Dave's nose and a meaningful glance passed between the two boys, now left standing on their own.

The group round Keith and Donovan fell silent as they took in the full meaning of the black boy being foster-brother to Chapman.

'Foster-brother?' queried Len Andrews.

'Yes, foster-brother,' replied Keith shortly, trying to bring the questioning to an end. He'd had enough now and wanted to meet up with Dave and Tony. He spelt it out slowly. 'He's my foster brother.'

'Is he?' said a voice from the throng. 'Is that why you don't want to know us any more?'

Keith swung round at the sound of the familiar voice. He knew before he looked that it was Dave.

'It must be nice having a little brown brother. Is he brown all over, Chapman? Is his bum as brown as his face?'

Suddenly Keith found it hard to breathe. His heart thumped and his chest went tight.

'Shut up, Dave,' said Tony, who was standing with an arm round Dave's shoulder. 'Don't be rotten.'

'Well, I only wondered,' said Dave. 'I'm just interested, that's all.'

He coloured a little before Keith's white, angry and betrayed stare.

'Watch it, Smith,' Keith managed to hiss out, 'or I'll put one on you!'

Dave broke away from the crowd.

'Oh, come on, Tone,' he shouted. 'Let's go. I'm scared stiff.'

He suddenly swung back on Keith. 'But I'll tell you, Chapman, when you get fed up with your brown brother don't come running back to be friends with us! If you're too busy for us today you can bloody stay like it!'

With a backward glance Tony followed Dave away, and some of the other went with them. A few minds were suddenly being changed as it became obvious that Keith could no longer draw strength from Tony and Dave.

'See you later,' said one, not sure yet, as he drifted away. Keith and Donovan might make a formidable partnership on their own.

'Just don't forget your old mates, Chapman,' said another, an emboldened boy who had never claimed Keith's friendship. Then someone at the back of the circle shoved everyone forward, but a heavy plastic ball kicked by one of the fourth-years landed in their midst and scattered the group, some to chase it and others to avoid the footballers, and the tension went out of the situation.

'Let them get on with it,' said Winnie Marchall, one of the few girls in the group. 'What's it all about anyway, Keith?'

Keith pulled a face. 'I dunno,' he answered. And truly, he didn't.

You can read the whole story of Keith and Donovan in
'The Trouble with Donovan Croft'.

# EXERCISES

*(for discussion or writing)*

*1.* What details suggest that this is the first day of term?

*2.* What do you think of the portrayal of the schoolyard scene, contained in the first three paragraphs?

*3.* What descriptive sentence do you think best and why?

*4.* What do you see as the main theme or themes of the whole extract?

*5.* Where would you locate the climax? Why?

*6.* Compile a character sketch of Keith. In other words what do we learn about this boy from the details given in the extract?

*7.* Compose a DIARY-STYLE entry for Donovan Croft, for that day.

*8.* What is the main idea in each of the first three paragraphs? Write it down.

*9.* Use your dictionary to find the meaning of any difficult words. Write them into your Word Copy.

*10.* Can you now fill in the following words.

| | |
|---|---|
| uneasy | A _ _ _ _ _ _ _ _ _ V _ |
| full of zeal for something | _ _ T _ _ _ _ _ _ T _ C |
| now and then; here and there | O _ _ _ S _ _ _ _ L |
| shouting | C _ _ _ O R _ _ _ _ |
| kept in check, controlled | R _ _ _ _ _ _ _ _ D |
| marked off in sections | P _ _ _ T _ _ _ _ D |
| difficult to overcome | F _ _ M _ _ _ _ _ E |
| mental strain or excitement | T _ _ _ _ _ N |

# DISCUSSION

*(for groups or class)*
*Have a discussion on gangs, groups, cliques. Are they good or bad? Are they necessary, etc.?*

# REPORT BACK.

*At work on the set of 'Fair City', R.T.E.*

# MEDIA/DRAMA

**1.** Would this story make good Television Drama? Why or why not?

**2.** In groups of 3 to 5, rehearse the dialogue for a school-yard problem or incident. Then act it out.

or

**3.** Study a TV drama programme:

There are many types of TV drama: play, situation comedy, mini series, televised book, etc. But by far the most popular are THE SERIES and THE SERIAL.

SERIES—a series is usually based around a star or group of characters who are the focus of each programme in the series. The activities they get up to each week (or the plots) are usually somewhat similar. Often the characters are either goodies or baddies. Each episode tells a complete story. Programmes such as Miami Vice, Knight Rider and MacGyver are series.

SERIAL—In a serial the story is continued from one episode to the next. It often ends on a very dramatic note, in order to entice you to watch the next episode. Examples of well-known serials are: Coronation Street, Glenroe and Neighbours.

**SOME ACTIVITIES:**

**a.** Watch an episode or two of Grange Hill or other school television drama.

Is it a series or a serial?

**b.** Trace the PLOT of the episode. Or was there more than one plot or story happening at the same time? If so give a brief outline or summary of each.

**c.** Was there CONFLICT in the episode? Describe.

**d.** Consider the CHARACTERS. Were there some good and some bad? Describe one of each. What suggested that they were good or bad? Consider actions, appearance (looks, clothes, gestures, facial expressions, etc.), tone of voice and other giveaways.

Perhaps some of the characters were more complex than just individual goodies and baddies. Consider this.

**e.** Look up the words STEREOTYPE and CARICATURE. Do they apply to any of the characters?

**f.** Were the characters REALISTIC—that is, are people like this in ordinary life?

**g.** What ISSUES did this episode deal with?

Look back to the concept of THEME in the first story.

**h.** Can you find out why TV drama serials are often referred to as 'soap'?

## P R O J E C T

(for groups of 4 or 5)

Plan an episode of a school-based series or serial.

Think of the plot or plots—THE STORYLINE.

Plan the outline first and later the details.

CHARACTERS—make them as individual and different from each other as you can manage.

Are they to be realistic?

SCENES—each story or plot will be broken down into scenes—decide on these.

Role play and later write the dialogue for each.

Act it out.

A still from *'Glenroe'*, R.T.E.

Behind the scenes *'Glenroe'*, R.T.E..

Some students have to overcome great handicap in order to learn. Such a one is Christopher Nolan. He suffered severe brain damage at birth and is unable to speak or walk as a result. Indeed he has hardly any control over the muscles of his body.

Yet with the aid of a 'Unicorn' stick strapped to his forehead and with his mother supporting his chin in her hands he wrote his autobiography, laboriously tapping it out letter by letter. It is called *Under the Eye of the Clock*. Here is an extract about his first school, the Central Remedial Clinic, Dublin where all the students have some form of handicap. He calls himself 'Joseph' here.

# Under the Eye of the Clock

*Christopher Nolan*

Making fun for the class became the custom and on this particular day handsome Eamonn Campbell donned the comic's robe. He let the air out of the tyres of the two wheels of Joseph's wheelchair. Then he defied Joseph to be able to tell the teacher. Miss Ryan entered the classroom after coffee-break and determined not to fail, Joseph set about making his complaint. He peddled furiously on the footrest of his chair in order to catch her attention. She glanced down at Joseph. He peddled more furiously building up to a great crescendo while at the same time keeping a wary eye on her face. She frowned and then an enquiring look lit up her face. Joseph then caught her gaze and with his eyes drew her sight downwards to his flat-rimmed wheel. He repeated his sweeping eye course until she walked down to stand before him and to look closely into his eyes. He drew her eyes downwards to his wheels. 'What's wrong, Joseph, is something wrong with your chair?' she asked. He nodded his offended nod and she glanced hard at his wheel. 'Oh you've got a puncture,' she said. Joseph looked into her face and swung her gaze to the other wheel.

Keeping his head turned towards the other wheel she walked around to the other side of his chair. 'Oh, someone let the air out of your wheels,' she observed. 'Who did that?' she demanded, but Joseph jumped into action and nodded accusingly at Eamonn. Eamonn denied having had anything to do with Joseph's wheelchair. 'Right,' said Miss Ryan, 'we'll have a trial by jury. A courtroom hearing we'll have, and I'll be the judge. The hearing got underway; the plaintiff was Joseph, the defendant was Eamonn; eyewitnesses were called to give evidence and the rigged jury were unable to give a unanimous verdict, so a split decision was sure to please both sides. The judge then rapped out her attention to order and with a gleam in her eye she quashed the sitting and asked the accuser and the accused to shake hands. Eamonn walked swiftly to Joseph's side and bending down he grasped his accuser's hand and shook it warmly. Then turning to Miss Ryan he suggested that he'd go in search of a pump to inflate the flat tyres for Joseph. From that day forward Eamonn claimed Joseph among his normal friends.

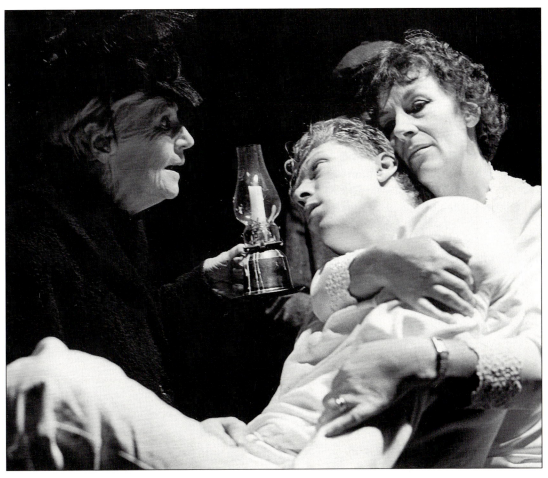

A moment from *'Torchlight and Laser beams'*, the stage version of Christopher Nolan's book.

## WRITTEN EXERCISES

*1. In your own words, very briefly describe what happened in the classroom, in this extract.*

*2. Make a list of all the new words and phrases you learned from this extract. Indicate which words were nouns and which were adjectives.*

## DISCUSSION

*In your groups, discuss the extract. What did you learn about handicapped pupils from it?*

## REPORT BACK

## P R O J E C T

Working in groups, research, write up and present a project on 'SCHOOL THROUGH THE AGES'. Here are some suggested headings but you can use others.

The first alphabet—early writing—the life of a scribe.

The Greeks—going to school in Athens and Sparta.

The Romans—what was a boy taught? What did girls learn?

The Celts, druids, fili, etc.—memory work.

The medieval monk—the work of the scriptorium—the important languages then were Latin and Greek.

The Renaissance scholar—read in your own language—the invention of printing.

Irish hedge schools—what was taught, how much did it cost? (Extract from Translations by Brian Friel).

The first dictionaries.

Nineteenth century schools in Ireland and Britain (Ch. 2 of Hard Times by Charles Dickens).

What do we learn today?

## R E V I S I O N

*TEST YOURSELF SECTION*

*1. Describe each of the following terms briefly (2 or 3 sentences):*

| | | |
|---|---|---|
| STORY | SERIES | DIARY |
| CHARACTER | SERIAL | DIALOGUE |
| PLOT | EPISODE | DRAMA |
| THEME | SOAP | |
| CLIMAX | | |

**2.** *Vocabulary: Can you remember the meaning of each of the following words? You met them all.*

| | | | |
|---|---|---|---|
| *TIMID* | *TOWERING* | *SEPARATED* | *CUSTOM* |
| *BARMY* | *'SNAP'* | *CONSISTED* | *COMPLAINT* |
| *AQUARIUM* | *CRUMPLED* | *APPREHENSIVE* | *CRESCENDO* |
| *NIMBLE* | *OBJECTION* | *RESTRAINED* | *PLAINTIFF* |
| *LETHAL* | *OCCASIONAL* | *SCANNED* | *DEFENDANT* |
| *CURRICULUM* | *OPTIONAL* | *PUNCTUATED* | *UNANIMOUS* |
| *VAULT* | *COMPENSATED* | *INQUISITIVE* | *VERDICT* |
| *POTENTIAL* | *FACILITATE* | *SULLENLY* | *INFLATE* |
| *PARLANCE* | *ENTHUSIASTIC* | *CHALLENGE* | *ACCUSER* |
| *TWILIGHT* | *POPULAR* | *TENSION* | *CONCERNED* |

**3. a.** *Write out the nouns in the following sentences:*
*When the lifeboat had been swung out, the captain came down from the bridge.*
*A sailor grabbed my mother's hand and helped her in.*
  **b.** *Pick out the verbs:*
*I saw my mother near me and yelled to her.*
*Then something hit me from above.*
*They dragged and pushed each other behind a tree while the great dark shape thudded into the lorry.*
  **c.** *Write out the adverbs in this sentence:*
*He was flung violently from the saddle and fell heavily to the road.*
  **d.** *Which are the adjectives here?*
*I sat in the cold room, sipping tepid tea, while gazing at the blue wallpaper.*
  **e.** *Which are the pronouns here?*
*Is he?' said a voice from the throng.*
*Is that why you don't want to know us any more?'*
  **4.** *Rewrite the following passage, dividing it into three paragraphs.*

In September 1925, when I was just nine, I set out on the first great adventure of my life—boarding-school. My mother had chosen for me a Prep School in a part of England which was as near as it could possibly be to our home in South Wales, and it was called St Peter's. The full postal address was St Peter's School, Weston-super-Mare, Somerset. Weston-super-Mare is a slightly seedy seaside resort with a vast sandy beach, a tremendous long pier, an esplanade running along the sea-front, a clutter of hotels and boarding-houses, and about ten thousand little shops selling buckets and spades and sticks of rock and ice-creams. It lies almost directly across the Bristol Channel from Cardiff, and on a clear day you can stand on the esplanade at Weston and look across the fifteen or so miles of water and see the coast of Wales lying pale and milky on the horizon. On those days the easiest way to travel from Cardiff to Weston-super-Mare was by boat. Those boats were beautiful. They were paddle-steamers, with gigantic swishing paddle-wheels on their flanks, and the wheels made the most terrific noise as they sloshed and churned through the water.

(from BOY by Roald Dahl)

# O R A L

*5. Prepare a one-minute or a two-minute speech on any of the following:*
*The value of school uniforms*
*The problem of school uniforms*
*All boys should study cookery*
*My favourite book*
*A poem I read*
*A view I like*
*My favourite time of day*
*A one-minute story*
*Schools should be abolished*
*An incident I witnessed*
*6. Aural: Listen to the speeches. What were the main points in each?*

## DEAR EXAMINER

Thank you so much for your questions
I've read them all carefully through
But there isn't a single one of them
That I know the answer to.

I've written my name as instructed,
Put the year, the month and the day
But after I'd finished doing that
I had nothing further to say.

So I thought I'd write you a letter
Fairly informally
About what's going on in the classroom
And what it's like to be me.

Mandy has written ten pages
But it's probably frightful guff
And Angela Smythe is copying
The answers off her cuff.

Miss Quinlan is marking our homework
The clock keeps ticking away
For anyone not in this classroom
It's just another day.

Mother's buying groceries
Grandmother's drinking tea
Unemployed men doing crosswords
Or watching 'Crown Court' on TV.

The drizzle has finally stopped here
The sun's just started to shine
And in a back garden in Sefton Road
A housewife hangs shirts on the line.

A class chatters by to play tennis
The cathedral clock has just pealed
A motor chugs steadily back and forth
Mowing the hockey field.

Miss Quinlan's just seen what I've written
Her face is an absolute mask
Before she collects in the papers
I have one little favour to ask.

I thought your questions were lovely
There's only myself to blame
But couldn't you give me something
For writing the date and my name?

*Gareth Owen*

# UNIT 2
## POETRY

# Introducing Poetry

There are many ways of enjoying poetry. You can read it for the story, if it is a narrative poem. Some poems you can read aloud and just enjoy the sounds of the words. You might study a few poems in some detail, discover how the poet constructed them, examine his choice of words, etc. and so enjoy the secret of the poet's craftsmanship. Or you may just wish to close your eyes and enjoy the colourful pictures or images the poet paints for us.

> **IMAGE**: An image is a mental picture which the poet creates for us with his words. It is usually very clear or vivid and we can easily imagine it if we close our eyes. We find a lot of images in poetry. This is why it is often more colourful than other forms of writing.

Here is a poem with many interesting images. Read it silently a number of times. Use your dictionary to find the meanings of any difficult words and write them into your Word Copy.

### THE TOMCAT

At midnight in the alley
A tomcat comes to wail,
And he chants the hate of a million years
As he swings his snaky tail.

Malevolent, bony, brindled,
Tiger and devil and bard,
His eyes are coals from the middle of hell
And his heart is black and hard.

He twists and crouches and capers
And bares his curved sharp claws,
And he sings to the stars of the jungle nights
Ere cities were, or laws.

59

Beast from a world primeval,
He and his leaping clan,
When the blotched red moon leers over the roofs,
Give voice to their scorn of man.

He will lie on a rug tomorrow
And lick his silky fur,
And veil the brute in his yellow eyes,
And play he's tame, and purr.

But at midnight in the alley
He will crouch again and wail,
And beat the time for his demon's song
With the swing of his demon's tail.

*Don Marquis*

# E X E R C I S E S

*1. After your teacher has read it aloud, try a dramatic choral reading. Each row should take a verse and read it aloud together. Decide which picture or image you want to stress in your dramatic reading. Do it a number of times until you think you have it nearly right.*

*2. Individually, decide which images or pictures you like best and why.*

*For example: What idea of the cat do we get from the image, 'As he swings his snaky tail'.*

*What does the image, 'the blotched red moon leers over the roofs', suggest to you?*

*Examine the other images.*

*3. Pick out the adjectives. What do they add to the images?*

*4. List the verbs used to describe the actions of the cat. Discuss how effective they are.*

> METAPHOR:  A metaphor is a type of image where two different things are compared, without using the words 'like', 'as' or 'than'. Example: 'His eyes are coals from the middle of hell'.  This image is made more colourful and interesting by the comparison between the cat's shiny eyes and the glowing coals from hell.  As well as describing colour it suggests something evil about the cat.

*5. Do you notice any other interesting metaphors in the poem?  Discuss what they suggest.*

*6. Listen to an extract from the musical, Cats. What words does it suggest which might be used to describe cats? Make a personal list—then share it with the class. Your teacher may wish to add other words. Add the new words to your own list.*

*7. Using appropriate images, write a colourful description of any animal you have seen or read about.*

*8. Listen to 'Macavity: the Mystery Cat', a poem by T.S. Eliot. Barry McGovern reads it on Inter. Cert. English course 1988 tape, produced by Paycock publications. Or read 'The Cat' by Gareth Owens, from 'Salford Road and Other Poems', published by Collins Young Lions.*

*9. PUBLIC SPEAKING: Working in groups, do some research on a wide variety of PETS. Each individual should then present some aspect of this to the whole class. Speeches could be 1, 2 or 3 minutes long—agree a common length.*

# H I N T S

*1. Plan well—think in paragraphs so that one point follows from another.*

*2. Think and write in pictures or images—it is easier for your listeners to remember an image or a good example.*

*3. Have a good opening to get their attention.*

*4. Write out your speech in full—approximately 120 words per minute. Then put the main points on a card, to prompt you if you forget.*

*5. Speak clearly and slowly—make certain you can be heard by all. But avoid a monotone. It is more effective to vary the level of your voice.*

*6. Look at your listeners—make eye contact. Try to avoid reading it all.*

*10. DEBATE: Read Seamus Heaney's poem 'The Early Purges' (page 118) which deals with country people's more practical unromantic attitude to animals. Read some short articles on blood sports such as coursing or bullfighting. Then hold a debate on some aspect of Animal Rights. Organise it formally with Chairperson, Timekeeper, two teams, etc. (see Hints for Debating, page 189).*

# POETRY NOTICE

One of the ways in which a poem differs from other forms of writing is that it gets its meaning across in images or pictures rather than in sentences. So forget all you have been taught about full stops, capital letters, subjects, predicates, proper sentences!

Think in **VERBAL PICTURES.** For example in a famous poem about a Highwayman, the road at night is described as 'a ribbon of moonlight'. This suggests a long winding narrow road, shimmering in the moonlight. By implication there is dark and danger on either side. It also might suggest that there is a long way to go to reach safety. Or it might suggest that the highwayman was thinking of his girlfriend as ribbons are normally associated with girls' hair. The poet suggested all this in four words rather than four lines!

> **SIMILE:** There is another kind of verbal picture or image, where the comparison is made very simply by using the words 'like', 'as' or 'than'. This is called a SIMILE.
>
> **Example:** 'I tossed a boot at the wailing cat and he shot off like a bat out of hell.'

# E X E R C I S E S

*1. Complete the following similes:*
*He felt a blow on his back like ...*
*The car hit the oily patch and whirled around as though ...*
*The teacher charged in the door like ...*
*When she saw the present her face lit up like ...*
*'That one is as tough as ...'*
*2. Have a simile competition to describe some of the following: a telephone; a lamp post; a chimney on fire; the road at night; a toothache; a penguin; an elephant; a giraffe; lunch hour; the sound of the school bell.*
*3. Study the following pairs of sentences. One sentence is just a factual statement, the other compares two things. Which sentence contains the metaphor in each case? Say what the metaphor suggests to you.*
*a. The lake was frozen at that time of year.*
*b. The girl froze in her tracks when she saw the Headmistress come into the disco.*

*a. The hawk was circling overhead.*
*b. That teacher has the eyes of a hawk.*

*a.* '*Did you iron out that problem yet?*'
*b.* '*I've just finished ironing that shirt, ya eejit!*'

*a.* *The truth has just dawned on me.*
*b.* *The dawn brightened up that sombre room.*

*a.* *The water from the pipe flowed down the walls.*
*b.* *All the stored-up anger just flowed out of him.*
*4. Create metaphors to describe:*
*a scarecrow • a tree covered in snow • the shock of a plunge into the cold sea.*
*a mouth watering smell • an eerie sound • wild happiness • fear •*
*surprise • relief.*

# Write Your Own Poetry

Everyone can write poetry.
Try some **ONE LINE METAPHOR POEMS.**

Hunger is a cave echoing inside me.

Wind is the singing of the trees.

Monday is ...

Summer is ...

Happiness is ...

Poetry is ...

Failure is ...

Swimming is ...

Night is ...

Saturday mornings are ...

Empty corridors are ...

Nightmares are ...

Or you could try some **RIDDLE POEMS.** First read
these poems by James Reeves and then try some two-line
(couplet) riddle poems. Don't worry about the rhyme.

## THE WIND

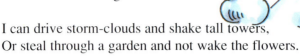

I can get through a doorway without any key,
And strip the leaves from the great oak tree.

I can drive storm-clouds and shake tall towers,
Or steal through a garden and not wake the flowers.

Seas I can move and ships I can sink;
I can carry a house-top or the scent of a pink.

When I am angry I can rave and riot;
And when I am spent, I lie quiet as quiet.

## S P E L L S

I dance and dance without any feet—
This is the spell of the ripening wheat.

With never a tongue I've a tale to tell—
This is the meadow-grasses' spell.

I give you health without any fee—
This is the spell of the apple-tree.

I rhyme and riddle without any book—
This is the spell of the bubbling brook.

Without any legs I run for ever—
This is the spell of the mighty river.

I fall for ever and not at all—
This is the spell of the waterfall.

Without a voice I roar aloud—
This is the spell of the thunder-cloud.

No button or seam has my white coat—
This is the spell of the leaping goat.

I can cheat strangers with never a word—
This is the spell of the cuckoo-bird.

We have tongues in plenty but speak no names—
This is the spell of the fiery flames.

The creaking door has a spell to riddle—
I play a tune without any fiddle.

You could try some **ADVERB POEMS.**

First read 'Slowly' by James Reeves and then try some 'Swiftly', 'Quietly' or other adverb poems.

### SLOWLY

Slowly the tide creeps up the sand,
Slowly the shadows cross the land.
Slowly the cart-horse pulls his mile,
Slowly the old man mounts the stile.

Slowly the hands move round the clock,
Slowly the dew dries on the dock.
Slow is the snail—but slowest of all
The green moss spreads on the old brick wall.

You can have great fun with ACROSTIC POEMS. First you write the word down the side and then the poem grows out from that. For example:

**P**oetry is
**O**bservisng the
**E**legant
**T**ree
**R**ippling in the wind
**Y**onder.

**Or**

**P**oetry class is
**O**ver for this
**E**vening
**T**hanks a lot
**R**umbled the
**Y**oung students.

Try some acrostic poems on these words:
ACROBAT, DAWN, DUSTBIN, FALLING, HOLI-DAYS, HOUSES, MUSHROOMS, RARE, SCHOOL, etc.

> Sometimes the poet tries to get a run of words all beginning with the same letter, in order to create a musical sound effect. This is called ALLITERATION.

There are many examples in the poem below. I particularly like 'Nervous Knots of Newcomers' and 'Scrumptious Sizzling Sausages Sighing to be Swallowed'. Which one do you prefer? Why?

## SCHOOL

Schoolboys scamper with smiling shining faces.
Girls in groups gape and gossip at the gate.
Nervous knots of newcomers.
Big books bulge in brown bags.
Car doors clash and clank and clatter.
Bells bring boys bustling, banging, bothering, bouncing.
Girls go grumbling and groaning along gangways.
Action at Assembly.
Crowds come clamouring into classsrooms.
Girls go and group for games.
Boys battle bravely with boredom.
In Maths some mutter in misery.
Slowly silence settles in school.
Bells bleat for dinner-break.
Great the galloping and gallumphing.
Grace ungracefully groaned.
Scrumptious sizzling sausages sighing to be swallowed.
Slurping and sloshing and slopping.
Great guzzling and greedy galloping.

*Janet, Paul and Christine*
*aged 12*

Now, using appropriate alliteration, write *a line* about each of these: music, sunshine, cold, school lunch, your favourite food, a sport you enjoy, the sea, sisters, brothers, an animal you like, or any other.

## THE HAIKU

This is a Japanese form of poetry, where the writer tries to capture the mood of something in THREE short lines. The first and third lines should have five syllables and the second line should have seven. (Remember a syllable is the smallest unit of sound in a word. See dictionary section page 251.) Here is a haiku by Ian Serraillier, about a mountain. Read it and check the syllables.

Alone I cling to
The freezing mountain and see
White cloud—below me.

These are some haikus about Christmas by Wes Magee.

## THE CHRISTMAS HAIKU

*A Candle*
That feather of flame
melting the window's ice skin
guides us through the night.

*New Star*
Atop the church spire
one hundred coloured bulbs flash
Christmas news in morse.

*Christmas Bells*
Urgent, they call us
across fields to a barn where
cows, a donkey stand.

*Holly Sprig*
Berries like blood drops,
and green leaves that remind us
Spring sleeps beyond the hill.

*Robin*
As heavy snow falls
he's a red-vested Batman
on the garden fence.

Now try it for yourself.  Write some haikus suggested by
the following photographs.

Here are other suggestions for themes:
Watching sunrise alone  •  Autumn evening  •  Church bells
A tree sways in the wind at midnight  •  A baby cries  •
The sound of a footstep on gravel  •  The first snowflakes  •
A stranded jellyfish  •  A football match lost  •  The new calf

Or on anything you like—remember to catch one simple
idea in your poem.
Read your work aloud.  Revise and print it out carefully
for display on the notice board.


## THE LIMERICK

The limerick too is fairly easy to compose.  Some of these you will have heard
already.

There was an old man of Nantucket
Who kept all his cash in a bucket;
    But his daughter named Nan,
    Ran away with a man,
And as for the bucket, Nantucket.

A thrifty yound fellow of Shoreham
Made brown paper trousers and woreham
    He looked nice and neat
    Till he bent in the street
To pick up a pin; then he toreham.

A chemistry student from Gillingham
Kept emptying jam jars and filling 'em
    With a poisonous jelly
    That was bright green and smelly
So he used it on teachers for killing 'em.

The cautious collapsible cow
Gives milk by the sweat of her brow;
    Then under the trees
    She folds her front knees
And sinks fore and aft with a bow.

I sat next to the Duchess at tea
It was just as I feared it would be
    Her rumblings abdominal
    Were truly phenomenal
And everyone thought it was me.

A tutor who taught on the flute
Tried to teach two young tooters to toot
　　Said the two to the tutor,
　　'Is it harder to toot, or
To tutor two young tooters to toot?

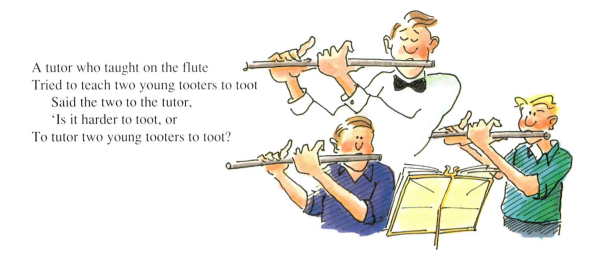

Now what in the world shall we dioux
With the bloody and murderous Sioux
　　Who some time ago
　　Took an arrow and bow
And raised such a hellabelioux?

The poet Edward Lear was famous for his limericks. Here is one from his 'A book of Nonsense':

There was an Old Man with a beard,
Who said, 'It is just as I feared—
　　Two Owls and and a Hen
　　Four Larks and a Wren,
Have all built their nests in my beard!

There are even limericks about limericks.

There once was an artist named Lear
Who wrote verses to make children cheer.
　　Though they never made sense,
　　Their success was immense,
And the Queen thought that Lear was a dear.

The līmerick is fūrtive and mēan;　　a
You must kēep her in closē quarantīne,　　a
　　Or she snēaks to the slūms　　b
　　And prōmptly becōmes　　b
Disōrderly, drūnk and obscēne.　　a

**NOTICE:**

**1. RHYME:** The 1st, 2nd and 5th lines all end with the same rhyming sound.

Lines 3 and 4 end with another rhyming sound. So if we call the 1st line 'a' we have a rhyming scheme of a, a, b, b, a.

**2. RHYTHM:** You will have noticed from your dictionary work that some syllables are stressed or accented and many more left unstressed, as we speak and pronounce the words. The stressed syllable is usually marked — and the unstressed ˘ or left unmarked. So we pronounce these words: LĪM/ĔR/ĬCK; COM/PŌSE; DĬC/TĬŎN/ĂR/Ў; IMM/ĒNSE.

So in a line of poetry or a limerick there will be a number of stressed sounds. If this is regular it is called RHYTHM, as it sets up a regular beat or rhythm. In a limerick we often find three stresses in the 1st, 2nd and 5th lines and two stresses in each of the 3rd and 4th lines. Look at the letters beside the last limerick.

# E X E R C I S E S

*1. See if you can find the rhythm in the other limericks.*
*2. Have a limerick competition in your class.*
*(Remember: compose your own and they must be laundered—clean!)*
*Here are some first lines if you want a push start.*
*There once was a gnu in a zoo ...*
*There was a young girl called Sue ...*
*I'd rather have fingers than toes ...*
*A poodle was charged by the law ...*
*The was a fat lady of Clyde ...*
*Or perhaps you feel like the writer in this poem:*

## POEM ABOUT WRITING A POEM

'Write a poem,' she says
'About anything you like.'
You can practically feel the class all thinking,
'On your blooming bike!'
A poem! I'll tell you one thing:
Mine's not going to rhyme.
A poem between now and playtime!
There's not the time.
In half an hour she'll say,
'Have you done? Hand papers in
And go out.'
I mean, does she have the slightest idea
What writing a poem's about?
I mean, it's agony:
It's scribbling thoughts
And looking for rhymes
And ways to end and begin;
And giving it up in total despair—
'I'm chucking it in the bin.'
But tomorrow it pulls you back again,
And hey, a bit of it clicks!
And you sweat with the words
But it's hopeless again
And it sticks.
And you put it away for ever ...

But it nags away in the back of your head
And the bits of it buzz and roam,
And maybe—about a century later—
You've got a kind of a poem.

*Eric Finney*

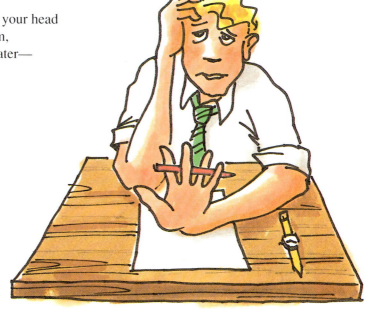

# More About Poetry

## Narrative Poetry

'Narrative poetry' is the term used to describe poetry which tells a story. There are many types of narrative poems such as: the ballad; the allegory; the epic; and others.

Here we are going to look at some BALLADS. The ballad was one of the earliest forms of story-poem. Many of these early ballads handed down to us are anonymous and were spoken or sung rather than written down. In the nineteenth and twentieth centuries many poets adapted and developed the ballad in written form. Now, of course, there are also many modern sung ballads.

Most ballads have a number of common characteristics:

**a** They are narratives. In other words, they tell a story which is usually very dramatic and gripping.

**b** The most common themes are DEATH, LOVE and WAR.

**c** The language is usually simple and they are often written in simple four-line stanzas.

**d** The descriptions are often very colourful, with striking images.

**e** The lines rhyme and the poem usually has a lively beat or rhythm to carry the story along at a good pace.

**f** There is often dramatic dialogue.

**g** Sometimes there is a repeated refrain or chorus.

## LORD ULLIN'S DAUGHTER

A chieftain to the Highlands bound
Cries 'Boatman, do not tarry!
And I'll give thee a silver pound
To row us o'er the ferry!'

'Now who be ye, would cross Lockgyle
This dark and stormy water?'
'O, I'm the chief of Ulva's isle,
And this, Lord Ullin's daughter.

'And fast before her father's men
Three days we've fled together,
For should he find us in the glen,
My blood would stain the heather.

'His horsemen hard behind us ride—
Should they our steps discover,
Then who will cheer my bonny bride
When they have slain her lover?'

Out spoke the hardy Highland wight,
'I'll go, my chief, I'm ready:
It is not for your silver bright,
But for your winsome lady:—

'And by my word! the bonny bird
In danger shall not tarry;
So though the waves are raging white
I'll row you o'er the ferry.'

By this the storm grew loud apace
The water-wraith was shrieking;
And in the scowl of heaven each face
Grew dark as they were speaking.

But still as wilder blew the wind
And as the night grew drearer,
Adown the glen rode armèd men,
Their trampling sounded nearer.

'O haste thee, haste!' the lady cries,
'Though tempests round us gather;
I'll meet the raging of the skies,
But not an angry father.'

The boat has left a stormy land,
A stormy sea before her,—
When, O! too strong for human hand
The tempest gather'd o'er her.

And still they row'd amidst the roar
Of waters fast prevailing:
Lord Ullin reach'd that fatal shore,—
His wrath was changed to wailing.

For, sore dismay'd, through storm and shade
His child he did discover:—
One lovely hand she stretch'd for aid,
And one was round her lover.

'Come back! come back!' he cried in grief
'Across this stormy water:
And I'll forgive your Highland chief,
My daughter!—O my daughter!'

'Twas vain: the loud waves lash'd the shore,
Return or aid preventing:
The waters wild went o'er his child,
And he was left lamenting.

*Thomas Campbell*

## GLOSSARY OF ARCHAIC WORDS

Stanza 1:  tarry—delay

Stanza 4:  bonny—beautiful

Stanza 5:  wight (pronounced 'wite')—person

winsome—delightful

Stanza 7:  apace—swiftly

water-wraith—water spirit

Stanza 8:  drearer—more gloomy

Stanza 12: sore—painfully

## EXERCISES

**Drama (for groups)**
*1. In your group choose a scene from the poem and compose a tableau or sculpture to represent it. Explain your work.*
*2. Prepare for a dramatic recital of the poem, to be delivered without a text.*

## OTHER EXERCISES

*3. What images are the most striking and why?*
*4. What are your favourite lines and why?*
*5. Can you beat out the stresses or rhythm of the lines? What effect does this have?*
*6. Write the story from the father's point of view.*

## Correct Writing—Dialogue

**NOTE:** Only the exact speech which comes out of a person's mouth is put in inverted commas.

**Example:** 'Come back!  Come back!' he cried in grief.

It begins with a capital letter and ends with a comma, full stop, question mark or exclamation mark, depending on the sentence.

Dialogue should say something important, express a deep feeling or new idea or advance the plot of the story.  Try to avoid writing empty filler phrases.

## E X E R C I S E S

*(for Pairs)*

*1. Script the conversation that might have occurred between Lord Ullin's daughter and her chieftain lover as they fled through the heather to the lochside.*

*2. Write the conversation, as you imagine it, between the father and the commander of his armed escort as they ride wearily homeward.  (You can use modern English words.)*

*3. Record a radio interview between a reporter and an observer of the tragic scene.*

### The Wreck of the Hesperus

It was the schooner Hesperus,
    That sailed the wintry sea;
And the skipper had taken his little daughter,
    To bear him company.

Blue were her eyes as the fairy-flax,
    Her cheeks like the dawn of day,
And her bosom white as the hawthorn buds
    That ope in the month of May.

The skipper he stood beside the helm,
    His pipe was in his mouth,
And he watched how the veering flaw did blow
    The smoke now West, now South.

Then up and spake an old Sailor,
    Had sailed the Spanish Main,
'I pray thee, put into yonder port,
    For I fear a hurricane.

'Last night the moon had a golden ring,
    And to-night no moon we see!'
The skipper he blew a whiff from his pipe,
    And a scornful laugh laughed he.

Colder and colder blew the wind,
    A gale from the North-east;
The snow fell hissing in the brine,
    And the billows frothed like yeast.

Down came the storm, and smote amain,
    The vessel in its strength;
She shuddered and paused, like a frightened steed,
    Then leaped her cable's length.

'Come hither! come hither! my little daughter,
    And do not tremble so;
For I can weather the roughest gale,
    That ever wind did blow.'

He wrapped her warm in his seaman's coat
    Against the stinging blast;
He cut a rope from a broken spar,
    And bound her to the mast.

'O father! I hear the churchbells ring,
    O say, what may it be?'
'Tis a fog-bell on a rock-bound coast!'—
    And he steered for the open sea.

'O father! I hear the sound of guns,
    O say, what may it be?'
'Some ship in distress, that cannot live
    In such an angry sea!'

'O father! I see a gleaming light,
    O say, what may it be?'
But the father answered never a word,
    A frozen corpse was he.

Lashed to the helm, all stiff and stark,
    With his face turned to the skies,
The lantern gleamed through the gleaming snow
    On his fixed and glassy eyes.

Then the maiden clasped her hands and prayed
    That savèd she might be;
And she thought of Christ, who stilled the wave,
    On the Lake of Galilee.

And fast through the midnight dark and drear,
    Through the whistling sleet and snow,
Like a sheeted ghost, the vessel swept
    Towards the reef of Norman's Woe.

And ever the fitful gusts between
    A sound came from the land;
It was the sound of the trampling surf,
    On the rocks and the hard sea-sand.

The breakers were right beneath her bows,
    She drifted a dreary wreck,
And a whooping billow swept the crew
    Like icicles from her deck.

She struck where the white and fleecy waves
    Looked soft as carded wool,
But the cruel rocks, they gored her side
    Like the horns of an angry bull.

Her rattling shrouds, all sheathed in ice,
    With the masts went by the board;
Like a vessel of glass, she stove and sank,
    Ho! ho! the breakers roared!

At daybreak, on the bleak sea-beach,
    A fisherman stood aghast,
To see the form of a maiden fair,
    Lashed close to a drifting mast.

The salt sea was frozen on her breast,
    The salt tears in her eyes;
And he saw her hair, like the brown sea-weed,
    On the billows fall and rise.

Such was the wreck of the Hesperus,
    In the midnight and the snow!
Christ save us all from a death like this
    On the reef of Norman's Woe!

*Henry Wadsworth Longfellow*

## GLOSSARY OF ARCHAIC WORDS

Stanza 2:    ope—open
Stanza 3:    flaw—a sudden gust
Stanza 4:    spake—spoke
Stanza 6:    billows—great waves
Stanza 7:    smote—struck
             amain—violently
Stanza 13:   stark—hard
Stanza 15:   drear—dreary or gloomy

# E X E R C I S E S

*1. Listen to the poem, read by your teacher. See if you can get the gist of it on a first hearing. Then read it yourself using the glossary and your dictionary to find the difficult meanings. Write them into your Word Copy.*

*2. You may need to hear it read aloud a number of times.*

*3. Pick out about ten lines that seem to you to describe the storm best and write them into your copy. They can be single lines here and there, if you wish. Learn them and prepare to recite them to the class. Exaggerate the sounds of the words so that you can almost hear the sea.*

**Example:** *'The snow fell hissing in the brine,*
*And the billows frothed like yeast.'*

*hissing—the sound of the word helps you understand the meaning.*
*billows—the sound of the word suggests a great bulge, like the wave it is.*
*the stinging blast—blast is a sharp explosive sound, and that is also what it means.*

> *This is a trick poets use to get the sound of something across . It is called ONO-MATOPOEIA—where the sound of the word is similar to the meaning of the word. If you want to use this word as an adjective you say it is 'onomatopoeic.'*

*So bring out all the onomatopeia when you say the poem aloud.*

*4. Did you notice how the poet made his descriptions more colourful by using comparisons in his images.?*

> *These are straight forward comparisons, using the words 'like' or 'as' and they are called SIMILES.*
> *Example: 'But the cruel rocks, they gored her side*
> *Like the horns of an angry bull.'*

*Pick out any other similes you thought were particularly good and say why.*

*5. Make a list of all the technical or special words about the sea, ships and sailing which you find in the poem. Write in the exact meanings. Have a class discussion and see if you can add to your list.*

*6. Then write a brief, concise and accurate report of the sinking as if you were an onlooker from a cliff. Your testimony might be valuable in a court case about salvage rights or insurance so get the sequence of events correct.*

*7. Have a discussion or debate on: 'The need for care in the water.' Prepare 2 or 3 minute statements.*

*8. Learn some sections of the ballad so that you can recite it, dramatically.*

*9. Listen to extracts from 'The Brendan Voyage'—an orchestral suite for uilleann pipes, composed by Shaun Davey and played by Liam O'Flynn. Choose an extract, or any other appropriate piece of music, which you think most suitable to use as background music to the ballad.*

*10. Stage a final dramatic reading, with background music. Record it.*

## NOTICE—SOUNDS IN POETRY

**1.** We saw already how ONOMATOPOEIA works. Now practise on your own. Can you find appropriate and imaginative onomatopoeic words for the following expressions.

The drip drop of the leaking tap

the ticking of the clock

the ruggedness of the terrain

the ............. of car tyres

the ............. of the frog

the ............. of the bell

the ............. of tiny feet

the ............. of crows

the ............. of hoof beats

the ............. of the waterfall

the ............. of cymbals

the ............. of the gas catching fire

the ............. of the saw

**2.** We also saw earlier how the poet often uses ALLIT-ERATION. You remember this occurs when words following each other begin with the same letter, so that letter sound is repreated for musical effect. For example: 'Around the rugged rocks, the ragged rascal ran'.

The repeated 'r' sound is harsh, rough, and so goes well with the images of sharp rocks and torn clothes.

We also saw some examples of this in the last ballad. Look at the second stanza again:

fairy-flax; dawn of day; month of May.

What is the effect of each alliteration here?

■■■■■■■■■■■■■■■■■■■■■■■■■■■■■■■■■■■

# Real-Life Voyages

**1.** Some fantastic adventures often happen in real life also. Here is an extract from Tim Severin's book, 'The Brendan Voyage', an account of a most extraordinary but successful Atlantic crossing.

On that wind-torn evening in late May 1976, it seemed to my tired mind that the wave pattern was changing. Instead of the seventh waves,* the sea appeared to be collecting its strength in random groups of three. The leading wave of each group would come rolling down on us, steeper and steeper by the moment, until it could no longer support its own mass. Its crest toppled forward, and then came sliding down the wave front in a self-generated avalanche of foam and released energy. When it struck, the boat shuddered and faltered. The helm twisted savagely in my hand, then went slack, and we were picked up bodily and rushed forward in the grip of the white water. In that dangerous instant the gale clawed at us, striving to slew the boat sideways so that she would be parallel to the advancing wave crests. Should that happen, we were lost. Then the second or the third great wave would sweep over the vulnerable length of the hull, and each time I feared it would be the last wave my crew and I would ever face.

No one could tell us how to steer our boat through the gale. No boat quite like her had been afloat for the past thousand years or so. To a casual observer our craft looked like a floating banana; long and slim, with her tapering bow and stern curved gently upward in an odd fashion. Yet her most extraordinary feature was only apparent if one examined her closely: the boat was made of leather. Her hull was nothing more than forty-nine oxhides stitched together to form a patchwork quilt and stretched over a wooden frame. It was this thin skin, only a quarter of an inch thick, flexing and shifting as the boat moved—just like the skin over a man's ribcage—that now stood between us and the fury of the Atlantic. Watching the waves, I recalled the bleak warning of one of the world's leading authorities on leather science before we started our voyage:

'Oxhide,' he had explained in his precise, university tone, 'is very high in protein. It resembles a piece of steak, if you like. It will decompose in the same way, either quickly or

* There is a superstition among sailors that every seventh wave is the worst and does most damage in a gale.

87

slowly, depending on various factors such as the temperature, how well it has been tanned to turn it into leather, and the amount of stress imposed upon it.'

'What happens when the leather is soaking wet in sea water?' I had asked.

'Ah, well. That I'm not sure,' he replied. 'We've never been asked to test it. But leather will usually break down more quickly if it is wet, though perhaps the salt in sea water may have a pickling effect. I really don't know ...'

'And what happens in the end?'

'Just the same as if you left a piece of steak out in the air on a saucer. In time it will turn into a nasty, evil-smelling blob of jelly. Just like a rotting piece of oxhide.'

The hull's turning to jelly was now the least of my problems. The gale was showing signs of getting worse; the waves were increasing in size. They were smashing into us more violently; and if the leather hull was not strong enough, the first result would be when the thread holding the oxhides together simply ripped through the weakened hides like tearing the perforations on a cardboard packet. Then the oxhides would peel away like petals, and the wooden frame underneath would spring open like a flower in a brief moment of disintegration. Privately, I doubted it would ever come to that. Much more likely was the possibility of a capsize. Our boat had no keel beneath her to hold her steady. If one of the tumbling wave crests caught her wrong-footed, she would be sent spinning upside down, and her crew tipped into the water, where there was no hope of rescue.

Why on earth, then, were my crew and I sailing such an improbable vessel in the face

The Brendan Voyage

of a rising gale? The answer lay in the name of our strange craft: she was called Brendan in honour of the great Irish missionary, Saint Brendan, who had lived in the sixth century. Tradition said that Saint Brendan had made a voyage to America, and this astonishing claim was not just a wild fairy tale, but a recurrent theme based on authentic and well-researched Latin texts dating back at least to A.D. 800. These texts told how Saint Brendan and a party of monks had sailed to a land far across the ocean in a boat made of oxhides. Of course, if the claim was true, then Saint Brendan would have reached America almost a thousand years before Columbus and four hundred years before the Vikings. Such a notion, declared the sceptics, was harebrained. To suggest that anyone could have crossed the Atlantic in a boat made of animal skin was unthinkable, impossible, a mere fantasy, and the idea of a leather boat proved it. But the Latin texts were absolutely positive about the boat being made of leather, and they even explained how Saint Brendan and his party of monks had built this vessel. The obvious way of checking the truth of this remarkable story was to build a boat in similar fashion and then see if it would sail the Atlantic. So there we were, my crew and I, out in the ocean to test whether Saint Brendan and the Irish monks could have made an ocean voyage in a boat of leather.

# QUESTIONS

*(write the answers)*

*1. In your own words, describe the boat.*

*2. What fears did the writer have?*

*3. Explain why they were sailing in this vessel.*

*4. Use your dictionary to find the meaning of new words and write them into your Word Copy.*

*5. Write out the verbs the writer uses which you feel convey the energy of the sea best. Find SYNONYMS for them.*

*6. Look at the third sentence again. What form of comparison does the writer use to convey the force of the wave? What does it suggest?*

*7. Make NOTES to record the main points of the passage.*

*8. Read a number of examples of the 'WEATHER FORECAST' from the newspaper.*

# Correct Writing - Punctuation

### Quotation Marks

**1.** Quotation marks (inverted commas) are used to show direct speech, i.e., when you are putting down the exact words that came out of a person's mouth: -

He said, 'I will come home immediately after school.'

Never use quotation marks with reported speech: -
He said that he would come home immediately after school.

Notice that a piece of speech is usually introduced, followed, or interrupted by a phrase of explanation. It is then separated from the rest by commas: -
Ann mumbled quietly, 'When is gym class today?'
'When is gym class today?' Ann mumbled quietly.
'I'm going to pack up now,' Sheila whispered, 'before the bell goes.'

Notice that if a question mark or exclamation mark is used it is put inside the quotation marks.

**2.** Quotation marks can be used for the titles of books, plays, films, etc. but they are usually printed in italics: -
John watched 'Neighbours' but he hated 'Coronation Street'. 'The Hobbit' is a terrific book.

**3.** You can use inverted commas to highlight a humorous or an ironic word (where you mean the opposite): -
Our 'free' holiday cost us about £1,000!
Instead of going to the concert I had a really 'exciting' evening doing homework.

Notice you may have to use single and double quotation marks if you want to quote a title or something inside direct speech. This will avoid confusion: -
'Last night, we saw Michael Jackson's "Thriller" for the tenth time!' he said.

Now look again at the dialogue writing in 'The Brendan Voyage' extract.

Script the conversation that might occur between two of the voyagers' relatives, back home. (Choose a role: son, daughter, brother, sister, etc.)

Or script the 'conversation' that might occur between two dolphins following the raft.

**4.** Read this extract of information on the notorious Grainne Mhaol and record the main points in spider diagram form (see Appendix A, page 245).

# GRACE O'MALLEY 1530-1600

According to tradition, the source of most of her history, Grainne Mhaol, 'Grace of the cropped hair', was a bold and independent leader. Described as 'a most famous feminine sea captain', she is reputed to have visited Queen Elizabeth I in London and spoken to her as one queen to another.

Born probably in County Mayo, she was of noted sea roving stock and spent her childhood on the islands off the western coast of Ireland. She married twice, first to an O'Flaherty and then in 1582 to Richard Burke, chief of his clann in Mayo. After his death in 1586, she was arrested by Sir Richard Bingham and accused of plundering the Aran Islands. A gallows was prepared for her execution. She was released on a pledge from her son-in-law, Richard Burke, and when he rebelled against the English, she fled to Ulster and sought sanctuary in the O'Neill stronghold. She was unable to return owing to the loss of her ships. Once again, she was pardoned by Queen Elizabeth and went back to Connaught, dying there in abject poverty a few years later. She is buried in Clare Island, Clew Bay, County Mayo.

Grace O'Malley's Castle, Clare Island, Co.Mayo

Not all ballads end with the death of the heroine.  Read
about the wily May Colvin.

## MAY COLVIN

False Sir John with fiery heart
To court his lady came;
She was her father's only heir,
May Colvin was her name.

He courted her in bower and hall,
He wooed her every day,
Until at last he'd wrung consent
To mount and ride away.

'Go fetch me some of your father's gold
And of your mother's too;
I'll take you to a northern land,
And there I'll marry you.'

She went to her father's treasure chest,
Where all his money was kept;
She took the gold and left the silver
While he soundly slept.

Then she went to her father's stables,
Undid the bolted door;
Twelve horses, white and dapple-grey
Stood champing on the floor.

She mounted on a milk-white horse,
He chose a dapple-grey;
And only her parrot in his cage
Saw them ride away.

They came at last to a lonely cliff
Washed by the waves, and high;
The rocks below were steep and sharp,
And none could hear her cry.

'Get off your horse,' cried false Sir John,
'And see your bridal bed.
Seven wives I've thrown to the waves,
And you'll be the eighth,' he said.

'Take off, take off your shining jewels,
So costly and so brave;
For they're too precious and too fine
To throw in the salt sea wave.

'Take off, take off your silken dress,
Your stockings and satin shoes,
Take off your gloves, your coat and vest—
They are too good to lose.'

'Then turn your back on me, false Sir John,
Look at the leaves of the tree.
It is not right for a gentleman
A naked woman to see.'

Loud he laughed, as he turned his back
To look at the leaves of the tree,
She twined her arms about his waist
And threw him into the sea.

'O, reach me your hand!' cried false Sir John.
'O, help me—I shall drown!
I'll take you home to your father's house
And safely set you down.'

'You'll get no help from me, Sir John,
No help at all,' said she.
'You could not lie in a colder bed
than the one you meant for me.'

She mounted on her milk-white horse
And led the dapple-grey;
She rode till she came to her father's house
Before the break of day.

Up and spoke her pretty parrot,
'May Colvin, where have you been?
And what has become of false Sir John?
With *you* he last was seen'.

'O, hold your tongue, my pretty parrot!
Tell no tales of me;
And your cage shall be made of beaten gold
And the bars of ivory.'

Her father was lying asleep in bed.
He woke with an angry yawn:
'What is the matter, you prattling parrot?
There are still two hours till dawn.'

'The cat was scratching the door of my cage,
Tormenting me, I say.
I was calling out to May Colvin
To chase the cat away.'

*Anonymous*

## E X E R C I S E S

*1. Write the entries in May Colvin's DIARY for the day before that day and the
day after the event.*
*2. Compose some LETTERS which Sir John might have sent to May and some
replies which she might have written.*

# Correct Writing

PERSONAL LETTERS

Here are some hints:

**1.** The formal structure of a letter is shown in the illustration on page 95. Practise it.

**2.** First plan a rough draft of your letter. Remember to include all the necessary information.

**3.** Choose your words to suit the relationship between you and the person receiving the letter. For example, the greeting is usually 'Dear' but it could be 'My dear', 'Dearest', 'Darling', 'Dear Friend', etc. 'Yours sincerely' might be considered too formal for some letters, so you might vary it to: 'All the best', 'All good wishes', 'With all my love'; 'Wishing you a swift recovery', 'In haste', etc. Likewise the words and phrases you choose for the body of the letter should be appropriate to the relationship. Use your dictionary or thesaurus to help you vary the expression.

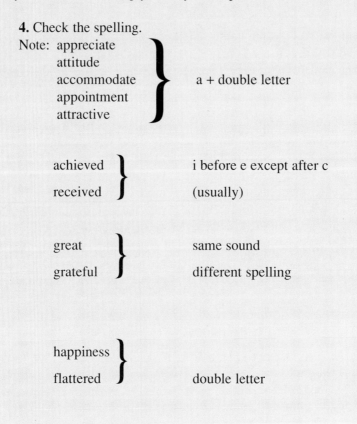

**4.** Check the spelling.

Note: appreciate
attitude
accommodate          a + double letter
appointment
attractive

achieved          i before e except after c
received          (usually)

great          same sound
grateful          different spelling

happiness
flattered          double letter

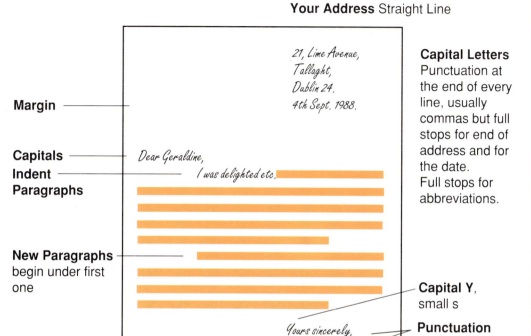

**Your Address** Straight Line

21, Lime Avenue,
Tallaght,
Dublin 24.
4th Sept. 1988.

**Margin**

**Capitals**
**Indent**
**Paragraphs**

Dear Geraldine,
I was delighted etc.

**New Paragraphs**
begin under first
one

**Signing Off**
under address

Yours sincerely,

John.

**Capital Letters**
Punctuation at
the end of every
line, usually
commas but full
stops for end of
address and for
the date.
Full stops for
abbreviations.

**Capital Y**,
small s

**Punctuation**
comma,
stop.

**Capital** for
name

Here are some words you might find useful:

| | | |
|---|---|---|
| gratitude; | special; | delighted; |
| pleasure; | choice; | remember; |
| surprised; | valuable; | memorable; |
| | rendezvous. | |

**Letter Competition**

Each student writes a letter as designated. Then, working
in groups or teams, a point will be deducted for each mistake
in an individual letter.

CORRECT WRITING CORRECT WRITING CORRECT WRITING CORRECT WRITING

# Stories and Tales

**1.** Have you heard any old stories, dramatic or strange, passed down by your grandparents or others, which sound like ballad stories? Prepare and tell one to the class.

**2.** Listen to some of the stories of a *seanchaí,* such as Eamon Kelly's 'In My Father's Time', published by Mercier Press. You will also find some strange stories in 'The Lucky Bag', a collection of stories published by Lucky Tree/O'Brien Press. 'Children of the Salmon' is an interesting collection of Irish folk tales, retold by Eileen O'Faolain and published by Poolbeg Press. 'The Shadow Cage and Other Tales of the Supernatural', by Philippa Pearse, published by Macmillan M Books, has great eerie stories.

**3.** Here is an example of the art of the *seanchaí.* Read the story and discuss the qualities which make it a good story. The extract is taken from 'Island Stories—Tales and Legends from the West', published by O'Brien Press.

# The Children of the Dead Woman

*Seán O'Sullivan*

There was a man long ago, and he was looking for a wife. He found one, but he was only a year married to her when she died, while giving birth to a child. Her mother was anxious to have the child to rear, but the father said that he would not give the child away to anybody. He would try to rear it himself. At that time, there were old women who earned their living by minding children; so the father got one of them to look after his own child. The only people in the house besides the child were this old woman and himself. He was a very strong man. Two months went by. The old woman slept in a bed beside the fire with the cradle nearby, so that she was able to attend to the child by night and by day.

One stormy evening, the father came home from his work. He took off his boots and sat beside the fire.

He took up the child, saying, 'You are doing well, my little orphan, and getting strong.'

'May God give you long life,' said he to the old woman. 'You are minding him well, to say that he is thriving so fast!'

'You don't know what I know,' replied the old woman. 'Every night since she died—at least, since I came here—that child's mother comes here. She eats some boiled potatoes and drinks some milk from the cupboard. The moment she comes in, she goes over to the cradle and kisses the child. Then she warms her hands at the fire before taking the boiled potatoes and milk from the cupboard. When she has taken some food, she comes to the cradle again, takes up the child, and feeds him at her breast. Then she washes him, puts dry clothes under him and lays him down in the cradle, kissing him. She then stands in the middle of the floor, looks up toward the room, where you are asleep, heaves a sigh, and goes out the door. She has done that every night since I came here. I see her, but I don't ask her any question.'

'Had I known that,' said the man, 'and had I seen her, I would have held her here or failed in the attempt.'

'You'll get your chance,' said the old woman. 'I will cough tonight when she comes. Have your ears open.'

That night he did not take off all of his clothes but lay on the bed, so that he would see her when she came and hold her.

Late that night, they heard the door opening. She came in and kissed the child; then she went to the cupboard, got the dish of potatoes and the naggin of milk—naggins were common vessels at that time—and ate quickly. She then stirred up the fire and warmed herself. (I'd say she was cold.) When she had warmed herself, she went to the cradle, took up the child, suckled him, washed and cleaned him, and put dry clothes under him. Then she stood in the middle of the floor and looked up toward the room. The old woman coughed, and the woman went out the door.

'Are you awake now?' asked the old woman.

'I am,' replied the man, coming down from the room.

'Did you see her?'

'I did, but I was too frightened to go near

97

her. And I thought that if I saw her at all, I'd hold her here.'

The two of them did not go to bed until it dawned. The man went next morning to the house of his wife's parents. Her three brothers were there, two of them were strong, hefty fellows, but the third was a weakling. The family welcomed him and asked him how the child was doing. He told them the child was thriving, that his mother came each night to wash and clean and suckle him.

'I saw her myself last night,' said he. 'She ate some potatoes and drank milk after attending to the child. Then she went out the door, and I was too frightened to move.'

'Bad luck to you,' said the eldest brother. 'If you saw her, you could have held her. If I were there, I'd not let her go.'

'Well, come over to me tonight then, and you'll see her,' said the husband. 'We'll see if you can hold her.'

'If I see her, I'll hold her,' said the brother.

They walked back to the house again. The old woman and the child were there. When they sat down, the dead woman's brother asked the old woman did his sister come every night. She said that she did.

'Well, if I see her tonight, I won't let her go,' said he.

Early in the night, the dead woman's husband and brother went up to the bedroom and kept watch to see if she would come. It wasn't long until they heard the door opening. Her brother saw her as well as the husband and the old woman. She went up to the fire and warmed her hands. (I suppose she was always cold.) When she had warmed herself, she went to the cupboard, took out the dish of potatoes and a naggin of milk and ate quickly. Then she went to the cradle, took up the child, and put him to her breast. She cleaned and washed him and put dry clothes under him. Then she stood in the middle of the floor, looked up toward the room, heaved a sigh, and went out.

'Are ye asleep?' asked the old woman.

'No,' they replied, as they came down from the room.

'Ye are the two most cowardly men I've ever met,' said the old woman.

(I must shorten my story for you now.) The same thing happened to the second brother.

'May the devil take ye!' said the third brother. 'If I were there, I'd hold her.'

'Bad cess to you! You're able to do nothing,' replied the two brothers.

'I'll tell ye what I can do,' said the youngest brother. 'If I saw my sister, I'd hold her and wouldn't let her go. If ye come along with me tonight , ye'll see that I'll hold her if I lay eyes on her.'

The three brothers went to the house that night. Before it was too late, they decided to go up to the bedroom. They lay down, the youngest on the outside, so that he could easily run down to the kitchen to catch his sister. It wasn't long until they heard the door opening, and in she came. They all saw her. She ran to the fire and warmed her hands. Then she went to the cupboard and took out the potatoes and milk. She seemed to be very hungry. After eating, she sat down and took the child from the cradle and put him to her breast; then she washed and cleaned him and put dry clothes under and about him.

As she put him back into the cradle, she kissed him three times. On the other nights, she had kissed him only once. She then stood up to leave. Weren't the four men great cowards that they made no move? Just then, up jumped the youngest brother, and he put his two arms around her. She screamed and begged him, for God's sake, to let her go. In the struggle, she lifted him up to the rafters, beseeching him to release her.

'I'll be killed if I'm not back in time,' she cried.

'The devil a foot will you put out of here,' said her brother.

She was dragging him about, almost killing him; so he shouted to one of his brothers to come to his assistance. The .pair of them struggled with her until she finally fell down on the floor in a dead faint. The youngest brother still kept his hold of her.

Next morning, her husband went with one of the brothers for the priest. When they came back, the priest prayed over her until ten o'clock, while her young brother held her. When she recovered her speech, she told the priest that that was to have been her last visit, as the fairies with whom she stayed were moving to Ulster that night. So she stayed with her husband and child, much the same as she had been before, except that she had a wild look in her eyes till the day she died. She bore nine sons to her husband after her rescue, and they came to be known as the children of the dead woman.

**4.** Compose a similar story or re-tell a story in prose or ballad form. Tape it. Revise it. Write a short version of it. Take great care to write the dialogue correctly.

**5.** Re-tell a well-known fairy story in as dramatic a way as possible.

**NOTE:** To read this well you need to be aware of the different kinds of RHYME. When words at the end of lines rhyme, it is called END RHYME. We met this already. But sometimes words rhyme inside the lines and this is called INTERNAL RHYME

Example: 'Now Sam Mc<u>Gee</u> was from Tennes<u>see</u>, where the cotton blooms and blows.

Why he left his <u>home</u> in the South to <u>roam</u> round the Pole God only knows.'

Only by stressing both internal and end rhyme will you get the full musical quality of this poem.

Now read it, silently first and then aloud.

## THE CREMATION OF SAM McGEE

There are strange things done in the midnight sun
    By the men who moil for gold;
The Arctic trails have their secret tales
    That would make your blood run cold;
The Northern Lights have seen queer sights,
    But the queerest they ever did see
Was that night on the marge of Lake Lebarge
    I cremated Sam McGee.

Now Sam McGee was from Tennessee, where the
    cotton blooms and blows.
Why he left his home in the South to roam round
    the Pole God only knows.
He was always cold, but the land of gold seemed
    to hold him like a spell;
Though he'd often say in his homely way that
    he'd 'sooner live in hell.'

On a Christmas Day we were mushing our way
    over the Dawson trail.
Talk of your cold! through the parka's fold it
    stabbed like a driven nail.
If our eyes we'd close, then the lashes froze, till
    sometimes we couldn't see;
It wasn't much fun, but the only one to whimper
    was Sam McGee.

And that very night as we lay packed tight in our
        robes beneath the snow,
And the dogs were fed, and the stars o'erhead
        were dancing heel and toe,
He turned to me, and, 'Cap,' says he, 'I'll cash
        in this trip, I guess;
And if I do, I'm asking that you won't refuse my
        last request.'

Well, he seemed so low that I couldn't say no:
        then he says with a sort of moan:
'It's the cursed cold, and it's got right hold till
        I'm chilled through to the bone.
Yet 'taint being dead, it's my awful dread of the
        icy grave that pains;
So I want you to swear that, foul or fair, you'll
        cremate my last remains.'

A pal's last need is a thing to heed, so I swore I
        would not fail;
And we started on at the streak of dawn, but God!
        he looked ghastly pale.
He crouched on the sleigh, and he raved all day
        of his home in Tennessee;
And before nightfall a corpse was all that was left
        of Sam McGee.

There wasn't a breath in that land of death, and
        I hurried, horror driven,
With a corpse half-hid that I couldn't get rid
        because of a promise given;
It was lashed to the sleigh, and it seemed to say:
        'You may tax your brawn and brains,
But you promised true, and it's up to you to
        cremate those last remains.'

Now a promise made is a debt unpaid, and the
        trail has its own stern code.
In the days to come, though my lips were dumb,
        in my heart how I cursed that load.
In the long, long night, by the lone firelight, while
        the huskies, round in a ring,
Howled out their woes to the homeless snows—O
        God! how I loathed the thing!

And every day that quiet clay seemed to heavy
     and heavier grow;
And on I went, though the dogs were spent and
     the grub was getting low;
The trail was bad, and I felt half mad, but I swore
     I would not give in;
And I'd often sing to the hateful thing, and it
     hearkened with a grin.

Till I came to the marge of Lake Lebarge, and a
     derelict there lay;
It was jammed in the ice, but I saw in a trice it
     was called the 'Alice May.'
And I looked at it, and I thought a bit, and I
     looked at my frozen chum:
Then, 'Here,' said I, with a sudden cry, 'is my
     cre-ma-tor-eum.'

Some planks I tore from the cabin floor, and I lit
     the boiler fire;
Some coal I found that was lying around, and I
     heaped the fuel higher;
The flames just soared, and the furnace roared—
     such a blaze you seldom see;
And I burrowed a hole in the flowing coal, and I
     stuffed in Sam McGee.

Then I made a hike, for I didn't like to hear him
     sizzle so;
And the heavens scowled, and the huskies howled,
     and the wind began to blow.
It was icy cold, but the hot sweat rolled down my
     cheeks, and I don't know why;
And the greasy smoke in an inky cloak went
     streaking down the sky.

I do not know how long in the snow I wrestled
     with grisly fear;
But the stars came out and they danced about ere
     again I ventured near;
I was sick with dread, but I bravely said: 'I'll
     just take a peep inside.
I guess he's cooked, and it's time I looked,' ...
     then the door I opened wide.

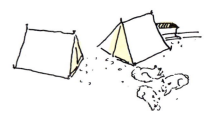

And there sat Sam, looking cool and calm, in the
    heart of the furnace roar;
And he wore a smile you could see a mile, and he
    said: 'Please close that door.
It's fine in here, but I greatly fear you'll let in the
    cold and storm—
Since I left Plumtree, down in Tennessee, it's the
    first time I've been warm.

*There are strange things done in the midnight sun*
    *By the men who moil for gold;*
*The Arctic trails have their secret tales*
    *That would make your blood run cold;*
*The Northern Lights have seen queer sights,*
    *But the queerest they ever did see*
*Was that night on the marge of Lake Lebarge*
    *I cremated Sam McGee.*

*Robert Service*

# EXERCISES

*1. In groups, prepare a DRAMATIC READING of this ballad, with different voices for characters, prologue and epilogue, etc. You might try accents if you feel confident enough. If it is good, record it.*

### 2. EPITAPHS

*Compose an epitaph for Sam McGee, to be inscribed upon his tombstone. Here are some humorous examples, to give you ideas.*

SAMUEL PEASE

Underneath this sod and beneath
these trees
Lies all that's left of Samuel Pease.
Pease ain't here,
It's just his pod;
He spilled out his soul
which flew to God.

Anon.

ARABELLA YOUNG

Here lies, returned to clay
Miss Arabela Young
Who on the first of May
Began to hold her tongue.

*Or you may wish to write a serious epitaph. One of the best known of Irish epitaphs is that of the poet W.B. Yeats.*

Cast a cold eye
On life, on death.
Horseman, pass by.

*What do you think it means? Write a similarly enigmatic one for Sam McGee.*

*3. You are his last surviving relative. Compose a notice of his death, for the newspaper. Look up some examples first.*

*4. Compose his obituary notice. Again look up some examples and examine the style of language used before attempting to write it.*

\* If you enjoyed this ballad, you might also like to read 'The Shooting of Dan Mcgrew', also by Robert Service.

\* There are many interesting novels about life in North America in the days of the pioneers. You might like to read one:

'Children of the Oregon Trail', by A.R. Van der Loeff

'Little House on the Prairie', by Laura Ingalls Wilder

'Shane', by Jack Schaefer

'White Fang', by Jack London

'Julie of the Wolves', by Jean George

## PROJECTS

**1.** Do you know any modern sung ballads? Tape one, say why you chose it and play it for the class.

**2.** Do you know any folk tales, myths or legends suitable for retelling in a dramatic way? Use the library to find a book that will help you. Here are some titles you might find useful:

'Irish Folk Tales', edited by Henry Glassie, published by Penguin.

'Irish Sagas and Folk Tales', by Eileen O Faolain, published by Poolbeg Press.

'The High Deeds of Finn MacCool', by Rosemary Sutcliff, published by Penguin (Puffin).

'Tales of Greek Heroes', by Roger Lancelyn Green, published by Penguin (Puffin).

'The Faber Book of Greek Legends', edited by Kathleen Lines.

'The Faber Book of North American Legends', edited by Virginia Haviland.

Choose your story, plan it, rehearse it in your groups and then have a DRAMATIC STORY-TELLING COMPETITION.

**3.** Choose any story or plot you think would make a good ballad. Decide on the characters and the plot. Plan it in episodes like verses. Think in images. Then attempt to write it.

Talk it over with your teacher and then rewrite it.

Have a great PUBLIC RECITATION when finished.

**4.** Write a poem about anything you like, in any style you like. don't worry about rhyme, rhythm and all that technical stuff—JUST THINK IN PICTURES.

# Find a Poem You Like

Find a poem you like. Think about it. Prepare and read it
to the class. Say why you choose it.

### SARKY DEVIL

Our teacher's all right, really,
But he can't stop making
These sarcastic remarks.

Nev Stephens, who's got no one to get him up,
Creeps in fifteen minutes late
Practically every morning—
Always with a new excuse.
And old Sarky says,
'Good evening, Stephens,
And what little piece of fiction
Have you got for us today?'

He even sarks the clever kids:
Says things like
'Proper little Brain of Britain, aren't we?'
And only yesterday when Maureen
(Who's brilliant at everything)
Complained of a headache,
He says, 'Perhaps it's the halo
Pinching a bit, Maureen.'

And then there's Bill Nelson
Who's just one of these naturally scruffy kids
Who can't keep anything clean—
Well, his homework book's a disgrace,
And Sarky holds it up
Delicately, by a corner,
At arm's length, and he says,
'Well, Lord Horatio,
Did you have your breakfast off this
Before or after the dog had a chew at it?'
Even the one who's getting sarked
Laughs—
Can't do much else, really;

And the rest of the class
Roars, of course,
And feels like one big creep.

It's a good job we understand
Old Sarky.

*Eric Finney*

## SCHOOL IN THE HOLIDAYS

A week of holiday reconciling me to work
I go up to school for the necessary books
And find the cleaning ladies in their jumble sale buys
Have established depots of buckets and bins
That the boys not there do not kick over
Along the corridor and the caretaker has reeled
Eels of flex out from the power points to the floor-polishers.
In my own classroom the portraits I have stood for
In felt-tipped pen and ink have been washed off
The wooden pages of desks towards the back:
Who was the Mary so many boys loved last term
And who wrote 'I hate Sir' and 'I love me'?
'They ought to have detention,' one lady says.
'And clean up the muck they've made,' wishing herself
Out of a job now she has everything
Spick as a sick room.  But what are they doing now?

Reading comics in bare feet in front of the fire
And letting their sisters go the errands, I should think.
Covering the carpet with records of pop
Like overlapping lilies on a pond
And behaving in some way or other like little men.

*Stanley Cook*

## TIMOTHY WINTERS

Timothy Winters comes to school
With eyes as wide as a football-pool,
Ears like bombs and teeth like splinters:
A blitz of a boy is Timothy Winters.

His belly is white, his neck is dark,
And his hair is an exclamation mark.
His clothes are enough to scare a crow
And through this britches the blue winds blow.

When teacher talks he won't hear a word
And shoots down dead the arithmetic-bird,
He licks the patterns off his plate
And he's not even heard of the Welfare State.

Timothy Winters has bloody feet
And he lives in a house on Suez Street,
He sleeps in a sack on the kitchen floor
And they say there aren't boys like him anymore.

Old man Winters likes his beer
And his missus ran off with a bombardier,
Grandma sits in the grate with a gin
And Timothy's dosed with an aspirin.

The Welfare Worker lies awake
But the law's as tricky as a ten-foot snake,
So Timothy Winters drinks his cup
And slowly goes on growing up.

At Morning Prayers the Headmaster helves
For children less fortunate than ourselves,
And the loudest response in the room is when
Timothy Winters roars 'Amen!'

So come one angel, come on ten:
Timothy Winters says 'Amen'
Amen amen amen amen.
*Timothy Winters, Lord.*
Amen.

*Charles Causley*

❋　　❋　　❋　　❋　　❋　　❋

## OH BRING BACK HIGHER STANDARDS

Oh bring back higher standards—
the pencil and the cane:
if we want education then we must have some pain.
Oh, bring us back all the gone days
Yes, bring back all the past ...
let's put them all in rows again—so we can see who's last.
Let's label all the good ones
(the ones like you and me)
and make them into prefects—like prefects used to be.
We'll put them on the honours board
... as honours ought to be,
and write their names in burnished script—

108

for all the world to see.
We'll have them back in uniform,
we'll have them doff their caps,
and learn what manners really are
... for decent kind of chaps!
... So let's label all the good ones,
we'll call them 'A's and 'B's—
and we'll parcel up the useless ones
and call them 'C's and 'D's.
... We'll even have an 'E' lot!
... an 'F' or 'G' maybe!!
... so they can know they're useless,
... and not as good as me.

For we've got to have the stupid—
and we've got to have the poor
Because—
if we don't have them ...
well ... what are prefects for?

*Peter Dixon*

✳    ✳    ✳    ✳    ✳    ✳

## DISTRACTED THE MOTHER SAID TO HER BOY

Distracted the mother said to her boy
'Do you try to upset and perplex and annoy?
Now, give me four reasons—and don't play the fool—
Why you shouldn't get up and get ready for school.'

Her son replied slowly, 'Well, mother, you see,
I can't stand the teachers and they detest me;
And there isn't a boy or a girl in the place
That I like or, in turn, that delights my face.'

'And I'll give you two reasons,' she said, 'Why you ought
Get yourself off to school before you get caught;
Because, first, you are forty and, next, you young fool,
It's your job to be there.
You're the head of the school.'

*Gregory Harrison*

## AUTUMN'S END

With upturned bellies lying cold
In habits black and striped with gold
Behind large windows of glass plate
Dead, swollen wasps accumulate.
Small monkeys in their Northern zoos
Grumble with unaccustomed 'flu's'.
Fat frogs harrumph and blurp in peace
On harvest bellies white as fleece
And in the wells the water's free
From beetle, bug and buzzing bee.
Soft salmon redden in the pools
And lazy squirrels shout: 'Down tools!'
Moist green leaves rest in rotting rust.
Hot donkeys roll no more in dust.

*John B. Keane*

## LEAVES

Who's killed the leaves?
Me, says the apple, I've killed them all.
Fat as a bomb or a cannonball
I've killed the leaves.

Who sees them drop?
Me, says the pear, they will leave me all bare
So all the people can point and stare.
I see them drop.

110

Who'll catch their blood?
Me, me, me, says the marrow, the marrow.
I'll get so rotund that they'll need a wheelbarrow.
I'll catch their blood.

Who'll make their shroud?
Me, says the swallow, there's just time enough
Before I must pack all my spools and be off.
I'll make their shroud.

Who'll dig their gave?
Me, says the river, with the power of the clouds
A brown deep grave I'll dig under my floods.
I'll dig their grave.

Who'll be their parson?
Me, says the Crow, for it is well-known
I study the bible right down to the bone.
I'll be their parson.

Who'll be chief mourner?
Me, says the wind,I will cry through the grass
The people will pale and go cold when I pass.
I'll be chief mourner.

Who'll carry the coffin?
Me, says the sunset, the whole world will weep
to see me lower it into the deep.
I'll carry the coffin.

Who'll sing a psalm?
Me, says the tractor, with my gear grinding glottle
I'll plough up  the stubble and sing through my throttle.
I'll sing the psalm.

Who'll toll the bell?
Me, says the robin, my song in October
Will tell the still gardens the leaves are over.
I'll toll the bell.

*Ted Hughes*

## THE WARRIOR OF WINTER

He met the star his enemy
They fought the woods leafless.
He gripped his enemy.
They trampled fields to quag.
His enemy was stronger.
A star fought against him.

He fought his losing fight
Up to the neck in the river.
Grimly he fought in gateways,
He struggled among stones.
He left his strength in puddles.
The star grew stronger.

Rising and falling
He blundered against houses.
He gurgled for life in ditches.
Clouds mopped his great wounds.
His shattered weapons glittered.
The star gazed down.

Wounded and prisoner
He slept on rotten sacking.
He gnawed bare stalks and turnip tops
In the goose's field.
The sick sheep froze beside him.
The star was his guard.

With bones like frozen plumbing
He lay in the blue morning.
His teeth locked in his head
Like the trap-frozen fox.
But he rejoiced a tear in the sun.
Like buds his dressings softened.

*Ted Hughes*

\* \* \* \* \* \*

## BOY AT THE WINDOW

Seeing the snowman standing all alone
In dusk and cold is more than he can bear.
The small boy weeps to hear the wind prepare
A night of gnashings and enormous moan.
His tearful sight can hardly reach to where
The pale-faced figure with bitumen eyes
Returns him such a god-forsaken stare
As outcast Adam gave to Paradise.

The man of snow is, nonetheless, content,
Having no wish to go inside and die.
Still, he is moved to see the youngster cry.
Tough frozen water is his element,
He melts enough to drop from one soft eye
A trickle of the purest rain, a tear
For the child at the bright pane surrounded by
Such warmth, such light, such love, and so much fear.

*Richard Wilbur*

## FIRST HAIKU OF SPRING

cuck oo cuck oo cuck
oo cuck oo cuck oo cuck oo
cuck oo cuck oo cuck

*Roger McGough*

✳   ✳   ✳   ✳   ✳   ✳

## BEECH TREE

I planted in February
A bronze-leafed beech,
In the chill brown soil
I spread out its silken fibres.

Protected it from the goats
With wire netting
And fixed it firm against
The worrying wind.

Now it is safe, I said,
April must stir
My precious baby
To greenful loveliness.

It is August now, I have hoped
But I hope no more—
My beech tree will never hide sparrows
From hungry hawks.

*Patrick Kavanagh*

## WORK AND PLAY

The swallow of summer, she toils all summer,
A blue-dark knot of glittering voltage,
A whiplash swimmer, a fish of the air.
    But the serpent of cars that crawls through the dust
    In shimmering exhaust
    Searching to slake
    Its fever in ocean
    Will play and be idle or else it will bust.

The swallow of summer, the barbed harpoon,
She flings from the furnace, a rainbow of purples,
Dips her glow in the pond and is perfect.
        But the serpent of cars that collapsed at the beach
Disgorges its organs
    A scamper of colours
    Which roll like tomatoes
    Nude as tomatoes
    With sand in their creases
    To cringe in the sparkle of rollers and screech.

The swallow of summer, the seamstress of summer,
She scissors the blue into shapes and she sews it,
She draws a long thread and she knots it at corners.
    But the holiday people
    Are laid out like wounded
    Flat as in ovens
    Roasting and basting
    With faces of torment as space burns them blue
    Their heads are transistors
    Their teeth grit on sand grains
    Their lost kids are sqalling
    While man-eating flies
    Jab electric shock needles but what can they do?

They can climb in their cars with raw bodies, raw faces
    And start up the serpent
    And headache it homeward
    A car full of squabbles
    And sobbing and stickiness
    With sand in their crannies

Inhaling petroleum
    that pours from the foxgloves
While the evening swallow
The swallow of summer, cartwheeling through
crimson,
Touches the honey-slow river and turning
Returns to the hand stretched from under the eaves—
A boomerang of rejoicing shadow.

*Ted Hughes*

## OH, I WISH I'D LOOKED AFTER ME TEETH

Oh, I wish I'd looked after me teeth,
    And spotted the perils beneath,
All the toffees I chewed,
    And the sweet sticky food,
O, I wish I'd looked after me teeth.

I wish I'd been that much more willin'
    When I had more tooth there than fillin'
To pass up gobstoppers,
    From respect to me choppers
And to buy something else with me shillin'.

When I think of the lollies I licked,
    And the liquorice allsorts I picked,
Sherbet dabs, big and little,
    And that hard peanut brittle,
My conscience gets horribly pricked.

My Mother, she told me no end,
    'If you got a tooth, you got a friend'
I was young then, and careless,
    My toothbrush was hairless,
I never had much time to spend.

Oh I showed them the toothpaste all right,
    I flashed it about late at night,
But up-and-down brushin'
    And pokin' and fussin'
Didn't seem worth the time—I could bite!

If I'd known I was paving the way,
    To cavities, caps and decay,
The murder of fillin's
    Injections and drillin's
I'd have thrown all me sherbet away.

So I lay in the old dentist's chair
    And I gaze up his nose in despair,
And his drill it do whine,
    In these molars of mine,
'Two amalgum,' he'll say, 'for in there.'

How I laughed at my Mother's false teeth,
    As they foamed in the waters beneath,
But now comes the reckonin'
    It's me they are beckonin'
Oh, I wish I'd looked after me teeth!

*Pam Ayres*

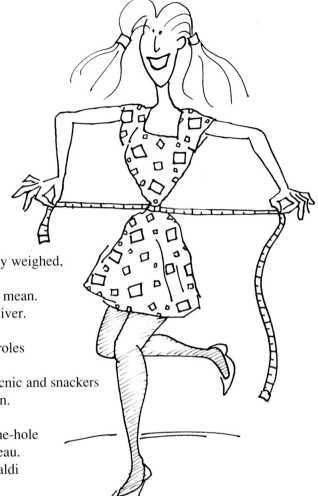

## THE SLIMMING POEM

I'm a slimmer by trade, I'm frequently weighed,
I'm slim as a reed in the river.
I'm slender and lean, and hungry and mean.
Have some water, it's good for your liver.

Don't give me cheese rolls or profiteroles
Don't show me that jelly a-shakin',
Don't give me cream crackers you picnic and snackers
Or great big ice-creams with a flake in.

Don't give me swiss roll or toad-in-the-hole
Don't show me that Black Forest gateau.
You sit and go mouldy you old garibaldi
Your pastry all riddled with fat.  Oh!

When I'm fat I feel weary and tubby and dreary
The stairs make me struggle and grunt dear,
And yet I'm so happy and punchy and snappy
When me hip bones are stuck out the front dear.

No, it's white fish for me, no milk in me tea
And if we don't like it we lump it.
No figs or sultanas, no mashed-up bananas
No pleasure and no buttered crumpet.

So don't get any bigger, me old pear-shaped figure
I can and I will become thinner.
So cheer up and take heart, pass the calorie chart,
let's see what we're having for dinner!

*Pam Ayres*

117

## THE EARLY PURGES

I was six when I first saw kittens drown.
Dan Taggart pitched them, 'the scraggy wee shits'.
Into a bucket: a frail metal sound.

Soft paws scraping like mad. But their tiny din
Was soon soused. They were slung on the snout
Of the pump and the water pumped in.

'Sure isn't it better for them now?' Dan said.
Like wet gloves they bobbed and shone till he sluiced
Them out on the dunghill, glossy and dead.

Suddenly frightened, for days I sadly hung
Round the yard, watching the three sogged remains
Turn mealy and crisp as old summer dung

Until I forgot them. But the fear came back
When Dan trapped big rats, snared rabbits, shot crows
Or, with a sickening tug, pulled old hens' necks.

Still, living displaces false sentiments
And now, when shrill pups are prodded to drown
I just shrug. 'Bloody pups'. It makes sense:

'Prevention of cruelty' talk cuts ice in town
Where they consider death unnatural.
But on well-run farms  pests have to be kept down.

*Seamus Heaney*

118

## BIRTH OF THE FOAL

As May was opening the rosebuds,
elder and lilac beginning to bloom,
it was time for the mare to foal.
She'd rest herself, or hobble lazily

after the boy who sang as he led her
to pasture, wading through the meadowflowers.
They wandered back at dusk, bone-tired,
the moon perched on a blue shoulder of sky.

Then the mare lay down,
sweating and trembling, on her straw in the stable.
The drowsy, heavy-bellied cows
surrounded her, waiting, watching, snuffing.

Later, when even the hay slept
and the shaft of the Plough pointed south,
the foal was born.  Hours the mare
spent licking the foal with its glue-blind eyes.

And the foal slept at her side,
a heap of feathers ripped from a bed.
Straw never spread as soft as this.
Milk or snow never slept like a foal.

Dawn bounced up in a bright red hat,
waved at the world and skipped away.
Up staggered the foal,
its hooves were jelly-knots of foam.

Then day sniffed with its blue nose
through the open stable window, and found them—
the foal nuzzling its mother,
velvet fumbling for her milk.

Then all the trees were talking at once,
chickens scrabbled in the yard,
like golden flowers
envy withered the last stars.

*Ferenc Juhász* from the Hungarian (trans. David Wevill)

## THE COBRA

This creature fills its mouth with venum
And walks upon its duodenum
He who attempts to tease the cobra
Is soon a sadder he, and sobra.

*Ogden Nash*

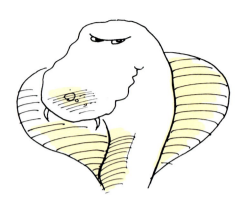

## THE COW

The cow is of the bovine ilk;
One end is moo, the other, milk.

*Ogden Nash*

The Walrus lives on icy floes
And unsuspecting Eskimoes.

Don't bring your wife to Arctic Tundra
A Walrus may bob up from undra.

*Michael Flanders*

## TIME OUT

The donkey sat down on the roadside
Suddenly, as though tired of carrying
His cross.  There was a varnish
Of sweat on his coat, and a fly
On his left ear.  The tinker
Beating him finally gave in,
Sat on the grass himself, prying
His coat for his pipe.  The donkey
(not beautiful but more fragile
than any swan, with his small
front hooves folded under him)
Gathered enough courage to raise
That fearsome head, lipping a daisy,
As if to say—slowly, contentedly—
Yes, there is a virtue in movement,
But only going so far, so fast,
Sucking the sweet grass of stubbornness.

*John Montague*

\*   \*   \*   \*   \*   \*

## THE POLAR BEAR

A polar bear who could not spell
Sat worrying in the snow.
'I wish,' he said, 'that I could tell
If *flow* is right or *floe*.'
But as he worried up there came
A hungry Eskimo
Who shot him and—it seems a shame—
That bear will never knoe.

*Edward Lucie-Smith*

121

# I HAD A HIPPOPOTAMUS

I had a hippopotamus; I kept him in a shed
And fed him upon vitamins and vegetable bread;
I made him my companion on many cheery walks,
And had his portrait done by a celebrity in chalks.

His charming eccentricities were known on every side,
The creature's popularity was wonderfully wide;
He frolicked with the Rector in a dozen friendly tussles.
Who could not but remark upon his hippopotamuscles.

If he should be afflicted by depressions or the dumps,
By hippopotameasles or the hippopotamumps,
I never knew a particle of peace till it was plain
He was hippopotamasticating properly again.

I had a hippopotamus; I loved him as a friend;
But beautiful relationships are bound to have an end;
Time takes, alas! our joys from us and robs us of our blisses;
My hippopotamus turned out a hippopotamissis.

My housekeeper regarded him with jaundice in her eye;
She did not want a colony of hippopotami;
She borrowed a machine-gun from her soldier-nephew Percy,
And showed my hippopotamus no hippopotamercy.

My house now lacks the glamour that the charming
creature gave,
The garage where I kept him is as silent as a grave;
No longer he displays among the motor-tyres and spanners
His hippopotamastery of hippopotamanners.

No longer now he gambols in the orchards in the Spring;
No longer do I lead him through the village on a string;
No longer in the mornings does the neighbourhood rejoice
To his hippopotamusically-modulated voice.

I had a hippopotamus; but nothing upon earth
Is constant in its happiness or lasting in its mirth;
No joy that life can give me can be strong enough to smother
My sorrow for what might-have-been-a-hippopotamother.

*Patrick Barrington*

# THE DIVER

I put on my aqua-lung and plunge,
Exploring, like a ship with a glass keel,
The secrets of the deep.  Along my lazy road
On and on I steal—
Over waving bushes which at a touch explode
Into shrimps, then closing, rock to the tune of the tide;
Over crabs that vanish in puffs of sand.
Look, a string of pearls bubbling at my side
Breaks in my hand—
Those pearls were my breath! ... Does that hollow hide
Some old Armada wreck in seaweed furled,
Crusted with barnacles, her cannon rusted,
The great *San Philip?*  What bullion in her hold?
Pieces of eight, silver crowns, and bars of solid gold?

I shall never know.  Too soon the clasping cold
Fastens on flesh and limb
And pulls me to the surface.  Shivering, back I swim
To the beach, the noisy crowds, the ordinary world.

*Ian Serraillier*

## SEA

I am patient, repetitive, multi-voiced,
Yet few hear me
And fewer still trouble to understand

Why, for example, I caress
And hammer the land.
I do not brag of my depths

Or my currents,I do not
Boast of my moods or my colours
Or my breath in your thought.

In time I surrender my drowned,
My appetite speaks for itself,
I could swallow all you have found

And open for more,
My green tongues licking the shores
Of the world

Like starved beasts reaching for men
Who will not understand
When I rage and roar

When I bellow and threaten
I am obeying a law
Observing a discipline.

This is the rhythm
I live.
This is the reason I move

In hunger and skill
To give you the pick of my creatures.
This is why I am willing to kill,

Chill every created nerve.
You have made me a savage master
Because I know how to serve.

*Brendan Kennelly*

## MUSHROOMS

Overnight, very
Whitely, discreetly,
Very quietly

Our toes, our noses
Take hold on the loam,
Acquire the air.

Nobody sees us,
Stops us, betrays us;
The small grains make room.

Soft fists insist on
Heaving the needles,
The leafy bedding,

Even the paving.
Our hammers, our rams,
Earless and eyeless,

Perfectly voiceless,
Widen the crannies,
Shoulder through holes. We

Diet on water,
On crumbs of shadow,
Bland-mannered, asking

Little or nothing.
So many of us!
So many of us!

We are shelves, we are
Tables, we are meek,
We are edible,

Nudgers and shovers
In spite of ourselves.
Our kind multiplies:

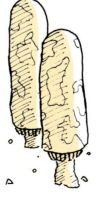

We shall by morning
Inherit the earth.
Our foot's in the door.

*Sylvia Plath*

# HYMN OF THE SCIENTIFIC FARMERS

We squirt the fields and scatter
Our phosphates on the land:
'Organic waste' and 'humus'
We do not understand.

We slaughter trees in thousands
To sell for what they're worth;
No stems to hold the water,
No roots to bind the earth.

Our farms will turn to deserts
Where not a crop can grow,
But long before that happens
We'll take our gains and go.

We'll strip the lanes of hedges;
No wild-flower must survive,
Nor bird find place to nest in—
Let only insects thrive!

We spray to kill diseases,
And once a cure is made
Some other pest is started:
But that is good for Trade.

We rob the flour of virtue,
We leave a rifled sack;
And then with new synthetics
We almost put it back.

We pump our fowls with hormones
As fast as fast can be;
Consumers die of cancer
But we're not there to see.

Our god is an Equation,
And Profit is our goal:
*'Exploit the parts like fury—*
*Forget about the whole.'*

*Clive Sansom*

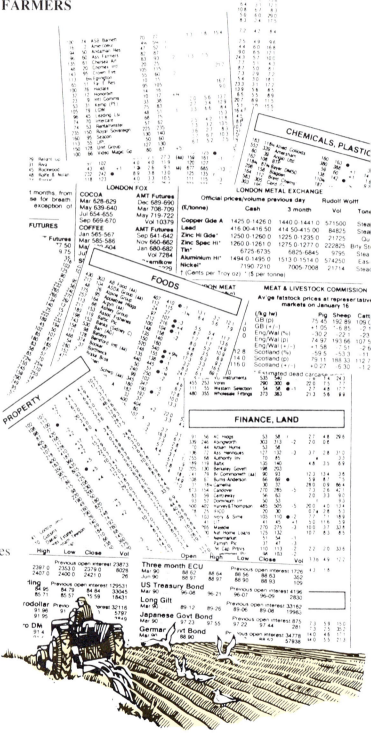

# TRAVELLING THROUGH THE DARK

Travelling through the dark I found a deer
dead on the edge of the Wison River road.
It is usually best to roll them into the canyon:
that road is narrow; to swerve might make more dead.

By glow of the tail-light I stumbled back of the car
and stool by the heap, a doe, a recent killing;
she had stiffened already, almost cold.
I dragged her off; she was large in the belly.

My fingers touching her side brought me the reason—
her side was warm; her fawn lay there waiting,
alive, still, never to be born.
Beside that mountain road I hesitated.

The car aimed ahead its lowered parking lights;
under the hood purred the steady engine.
I stood in the glare of the warm exhaust turning red;
around our group I could hear the wilderness listen.

I thought hard for us all—my only swerving—
then pushed her over the edge into the river.

*William Stafford*

127

## EVEREST CLIMBED

### The Icefall

It was April when they came to the Icefall—Hillary,
His coolies and Sherpas, fifty strong.
In the forest of ice they camped, upon Khumbu,
In the white moon-world where no grass, nothing grew.
And the snow fell all day long.  They were cold
And wet, some of them snow-blinded,
Short of tents and shelter—but nobody minded.
With the weather at freezing (or a shade below)
They turned their backs to the wind, crouched behind
boulders and stones,
Or lay content as huskies, curled in the snow.
Next morning, when the snow had done with falling,
They kicked their way through the crust.  And the climbers
Plodded on till, turning the valley head, they beheld
A white cascade of water, waves down the mountain
Leaping and whirling!  But the giant fountain
In frosty plunge appalling
Had frozen, to silence quelled, cold as the tomb.
It was the Icefall, grim guardian of the Western Cwm,
The green-white monster with a hundred mouths
And jaws abysmal and fangs of ice.  Near the way
Of the avalanche he lay,
Sprawled between Lhotse and Nuptse, sleepy-seeming,
Till down from those bastions the thunder came screaming
In billow-cloud of snow, with loud echoes in the summits booming
And rumbling, booming and rumbling.  And boulders of ice collided,
Split to a million pieces which the yawning mouths devoured,
Groaning for more.  Now upon their greed a white spray subsided,
While from deep caverns and creeks
Slowly the silence and the fear
Surged back ... But Hillary looked aloft and raised a cheer—
For April was sweeping the snow from the peaks!

Then Hillary attacked.  Snow falling, wind howling,
Five days he fought, with axe and hoisting gear,
Ladder of aluminium, ladder of rope
And timber for bridging.  Time and again
They were beaten back—
When cliff and wall crumbled, when avalanche
Wiped out a hundred feet of track,
By crevasse and gaping chasm, by toppling pinnacle
And serac overhanging.  But they fought back.
Hack, hack at the ice!  Over that ridge now—
Here's a flag to mark it—keep to the left of this—
We'll fix a line to the wall there—watch for the abyss.
Hack, hack at the ice!  It was the same every day
Till they pitched a couple of tents on a shelf half way.
Hack, hack at the ice!  More ridges,
Crevasses and pinnacles and chasms and bridges.
Hack, hack at the ice!  or wade in the snow knee-deep
And battle to the top.  At 20,000 there was room,
Just room to pitch a tent and, over the brink above, peep
Into their dreams and longings, into the Western Cwm.

*Ian Serraillier*

## WINDY NIGHTS

Whenever the moon and stars are set,
     Whenever the wind is high,
All night long in the dark and wet,
     A man goes riding by.
Late in the night when the fires are out,
Why does he gallop and gallop about?

Whevener the trees are crying aloud,
     And ships are tossed at sea,
By, on the highway, low and loud,
     By at the gallop goes he.
By at the gallop he goes, and then
By he comes back at the gallop again.

*Robert Louis Stevenson*

\*    \*    \*    \*    \*    \*

## MIDNIGHT

Midnight
The graveyard is silent.
The howling wind rushes by.
I hear a noise and spin around,
around and around.
There it is again; tap, tap, tap,
Looking behind a gravestone,
I see a vision of a man.
With a hammer and chisel
I ask him what he is doing,
He replies, 'They spelt my name wrong.'

*Baljit Kang (11)*

130

## 'OUT, OUT—'

The buzz saw snarled and rattled in the yard
And made dust and dropped stove-length sticks of wood,
Sweet-scented stuff when the breeze drew across it,
And from there those that lifted eyes could count
Five mountain ranges one behind the other
Under the sunset far into Vermont,
And the saw snarled and rattled, snarled and rattled,
And it ran light, or had to bear a load.
And nothing happened: day was all but done.
Call it a day, I wish they might have said
To please the boy by giving him the half hour
That a boy counts so much when saved from work.
His sister stood beside them in her apron
To tell them 'Supper'.  At the word, the saw,
As if to prove saws knew what supper meant,
Leaped out at the boy's hand, or seemed to leap—
He must have given the hand.  However it was,
Neither refused the meeting.  But the hand!
The boy's first outcry was a rueful laugh,
As he swung toward them holding up the hand
Half in appeal but half as if to keep
The life from spilling.  Then the boy saw all—
Since he was old enough to know, big boy
Doing a man's work, though a child at heart
He saw all spoiled.  'Don't let him cut my hand off—
The doctor, when he comes.  Don't let him, sister!'
So.  But the hand was gone already.
The doctor put him in the dark of ether.
He lay and puffed his lips out with his breath.
And then—the watcher at his pulse took fright.
No one believed.  They listened at his heart.
Little—less—nothing!—and that ended it.
No more to build on there.  And they, since they
Were not the one dead, turned to their affairs.

*Robert Frost*

131

## THERE ARE FOUR CHAIRS ROUND THE TABLE

There are four chairs round the table,
Where we sit down for our tea.
But now we only set places
For Mum, for Terry and me.

We don't chatter any more
About what we did in the day.
Terry and I eat quickly,
Then we both go out to play.

Mum doesn't smile like she used to.
Often, she just sits and sighs.
Sometimes, I know from the smudges,
That while we are out she cries.

*John Foster*

## I, TOO

I, too, sing America.

I am the darker brother.
They send me to eat in the kitchen
When company comes,
But I laugh,
And eat well,
And grow strong.

Tomorrow,
I'll sit at the table
When company comes.
Nobody'll dare
Say to me,
'Eat in the kitchen,'
Then.

Besides,
They'll see how beautiful I am
And be ashamed—

I, too, am America.

*Langston Hughes*

## DEAR MAUREEN

Dear Maureen,
I am a lamp-post.
Every Saturday evening at five o'clock
three boys
wearing blue and white scarves
blue and white hats
waving their arms in the air
and shouting,
come my way.
Sometimes they kick me.
Sometimes they kiss me.
What should I do
to get them to make up their minds?
Yours bewilderedly,
Annie Onlight.

*Michael Rosen*

## THE HUNCHBACK IN THE PARK

The hunchback in the park
A solitary mister
Propped between trees and water,
From the opening of the garden lock
That lets the trees and water enter
Until the Sunday sombre bell at dark

Eating bread from a newspaper
Drinking water from the chained cup
That the children filled with gravel
In the fountain basin where I sailed my ship
Slept at night in a dog kennel
But nobody chained him up.

Like the park birds he came early
Like the water he sat down
And Mister they called Hey mister
The truant boys from the town
Running when he had heard them clearly
On out of sound

Past lake the rockery
Laughing when he shook his paper
Hunchbacked in mockery
Through the loud zoo of the willow groves
Dodging the park keeper
With his stick that picked up leaves.

And the old dog sleeper
Alone between nurses and swans
While the boys among willows
Made the tigers jump out of their eyes
To roar on the rockery stones
And the groves were blue with sailors

Made all day until bell time
A woman figure without fault
Straight as a young elm
Straight and tall from his crooked bones
That she might stand in the night
After the locks and the chains

All night in the unmade park
After the railings and shrubberies
The birds the grass the trees the lake
And the wild boys innocent as strawberries
Had followed the hunchback
To his kennel in the dark.

*Dylan Thomas*

**Test Yourself**

*1. Briefly describe or give an example of each of the following terms:  (2 or 3 sentences will do)*

FICTION

NON-FICTION                        METAPHOR

BIOGRAPHY                          SIMILE

AUTOBIOGRAPHY                      RHYME

SYLLABLE                           RHYTHM

HAIKU                              ONOMATOPOEIA

LIMERICK                           ALLITERATION

NARRATIVE POETRY                   ASSONANCE

BALLAD                             SYNONYMS

HERO/HEROINE

IMAGE

*2. Write the correct versions of the following:*
  *— and what happens in the end*
  *— ah well that im not so sure he replied*
  *— weve never been asked to test it*
  *— well if i see her tonight i wont let her go said he*

*3. Write out the address and signing off sections of a personal letter.*

*4. Can you remember the meanings of the following words?*

NARRATIVE                         PATCHWORK

BLOTCHED                          AUTHENTIC

CROUCH                            PERFORATIONS

MONOTONE                          BLEAK

EVALUATE                          HARE BRAINED

VERBAL                            FANTASY

SYLLABLE                          BONNY

MORSE                             WATER WRAITH

QUARANTINE                        TEMPESTS

TARRY                             LAMENTING

CASUAL                            AVALANCHE

TAPERING                          FALTERED

PRECISE                           CRESTS

PROTEIN                           PARALLEL

| | |
|---|---|
| OBSERVER | GESTURED |
| VULNERABLE | ANXIOUS |
| SANCTUARY | INTERRUPTION |
| PUNCTUATION | THRIVING |
| RURAL | ASSISTANCE |
| ABBREVIATION | SLEIGH |

*5. Oral: Group Discussion*

*a. In your groups discuss the qualities of a good ballad and REPORT BACK*

*b. Prepare and tell a DRAMATIC STORY (of not more than 2 minutes length).*

*6. Aural*

*Listen to some letters read out. Write down the main points of one of them and compose an answer.*

# UNIT 3

## THE MASS MEDIA

# The Mass Media

## What Does This Mean?

A MEDIUM is anything which conveys information from one person to another. For example: telephone, telegram, telex, letter, book, smoke signal, dance, etc. are all media.

MASS MEDIA is the term used to describe inventions which convey information to great masses of people, at the same time. Radio, Television, Newspapers, Cinema are the most obvious examples. Some of these are PRINT mass media and some are ELECTRONIC.

List all the different mass media you can think of.

To which mass medium do you give most time each week? Why do you prefer it?

We had a brief look at TV Drama in Unit I. Here we will take a look at one of the Print mass media: NEWSPAPERS.

## What Is News?

(for groups of 4 or 5)

**1.** In your groups relate three items of news you heard today and one item you passed on to someone else. Why was it news?

**2.** Each student should recall three items of interest which happened to him/her in the past week. List them on paper and give a brief summary to the group. The group then chooses the top five newsworthy items.

A famous American newspaper editor, Charles Dana, once said: 'When a dog bites a man, that's not news. But when a man bites a dog, that's news'. It is generally agreed that if it is to be described as news, a story must be: NEW; IMPORTANT; INTERESTING; DRAMATIC; UNUSUAL; UNEXPECTED, etc. Could your top five stories be classed under any of these headings? DISCUSS.

**3.** Each group should now list the top THREE news items which occurred in the class or involved class members during this week or last week (decide which). Report back, giving reasons for choice.

**4.** List the TOP FIVE stories on a current Radio or TV News bulletin. Why do you think they were news?

# Newspapers

## FINDING YOUR WAY

(For this exercise each student will need a copy of a daily newspaper. Plan this beforehand so that all group A will have The Times, group B The Irish Press, group C The Independent, group D The Cork Examiner, and so on. Keep these newspapers in your classroom. We can use them again in the Advertising Section).

## EXERCISES

*1. Examine your newspaper and list the different types of news items you can find: for example, sport, foreign news, local news, Radio and TV guide, business news etc. Can you find the Classified Advertisements, Death Notices, Obituaries, Editorial (where we get the Editor's opinions on something topical), Features (long articles with lots of background information), Letters to the Editor, etc.?*

*2. How much space is given to each category you find? Counting the pages will give you a rough guide. (but newsprint is measured in COLUMN INCHES. So if you want to check a particular article, use a ruler to measure down the columns). Compare the different papers' coverage of particular categories of news. Which has most sports coverage? Which has most women's pages? Which has most foreign news? Which has most advertising, etc., etc.*

*3. Choose any front page story and decide on three reasons why it made the front page.*

Notice the two sizes of newspaper. The larger one is called BROADSHEET and the smaller TABLOID.

Are there any other differences between these types of newspaper, apart from the size of page? Discuss this in your groups and REPORT BACK.

## NOTICE SOME FEATURES OF A NEWSPAPER

THE MASTHEAD is the very distinctively printed name of the newspaper.

# THE IRISH TIMES

# Irish Independent

**IRISH Press**

THE TRUTH IN THE NEWS

**THE STAR**

**The Cork Examiner**

COLUMNS of print are used to make it easy to read. Some items are put in little boxes called BOXED COLUMNS. This helps the reader to pick out news items. Example

than seven internationals that day, Ashley Grimes, a substitute, replacing Gerry Ryan.

As a teenager, O'Connor started his senior career with St. Patrick's Athletic, moved to Athlone Town for a short while before Dalymount Park this season, at the invitation of Billy Young, and is now in charge. "I think it is one of the top jobs in football. It's a great challenge. I'll give it my best and hope something will come out of it, he says.

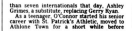

● PADRAIG O'CONNOR ... great pedigree.

has himself been asked by the English FA to explain his own newspaper criticism of his players.

## DAVID WAITS

**DAVID ROCASTLE shrugged off his weekend drama yesterday to challenge for an England place against World Cup hosts Italy at Wembley tomorrow.**

The Arsenal midfield man was in a state of shock after swallowing his tongue during Saturday's game at Millwall.

But Rocastle played a full part in England's opening training session at fog-bound Bisham Abbey yesterday and was anxious to hang-on to his starting slot.

Rocastle, however, will have to wait to discover whether he will be in the starting line-up because John Barnes is back after missing the trip to Katowice. If manager, Bobby Robson, decides to opt for two wingers then Rocastle would be unlucky.

Barnes has a slight foot

## Coyle concern

LIAM COYLE, Derry City's exciting striker, could be out of football much longer than was anticipated.

An exploratory operation in Hull, where he has gone for treatment, should reveal the full extent of the damage.

Coyle hasn't played a since twisting his knee against Dundalk on September 17, and says club chairman Ian Doherty, "the knee injury is more complicated than we first imagined. It's causing quite a bit of concern.

Coyle, 21, was playing so well last season that a number of English clubs

were beginning to show an interest, notably Manchester United.

It now seems unlikely that he will make a comeback before Christmas.

Dundalk's striker Roddy Collins, who missed the team's last four games, may be out of football for another couple of weeks. An ankle injury has sidelined the big, bustling striker.

But Joey Malone, out of last Sunday's side because of a hamstring problem, should be available for the clash with Shamrock Rovers at Dalymount Park.

**TONIGHT'S SOCCER**

(7.30 unless stated)
BARCLAYS LEAGUE
DIVISION FOUR
Torquay v Gillingham
UEFA U-21 CHAMPIONSHIP
Group Five
Scotland v Norway (at St. Johnstone)
B INTERNATIONAL
England v Italy (at Brighton)
LITTLEWOODS CUP
Third Round Second Replay
Bolton v Swindon
ZENITH DATA SYSTEMS CUP
First Round
Sunderland v Port Vale (7.45)
Second Round
Charlton v Leicester (7.45)
IRISH ROADFERRY CUP
Quarter-finals
Coleraine v Ards
Glentoran v Portadown

HOPPING TO IT . . .

**HOWARD'S WAY IS NOT OUR WAY SAY BASQUES**

HEADLINES are used to catch the reader's attention.
There are many styles of headline.

**1.** Most good headlines give the main point of the story.

**Examples**

## TYRE WORKERS VOTE

**WORKERS** at the giant Semperit tyre factory in Dublin yesterday voted on the Labour Court proposals for new working arrangements at the plant.

The company has threatened to withdraw a £25 million investment package which would create 150 new jobs at the plant if changes in working practices were not accepted.

The company wants workers to switch from three to four-shift working.

The result of the ballot will be released today, a spokesman for the ITGWU said.

# Results by express post

AROUND 60,000 Leaving Cert. students face a further delay before they get their results. They will have to wait until tomorrow afternoon or most likely Saturday morning to hear how they fared.

Education Minister Mary O'Rourke confirmed last night that the results would be ready for posting tomorrow and that An Post had agreed to a special delivery to all 800 post-primary schools before noon on Saturday.

Mrs. O'Rourke said they were anxious to get results to schools as quickly as possible and any school that wished to collect the results in Athlone could do so.

The Department has also been in touch with managerial groups to arrange for personnel to be available in the schools to receive the results. If nobody is available when the post is delivered the results will be returned to the post office where they can be picked up by the school authorities.

The postal delay will not affect the issuing of college offers through the Central Applications Office. The first round will be published in the *Irish Independent* on August 26 and the first round for the Carlow Regional Technical College early next week.

## CIE BUSES BURNT OUT

VICIOUS vandals set fire to three double decker buses yesterday costing CIE almost half a million pounds in damages.

The arsonists set fire to the three buses in Skerries and two of the three buses were burnt out while the third was badly damaged.

A spokesman for the company said two of the buses, which cost £150,000 each were beyond repair while there was some possibility of fixing the third.

143

**2.** Some use puns to catch your eye.

**Examples**

TESSA SANDERSON fired a final broadside at Britain's athletics chiefs before flying out yesterday for the pre-Olympic training camp in Japan.

"I was very upset by the way I was treated at the trials," said the Olympic javelin champion. "I was made to feel as though I wasn't really part of the team."

Sanderson is furious with the selectors who stood and watched her struggling against pain

# Furious Tessa fires parting shot

to compete in the trials in Birmingham last month.

She had a badly damaged Achilles tendon

Sanderson broke down before throwing, but was selected anyway because Sharon Gibson was the only competitor at the trials to achieve the

Olympic qualifying distance. Fatima Whitbread got the third place.

Sanderson said: "I will be competing for Great Britain, but above all I will be competing for myself. I'm going as an athlete to enjoy myself"

● Cram cheer: P30

# Yeats story a grave error

HORSEMEN or anyone else passing by the grave of William Butler Yeats should be in no doubt the poet's remains are interred in Drumcliffe, Co. Sligo, his only son said yesterday.

A new biography of a friend of the poet claims that the bones of an anonymous Frenchman lie in the famous plot. But the claim is nothing more than sensation-mongering, asserted Michael Yeats.

The biography of Hannah Gluckstein, painter and photographer, claims Yeats' widow, George, mistakenly chose a pauper's grave at Roquebrune in the south of France, where the poet was buried in January 1939.

According to Elizabeth Sich of publishers Unwin Hyman, this section of the graveyard was cleared every few years. The book claims the blunder was covered up.

But a scornful Michael Yeats said his mother had excellent French and explained at the time of her husband's first burial that she wanted to bring the body back to Ireland within a few months.

"The French are demons about protocol. All the necessary steps were gone through to ensure it was the correct body," insisted Mr. Yeats.

**3.** Some use humour to get attention.

**Examples**

# The £5m. storm in a cereal bowl

BREAKFAST cereals giant Kelloggs has landed itself in a storm in a cereal bowl.

Its £5 million TV advertising campaign claims Kelloggs' new wonder cereal Common Sense oat bran flakes reduce cholesterol levels in the body.

Not so, say medical experts who have branded the possible life-saving properties as "pure hype."

Now scientists have been called in to investigate the claims in the TV campaign.

The Advertising Standards Authority ordered its own tests as the £66.5 million war between the breakfast companies hotted up.

In the advertisement's early stages the ITV Association, which scrutinises campaigns before they are filmed, forced several changes.

The Independent Broadcasting Authority also made modifications after consulting its medical specialists.

The Coronary Prevention Group said: "We are unhappy because the advert should stress oat bran has to be consumed as part of a low fat diet to be effective.

"It's no good eating it with a dollop of cream on top or a fry-up to follow."

# Stokers pay issue boils over

ON the first working day after the Dail 'rose' for the summer break, a truck arrived at the Kildare Street services entrance to the complex of government buildings between that street and Merrion Square. Three years after it was first mooted, a natural gas-burning boiler was to be installed for the heating system in the complex.

But despite the long advance notice, the Office of Public Works had not reached agreement on redeployment of three of the five workers who have stoked the existing 25-year-old boilers with turf: Official confirmation of the intended changeover had come only in June.

When the heating contractors, H A O'Neill arrived to do the installation, the stokers walked out. And they have been on strike since then.

A Labour Court recommendation has been rejected by the stokers' union, the NEETU, because it does not take account of the impact on pensions and gratuities of the drop in weekly wages of the three men to be redeployed.

The Office of Public Works calculates it can save £100,000 a year by switching to gas. And the stokers accept the change makes sense.

But the three redeployed stokers who have worked a roster of 24-hours-a-day 364-days-a-year to keep the boilers burning — including a single boiler in summer for hot water — would be losing at least £100 in their weekly pay packet. And with a total of 133 years' service between them they are keenly aware of what the loss in earnings would do to their pensions.

**4.** Some play on the sounds of words, using ALLITERA-TION (where the first letter is repeated) or ASSONANCE (where the vowel sound is repeated).

# CORK COOL, CALM AND CONFIDENT!

## MEATH AND THE MODERN MASTERS

# HANDY ANDY!
## No go for Coe!-

## CRAM SLAM

**From JACK STEGGLES**

● STEVE CRAM last night flashed a warning to the rest of the world with a marvellous win over 1500m here in Brussels.

● The Geordie destroyed the rest of the field, including Olympic team-mate Peter Elliott,

to win in 3 mins 30.97 secs. Elliott finished second.

● That's the fastest in the world this year and the third fastest

Cram has ever run in his life.

● Fatima Whitbread gave the British Olympic selectors a scare when she collapsed in pain after spiking her leg during the javelin.

**BOOST: Cram**

A LIMITED number of tickets for the Dublin versus Cork All-Ireland Football semi-final will go on sale today.

A Dublin County GAA Board spokesman said the ground tickets would be available at 10 a.m. at the Nally Stand.

The batch of tickets is the last of 68,000 to go on sale. Most are distributed through clubs nationwide. The spokesman, Donal Hickey, said that unless some were returned, today's tickets would be the last available to fans.

He said everyone was entitled to two tickets and a limited number would go on sale.

"However, we are not sure exactly how many will be available," he added.

On Tuesday, 3,000 tickets sold out in less than two and a half hours at Croke Park.

THE Indian Prime Minister, Mr Rajiv Gandhi, has run over and killed a peacock — India's national bird — as it gave a mating display to a female in the middle of the road. Anyone who kills a peacock is technically liable to prosecution, but Delhi police say no charge has been laid against Mr Gandhi. The *Statesman* newspaper said police were considering charging the peacock with suicide and the peahen for aiding and abetting. — (Reuter)

SUNBURNED, red-eyed and worn-out, father of three John McDonald sprinted into Clerys department store today and grabbed a mink jacket at a knock-down price of £88.

The jacket, with a normal retail price tag of £1,988, was the bargain of the summer sale.

After two nights sleeping on O'Connell Street, unemployed John, of Newtownmountkennedy, beat a queue of about 80 people to the fur department on the first floor.

Then, with the pastel jacket draped over his shoulders he admitted: "Its my reward to my patient wife, Catherine, who allowed me to eat, drink and sleep football last week."

THE type of ship used by Columbus is to sail once more — out of Ireland. The 15th century ship will be built under a FÁS scheme with the aid of plans, timber and fittings presented by the Portuguese Navy to the Dublin Nautical Trust yesterday.

The Portuguese used the Caraval ship to explore the world in the 15th century and two accompanied Columbus on his voyage to discover America.

It will take two years to build and it is hoped to sail her to Lisbon in 1992 for the celebrations of the 500th anniversary of the discovery of America.

When finished it will join oher famous ships in the Dublin Nautical Trust's Maritime Heritage Centre in the Inner Canal basin at Ringsend. The other ships including the Mary Stanford lifeboat which rescued the crew of the Daunt lightship in 1936, are being restored under a FÁS scheme.

**5.** Some headlines go completely overboard. They exaggerate an event. Or they use emotional language. Discuss the suggestions conveyed by some of the words in the following headlines. Construct more accurate headlines.

**Examples**

# HI-DE-HI HORROR

**MORE THAN 300 Irish holiday-makers yesterday re-lived their 60-seconds of horror as a freak hurricane tore their holiday village to shreds.**

They described scenes reminiscent of a wartime blitz as the tail-end of Hurricane Dean ripped through their idyllic Welsh holiday camp.

**HOLIDAY CAMP TERROR NIGHT: PAGES 8 & 9**

Last night many of the shocked families arrived back in Dublin after the night of terror when their holidays were shat-

## 300 Irish caught in holiday blitz

tered by the freak tornado.

They described the scenes of devastation as high winds ripped through their camp as most of them sat down to dinner.

● Shards of glass and lumps of debris flew everywhere as hundreds

of chalets were devastated by the 86 mph winds

● Roofs of buildings and trees fell around frightened holidaymakers as they tried to flee to safety

● Thousands were left homeless and had to

■ TO PAGE 2

148

# Irish undaunted by British storm

DESPITE damage at the holiday camp in Pwllhei, almost 350 Irish tourists are to go ahead with their Butlins holiday in Wales.

Mr. Tony Kelly, of PAB Travel, said yesterday that following assurances from Butlins he would be taking 150 tourists over this weekend. Mr. Tony Griffiths, of Solar Travel, said none of his 200 tourists had pulled out.

"The Butlins people have assured me that everything will be in perfect order by Saturday, and I am satisfied that they will meet their commitments," he said.

On Tuesday, 150 tourists affected by the storm returned to Ireland. Any family seeking additional information may contact Butlins at 03-08832-6647.

# A Paddy goes to Queen Mum's head!

WHEN Britain's Queen Mum feels down in the dumps nowadays she has the option of turning to a Paddy for a booster!

But although the old dear is known to be fond of a drop of the hard stuff, the Paddy in this case is a real live Irishman!

He's hypnotherapist Tony Sadar from Dublin's Cabinteely.

Tony, who specialises in treating people suffering from emotional and confidence problems, recently sent Her Majesty a copy of his cassette, 'Sound of Inspiration', on the occasion of her 88th birthday.

And the Queen Mum was apparently so impressed by the tape, which contains a number of inspirational songs and Tony's soothing voice, she sent him a special 'Thank You' letter this week.

The acknowledgement from her residence, Clarence House, was signed by Her Majesty's 'Lady in Waiting', Frances Campbell Reston, who informed Tony: "Queen Elizabeth, the Queen Mother, has asked me to thank you for remembering her on the occasion of Her

• Queen Mum

Majesty's 88th birthday. "The Queen Mother greatly appreciates your cassette, 'Sounds of Inspiration'."

Tony, who has now opened a London office, told SUNDAY WORLD yesterday: "Since I launched the tape I've received hundreds of letters from people telling me that it has given them a lift when they've been feeling down."

**NOTE:  IT IS IMPORTANT NOT TO MISLEAD.**

## Photographs

NOTICE also how photographs are used to break up the monotony of the page, and to draw your attention to an item. CAPTIONS are used to explain the photographs.

# Conservatives face first test in the North

The North Down Conservatives, who won their battle to secure recognition from the Conservative Party in Britain last week, fight their first by-election as affiliated Tories in Castlereagh East tomorrow. FERGUS PYLE, Northern Editor, assesses their chances

## Abstentions ensure defeat of WP planning inquiry motion

By Frank McDonald
Environment Correspondent

## Robinson calls for 'loopholes' to be closed

## Talks on EC tax rates fail again

By Colm Boland

## Orange Order calls for people power protests

From Fergus Pyle
Northern Editor

Mr Pádraig Ó Connaill (75) of Inchicore, Dublin, inside the District Court yesterday.
(Photograph: Eddie Kelly)

## Summons over TV licence is struck out

## Trawler sunk in collision in fog

Pianist Ms Darina Ní Chuinneagain from Mount Merrion, Co Dublin, who last night received the Kaldor Achievement Award, designed to encourage young people in the pursuit of excellence. (Photograph: Jack McMahon)

## O'Malley denies misleading public on petrol prices

## Bishop warns on illegal emigrants

## Court case on radio planned

## Jail sentence for hygiene breaches

## B&I improvement considered

## Man cleared of assault on girlfriend's daughter

## Heavy fog strands anxious football fans at airport

## Early celebrations by the Irish fans in Malta

From Peter Byrne in Malta

## THE TRUTH, THE WHOLE TRUTH AND...

Some people think that because something is printed, it must be a fact. But can we believe everything we read in a newspaper or see on the TV news? While many newspapers try to do a good job of fair reporting, there are some factors we should think about:

**a.** A reporter, though well-meaning, might not have got the complete story. For example, he or she might have managed to interview only one of the witnesses to an accident. If that witness turned out to be unreliable or biased (disliked lady drivers, for instance) then ...

**b.** A newspaper must sell. Dramatic stories and sensational headlines catch readers. So there is always the temptation to hype up stories. Example—The Minister's statement of 'No comment' on the enquiry might be reported as 'Ominous silence on enquiry.' Does this suggest more than was actually said?

**c.** You yourselves probably could not agree completely on what was important news. All news, whether on radio, TV, or in newspapers is SELECTED. The Editor or someone responsible decides what goes in the programme and what is left out. So we get what he or she thinks is newsworthy.

**d.** Newspaper owners have views, support political parties, and may be for or against certain issues and causes etc. Does this influence what is printed?

## WRITING FOR A NEWSPAPER

News items, in a modern newspaper, are written in a particular style. The reporter tries to get all the main facts into the first two paragraphs. These facts are known as THE W QUESTIONS—what, when, where, who, and why. The following paragraphs are then filled out with the extra detail or background information or quotes. This is known as THE INVERTED PYRAMID

One of the reasons for this is that the sub-editor may have to cut an article so that it will fit in. The last paragraphs can now be cut without losing much of the story.

## E X E R C I S E S

*1. Choose a news item from your paper. Read it and ring each of the w questions as you find it. Is there anything of real importance in the final paragraph?*
*2. Write an INVERTED PYRAMID style account of some school event you attended or participated in recently. Write a headline for it.*

## MAKE YOUR OWN NEWSLETTER

### What Kind?

There are a number of different end products you might aim for.

**A.** Each student could make his/her own newsletter for display on the notice board. This could be either typed or neatly handwritten or hand-printed. HANDWRITING skills would be very important in such a project. You could have a competition for the most artistic and neatest newsletter. You might use Letraset for the headlines but this could become expensive. Use A3 size paper, divided into 3 columns of print, or A4 size with two columns of print.

**B.** Each discussion group of 4 or 5 pupils might produce a short newsletter and have a competition to decide the best. Or see which sells best!

**C.** The class might co-operate to produce a class newsletter, for sale in the class or to first and second years. Again it can be neatly written or typed.

**D.** The class might wish to produce a more professional effort, for sale to the junior years or indeed to the whole school. This would have to be typed. Can someone in your family help with the typing? Can you get the newsletter photocopied or duplicated cheaply?

Perhaps there could be a competition among two or more classes, trying to outsell each other!

Have a class discussion and decide what type of paper you want to produce. Remember the rules of good discussion. Everybody must be involved. You will need EDITORS; REPORTERS; SUB-EDITORS; DESIGN AND LAYOUT STAFF; ADVERTISING STAFF; PRODUCTION STAFF. You may think of other jobs?

**EDITORS** make the final decisions about what goes in, ensuring that it isn't rude, offensive or untruthful. They should check with the teacher on this. They also encourage everybody else.

**REPORTERS** find the news, write it and even rewrite it. For your production they probably will also write feature articles, interviews, horoscopes, recipes, indeed whatever else goes into the newsletter.

**SUB-EDITORS** proof-read the articles (correct the mistakes), compose headlines and cut the story, if necessary.

**DESIGN AND LAYOUT STAFF** design the pages; draw or print the masthead, headlines and photograph captions. They also do crosswords and cartoons etc. They draw advertisements or paste them in from cut-outs. If not using Letraset or type they will need to practice capital letters (called UPPER CASE) and small letter hand printing (called LOWER CASE).

*Renagh Holohan, Assistant News Editor, The Irish Times seeks out a reporter in the Irish Times newsroom to take a news story over the telephone.*

*Ronan Foster, Media Correspondent, The Irish Times, interviews students for a story for the following day's paper.*

The afternoon news conference at 4 o'clock in the Irish Times presided over by Editor, Conor Brady. The conference is attended by the editorial heads of all departments to decide what will be carried in the following day's paper.

The caseroom where the paper is 'made up' during the late afternoon and evening. Sub-editors decide on the layout of the paper and their instructions are being carried out by Paul Barry and Paul McCarthy (men in the picture).

The night's work done and the first Irish Times are taken off the printing machines. Mark Burke and Christy McCann catch up on the following day's news - at 2 o'clock in the morning.

## SOME IDEAS

You might include some of the following types of article:

Up the minute school news of all kinds, whether academic, personal, sporting or social; reports on special achievements, accidents, vandalism, etc.

Features on special aspects of school life, clubs, excursions, interviews with teachers or new pupils, etc.

Local news.

Poetry, short stories and other creative pieces.

Reviews of books, films, videos, concerts.

X words, quizzes, word sleuths etc.

Advertisements.

Letters to the Editor, etc., etc.

### Notice

You will get practice at many different styles of writing.

You need to take great care with your HANDWRITING.

### You will need

To arrange a big class conference in order to gather ideas and decide functions.

Patience and the ability to write, rewrite and rewrite until it is good. Remember to get all your rewriting done before the typing stage.

**Deadlines.** Deadlines are vital to newspapers as news goes stale very quickly. Set deadlines for each stage of the project: first draft; rewrite stage; design stage; and selling stage.

### Books To Help

Expert help and many useful hints can be found in:

**1.** 'Introduction to the Mass Media' I, by David Owens and Patrick Hunt, published by Veritas.

**2.** 'Young Citizen' Magpack, available from the Young Citizen, Institute of Public Administration, Dublin.

**3.** 'Write Your Own Newspaper', by L.R. Green and H.M. Sawyer, published by Macmillan Education.

### Proof Reading

You can of course, correct work in the way you have always done it. But you might like to use some of the official codes used to correct the test copy or proof.

| Code in Margin | Error | Meaning of Code | Correct Version |
|---|---|---|---|
| ⊙/ | J M. Barrie | *Full stop missing* | J. M. Barrie |
| cap/ | john Moloney | *Capital letter or Upper Case* | John Moloney |
| lc / | a Bright morning | *lower case—should not be capital* | a bright morning |
| :/ | The teacher said/ | *Punctuation must be changed* | The teacher said: |
| s/ | advertizements | *Cross out this letter and put s or whatever it should be* | advertisements |
| tro | recieve | *words or letters should be reversed* | receive |
| b/ | probaly | *letter or word left out* | probably |
| ϑ | busyiness | *leave out this letter or word* | business |
| N. p. | ...he fell. Hours later... | *new paragraph* | ...he fell. Hours later... |
| Run on | he shouted: 'We'll try again later' | *no new paragraph* | he shouted: 'We'll try again later' |
| # | all day long | *leave a space* | all day long |
| ⌣ | al ready | *Join up* | already |

## CHOOSING WORDS

Sometimes words seem to mean the same thing. A word that has a similar meaning to that of another word is called a synonym. But even synonyms have shades of difference in their meanings. For example:

Sinead disliked/disapproved of/hated/detested/loathed doing homework.

The meaning of the sentence changes, depending on the word you choose.

'Disliked' is probably the most straightforward, neutral expression. 'Disapproved of' suggests that she felt homework in general was a bad practice. Perhaps she was of the opinion that all study should be done in school.

'Hated/detested/loathed' suggest much stronger degrees of feeling. 'Loathed' is probably the strongest of these.

So, when writing, we have to choose our words carefully because each word may carry different suggestions or connotations. Our choice of words can reveal our attitude to something. This is true whether one is writing a poem or a news story.

# E X E R C I S E S

*A. Read the following sentences carefully and decide which words to use. Then write a paragraph of explanation on each choice. You can use your dictionary.*
*1. The* <u>solemn/sullen-faced</u> *child was to be seen, nearly every day, outside the Principal's Office.*
*2. He owned* <u>great/vast</u> *estates in the country, yet he didn't pay any taxes.*
*3. The badminton player* <u>hit/smashed</u> *the shuttle at the umpire and* <u>spoke loudly to/shouted at</u> *him.*
*4. The students involved in the row were* <u>asked to leave/expelled.</u>
*5. The* <u>youth/young man,</u> *who was* <u>jobless/unemployed</u> *appeared in court, charged with causing a* <u>disturbance/riot</u> *outside the cinema.*
*6. International cyclist Tom Donnelly was married yesterday to* <u>beautiful/pretty</u> *Deirdre Malone, a* <u>secretary/typist</u> *with 'The Moon International Company'.*
*B. What is the attitude of the writer, in the following paragraph? Which words in particular convey that attitude? Find synonyms for them and rewrite the article.*

*'Brilliant American Butch Reynolds charged into athletics history this week when he shattered the 20-year-old world 400 metres record. Reynolds, a favourite for a gold medal at Seoul, tells Tom O'Riordan how he followed the footsteps of legendary Jesse Owen to glory. Page 21'*
*Irish Independent, 20th August 1988*


## SENSATIONALISM

Sometimes newspapers use exaggerated language and imagery in order to attract attention. You can find a great many violent images used for shock effect: Axe; Cut; Chop; Clash; Plunge; Plummet; Hurtle; Soar etc.

**Examples:**
Threat to axe religion teachers.
Staff axed in Tulla hospital.

Hospital axe hits patients.
Support for Popular Party plummets.
Inflation Soars, etc.

Notice how this type of headline can change and distort the message. For instance, the first three examples are actually headlines to articles about shortage of money but they suggest all sorts of possibilities! The reader can get weary of this.

# Spelling Guide

If you are unsure about your spelling, then check with this SPELLING GUIDE, or ask your teacher.

## PLURALS OF NOUNS

### FOR MOST NOUNS ADD "S"

| | | |
|---|---|---|
| girl | — | girls |
| boy | — | boys |
| stone | — | stones |
| book | — | books |

### ADD "ES" TO SOME WORDS WHERE IT WOULD BE DIFFICULT TO PRONOUNCE THEM WITH JUST AN 'S'.

| | | |
|---|---|---|
| bus | — | buses |
| buzz | — | buzzes |
| six | — | sixes |
| church | — | churches |
| thrush | — | thrushes |

**Note:** These are words ending in S, Z, X, CH, SH

Can you think of others?

### NOUNS ENDING IN -F or -FE CHANGE TO VES

| | | |
|---|---|---|
| half | — | halves |
| loaf | — | loaves |
| calf | — | calves |
| wife | — | wives |

### Exceptions:

| | | |
|---|---|---|
| chief | — | chiefs |
| grief | — | griefs |
| roof | — | roofs |

### NOUNS ENDING IN -Y  ADD S
**a.** ending in vowel + y

| | | |
|---|---|---|
| boy | — | boys |
| bay | — | bays |
| donkey | — | donkeys |
| abbey | — | abbeys |
| monkey | — | monkeys |

**b.** ending in consonant +y change 'y' to 'i' and add es

| | | |
|---|---|---|
| baby | — | babies |
| daisy | — | daisies |
| lorry | — | lorries |
| fly | — | flies |
| sky | — | skies |

CORRECT WRITING CORRECT WRITING CORRECT WRITING CORRECT WRITING

## NOUNS ENDING IN O ADD "S"

**a.** ending in vowel + O

| | | |
|---|---|---|
| radio | — | radios |
| stereo | — | stereos |
| video | — | videos |

**b.** consonant + O

| | | |
|---|---|---|
| cargo | — | cargoes |
| echo | — | echoes |
| hero | — | heroes |
| potato | — | potatoes |
| tomato | — | tomatoes |

## Exceptions

| | | |
|---|---|---|
| biro | — | biros |
| grotto | — | grottos |
| halo | — | halos |
| piano | — | pianos |
| solo | — | solos |

## UNUSUAL PLURALS

| | | | | | | |
|---|---|---|---|---|---|---|
| foot | — | feet | | ox | — | oxen |
| man | — | men | | child | — | children |
| woman | -- | women | | sheep | — | sheep |
| mouse | — | mice | | salmon | — | salmon |
| | | | | deer | — | deer |

Can you think of others?
Have a competition.

# IE or EI

Usually i before e, except after c.

| | |
|---|---|
| achieve | |
| brief | |
| grief | ceiling |
| niece | deceive |
| priest | receive |
| shield | perceive |
| siege | |

How many more can you think of?

## Exceptions

**a.** where it is an 'ay' sound

eight
reign
sleigh
neighbour

**b.** odd ones!

either
neither
foreigner
seize
weird

Can you think of others?

## Adding Bits

If we add a bit at the beginning of a word, that is called a PREFIX, and if we add at the end, that is known as a SUFFIX.

Consider

| IN | ATE |
|---|---|
| (Prefix) | (Suffix) |
| in‎adequate | consider‎ate |

---

**1.** If the word ends in a silent -e drop the e before adding a suffix beginning with a vowel.

| | |
|---|---|
| argue | arguing |
| cure | curable |
| fame | famous |
| have | having |
| refuse | refusal |

**Some Exceptions**

| | |
|---|---|
| canoe | canoeing |
| courage | courageous |
| advantage | advantageous |
| notice | noticeable |
| knowledge | knowledgeable |

---

**2.** If the word ends in a consonant + y, change the "y" to "i" before any suffix except "ing".

| | |
|---|---|
| marry | married (but marrying) |
| try | tried (but trying) |
| beauty | beautiful |
| mystery | mysterious |
| empty | emptiness |
| study | studied (but studying) |

**Some Exceptions**

| | |
|---|---|
| dry | dryness |
| shy | shyness |
| day | daily |
| pay | paid |
| say | said |

} vowel + y, yet it changes nevertheless

---

**3.** Doubling the final letter

A word ending in a single consonant, which is preceded by a single vowel, doubles the consonant, when adding an ending that begins with a vowel.

| | | |
|---|---|---|
| drop | dropped, | dropping |
| hum | hummed, | humming |
| rob | robbed, | robbing |
| run | runner, | running |
| begin | beginner, | beginning |
| commit | committed, | committing |
| permit | permitted, | permitting |

**Exception**

limit — limited

## 4. Adding—ful to nouns

Note: one l

| | |
|---|---|
| beauty | beautiful |
| success | successful |
| hope | hopeful |

## 5. Adding 'ly'

Most words don't change

| | |
|---|---|
| bold | boldly |
| warm | warmly |

If the word ends in -l, just add -y

| | |
|---|---|
| full | fully |

If the word ends in -y, change to -i, before the -ly

| | |
|---|---|
| happy | happily |

## 6. Adding 'ally'

To make adverbs, add -ally, to adjectives ending in -ic,
even though the -al is not sounded.

| | |
|---|---|
| basic | basically |
| realistic | realistically |

### Exception

| | |
|---|---|
| public | publicly |

### IS IT?

Here are some words, often used, which frequently cause difficulty.
Learn them and have a spelling competition. Try the L.C.W.C. method.
That is Look, Cover, Write, Check. See if it helps.

| | | |
|---|---|---|
| ACKNOWLEDGE | FEBRUARY | PRIVILEGE |
| ARGUMENT | GOVERNMENT | PROCEED |
| CEMETERY | INOCULATE | RECOMMEND |
| COMMITTEE | LIBRARY | SCIENCE |
| CONSCIENCE | NECESSARY | SUCCEED |
| EMBARRASSMENT | OCCASION | WEIRD |
| EXISTENCE | PARLIAMENT | |

Most newspapers have a crossword as a regular feature. Read the clues and fill in the blank spaces with the words the clues point to.

**Across**

1. An edition of a newspaper (5)
5. Used to get newspapers to a train (1,3)
6. Not always as grumpy as they sound (7)
7. Time for opera without the op (3)
10. You are my lucky star (9)
11. Subjects, if you like (6)
15. What a sub-editor makes (4)
16. A reporter must .... it down (4)

**Down**

2. You paste things into this (9)
3. The man or woman in charge (6)
4. Not two or more newspapers (3)
5. A reporter is always anxious for a good one (1, 5)
8. You will read these in the papers (7)
9. In a newspaper, the National Coal Board could be shortened to the ... (3)
12. The magazine's very much the -thing (2)
13. Short for company. (2)
14. Short for street (2)

**Solution**

Across 1. issue 5. a van 6. critics 7. era 10. horoscope 11. topics 15. cuts 16. note
Down 2. scrapbook 3. editor 4. one 5. a story 8. reports 9. NCB 12. in 13. Co. 14. St

163

# A Brief History of News

## ———————— BEFORE NEWSPAPERS ————————

### What's on at the Colosseum?

One day in the year 131 BC, those Romans whose business took them into the Forum (a public meeting place in the centre of Rome) were surprised to see notices on display. One set of sheets, the *acta senatus* ('events in the Senate'), gave information about recent and coming legislation. The other, the *acta publica* ('public events'), offered a general report of what was happening in the city. These simple, handwritten bulletins, called together the *acta diurna* ('daily events') which the government introduced to inform the people, were posted regularly for 145 years. They reported public decrees, legal notices, the births, deaths and marriages of important people, the successes of the Roman armies, celebrations, performances, and even who had won or lost at sports and in the gladiatorial contests at the Colosseum.

In addition to the copies posted in the Forum, hundreds more were sent to cities and garrisons throughout the Empire. Those who could not read listened as the bulletins were read aloud, or heard the news by word of mouth later. The *acta diurna* are the earliest known form of what we call newspapers. When they ceased, towards the end of the Roman Empire, the idea was to disappear in the West for well over a thousand years.

That this should be so is strange, given people's urge to find out, and pass on, news. Various forms of official news dispatch have been devised throughout history.

### Marathon Man

In ancient Greece, *couriers* ('runners') literally ran with the latest news between the great cities or from one general to another. The most famous instance of this was the runner who in 490 BC died of exhaustion after carrying from Marathon to Athens (a distance of 40 kilometres) the news that the Persians had been defeated by the Athenians.

The Greeks also used torches (or fire), heliographs (sun signals, using polished metal as mirrors), and a primitive type of semaphore. Carrier pigeons have been used at different times, starting with the Egyptians about 300 BC. Other peoples have used smoke signals, message sticks, drums, secret symbol languages and many more ways of sending messages. From the time writing was invented (about 3000 BC), news could be sent by messenger, provided you were wealthy or important enough to have one.

In about AD 750 the Chinese Emperor Hsuan-tsung started sending out special court officials twice a year to report on important events and conditions within the country. The 'annals' were written up and distributed to important people in the court. In addition, a more general 'great report' was prepared in multiple copies, every month. This later became a weekly publication (in 1360) and finally a daily (1830). It continued for more that a thousand years, coming to an end in 1911, at which time it was called the Peking Gazette. Even though it was always more an official gazette than a newspaper as we understand it (having no general news and a very limited distribution), its long life is nonetheless remarkable.

### Saying the News

In Europe during the Renaissance, *town criers* were paid to read aloud the latest bulletins from government or municipal councils. A more popular version of talking newspapers became common in a number of countries. News-hawkers were a bit like today's buskers, except that they spoke the news instead of singing. First they attracted an audience by making a loud noise (in China they beat a gong) and holding up a placard with news 'headlines'. They then told the news to the crowd that had assembled and, they hoped, received some coins in payment. European poets and minstrels appear to have added to their other entertainments reports of goings-on they had picked up in their travels. This tradition was widespread and lasted a long time. The latest, and most sophisticated, of these oral newspapers were the French *nouvellistes* ('newsmen') of the 1600s and 1700s, fully fledged professional reporters who differed from 'real' journalists only in that they publicly spoke, rather than wrote, their stories.

## E X E R C I S E S

*1. Use your dictionary to find the meanings of any difficult words and write them into your Word Copy.*

*2. In spider diagram form, record all the examples of spoken news mentioned by the author.*

### The First Newspapers

All this began to change with the invention of movable type printing in 1455. Printers soon realised that money could be made from simple *broadsheets* (so called because they were sheets of paper the full size of the press) that described events of special importance: the results of a battle, the crowning of a monarch, the burning of witches, or, in 1493, a letter from a sailor called Columbus who claimed to have discovered a new land.

Another version that became popular was the newsbook or news pamphlet. One such was a four-page pamphlet published in 1513 called 'The Trew Encountre', an eyewitness account of the Battle of Flodden Field.

*Newsletters* that were either handwritten or carved on a wooden block had been popular for some time before, but the difficulties were obvious. Type offered speed and a much greater number of words on a sheet of paper. The whole idea began to gather momentum.

In 1568, the Fugger merchant house of Augsberg (Germany) started selling regular *Zeitungen* (newsletters) to the general public. They were based on the internal reports of the Fugger staff throughout Europe and were almost certainly the first commercial printed newspapers. Soon the idea spread to other countries. In Italy, these sheets were called *gazzettanti* (after the price, a coin called a *gazzetta*, worth about a cent), from which comes our modern word gazette. Technical improvements followed. Printing on both sides of the broadsheet, then folding it down the middle, produced a smaller, four-page newspaper. Our newspapers today are still made to the same two basic sizes: *broadsheet*, with one fold, and *tabloid*, which is the size obtained when you fold again.

In 1609, the first regular, weekly, titled newspapers describing current events began to appear in Germany. The first English newspaper was the Courant or Weekly News, which began in 1621. The first daily was the Daily Courant, established in 1702.

Although they were a vital beginning, these early newspapers were still primitive. Their layout was like that of the books of the time. Articles were very long, rambling and 'learned'. Both the name of the person who had written the report and how old the news was were left unmentioned. There were, of course, no trained journalists, no foreign correspondents, almost no editing. Most reports were penned by anonymous writers who based their accounts on private, 'leaked' information, third-hand accounts, or even gossip. In most cases, both writers and printers made their living by other work as well. It was not until the London Times (established in 1785 as The Universal Register, and changing to its present name three years later) took the daring step of appointing a paid agent to do nothing but cover the French Revolution (the biggest news of the time) that reporting began to move towards the regular and more or less reliable system of covering events, that we know to-day.

An important spur to this advance was the newspapers' growing financial strength. Early newspapers had financed themselves just by the purchase price, the way books do. But late in the seventeenth century, the idea of offering advertising space appeared. With the extra revenue this created, newspapers were able to expand their operations and often to lower the price. So important were advertisements to become that within a short time the front page of all papers consisted entirely of advertise-

ments. This lasted for 150 years. Modern newspapers no longer have a front page of advertisements, but even today, it is advertising that really supports the newspaper industry.

REPRODUCTION OF THE FIRST DAILY NEWSPAPER EVER PUBLISHED IN ENGLAND

---

# EXERCISES

*1. Explain the origins of the following terms:*
*Broadsheet, Tabloid, Gazette, Newsletter.*
*2. Name a. The first English weekly : b. The first English daily.*
*3. When did newspaper advertising first appear?*
*4. According to the author, what were the principal failings of the 17th and early 18th century newspapers?*
*5. Use your dictionary to find the meanings of the difficult words and write them into your Word Copy.*

# Correct Writing
## APOSTROPHE

**1.** It is used to show where letters or figures are left out.

I'm sick of this school, already. (I am)

He didn't do his homework. (did not)

We're going on holidays soon. (we are)

They're very good at cookery. (they are)

I'd like ice-cream. (I would)

I came to this school in '89. (1989)

etc., etc.

**2.** It is used to show possession or belonging.

Paul's bag

Mary's racket

The dog's collar

A day's drive

**Notice:** When a possessor or owner is singular, the apostrophe comes before the s.

The boy's book—(the book belonging to the boy)

The boy's books—(the books belonging to the boy)

When the possessors or owners are plural and the word ends in s, the apostrophe comes after the s.

The boys' book—(the book belonging to the boys)

The boys' books—(the books belonging to the boys)

**Exception A**

If the plural word does not end in s, then you add an s and put the apostrophe before it. But it will be obvious that the plural is meant.

The children's party was a great success.

The women's room is locked!

**Exception B—its, it's**

There is no apostrophe with 'its' when it means belonging:

For example: The tree shook its branches in the wind.

But there is an apostrophe when it means 'it is', as there is a letter left out:

For example: 'It's only the tree, shaking in the wind', she said.

Don't use apostrophes just to indicate the plural of something. Your page could look like it has measles!

# EXERCISES

*1. Find and explain the single example of an apostrophe used in the extract 'First Newspapers'.*

*2. Rewrite the following, inserting apostrophes where necessary:*
*'Its about time you helped out at home, young fellow! You could take that poor dog for its walk, for instance. Its not had any exercise since its nails were clipped. Theres nothing wrong with its feet now, you know.'*

*3. Read the following poem by Roger McGough and then write a short poem about a full stop or a question mark.*

twould be nice to be
an apostrophe
floating
above an s
hovering
like a paper kite
in between the its
eavesdropping, tiptoeing
high above the thats
an inky comet
spiralling
the highest tossed
of hats

*Roger McGough*

## THE GREAT LEAP FORWARD

The nineteenth century saw a real boom in newspapers. Britain, as leader of the Industrial Revolution, was in the forefront of this sudden expansion. It happened for a number of reasons. New techniques in printing technology came with the introduction of steam power. Steam-operated presses were very much faster than the old hand-presses, of course, and with bigger circulations, costs were reduced. The invention of paper-making machines in 1803 further stimulated the industry, though progress was slow until the old practice of pulping cotton was abandoned in the 1870s in favour of paper made from cheap, plentiful wood pulp. In the 1860s, the larger papers began to use continuous rolls of paper, which could be printed simultaneously on both sides, suddenly giving them huge outputs like 10,000 copies per hour. Instead of being the privilege of a small wealthy class, the 'penny press' could become the first genuine mass medium.

This process was hastened by a rise in the level of literacy and general education. State aid to education was introduced in 1832, and in 1870 the law made schooling compulsory, free and universal (i.e. for everyone).

Furthermore, the authorities, who had for centuries tried to contain the spread of information and to censor news, finally accepted newspapers. They could now be seen, not as a threat to governments, but as educators of the people, supporters of trade and the Empire. In 1833, English taxes on newspapers were reduced, and again in 1855. By 1861, they had been removed completely. Nine years later, the coming of universal education meant that every citizen from then on would be able to read the paper. The great modern age of newspapers had begun.

## THE MODERN AGE

Though printing itself was now quite sophisticated, the layout of newspapers remained for a long time very much in the old style - cramped and monotonous. Everything was printed in narrow columns going right down the page, with few paragraph breaks, no photographs, few pictures (by our standards) and tiny headings not much bigger than the text. You actually had to look for the news. The whole of the front page was still devoted to tiny advertisements. The first cross-column streamer headline did not appear in Britain till 1895, although the American papers were more adventurous earlier.

By the beginning of this century, photographs were being reproduced alongside engraved pictures, and, in the popular papers at least, the advertisements were moving off the front page. The idea of a newspaper displaying its contents on the front page in headlines and pictures was emerging. The dramatic events of the First World War speeded up this process as did the increasingly cutthroat competition between the big-circulation dailies. Soon banner headlines in large type were being set across the entire page in an effort to capture readers. Variety was more and more used, both in typefaces and illustration.

Layout was becoming more horizontal (the way the eye 'skims' best) instead of vertical. Though these changes were very slow in coming (the London Times did not abandon its front page of advertisements until 1966), they eventually produced what we think of as the look of a modern newspaper.

Recent decades have seen serious competition from radio and especially television. Many papers have ceased publication, and there have been a lot of mergers (company amalgamations) between the survivors. Advances in typesetting technology—especially computerization—have had a significant impact. The look of newspapers has changed greatly in just a couple of hundred years. The newspapers of the future may look very different again.

# EXERCISES

*1. What do you think are the key sentences or ideas in the first paragraph of this extract?*

*Which sentences are just examples and can be left out of a summary?*

*2. What was the change of heart the government had about newspapers? How did this change of heart show itself in practice?*

*3. Make notes on the main changes that have come about in newspaper layout, as stated in the MODERN AGE section of the extract.*

*4. Can you link the following words with their correct meanings?*

| 1 | BOOM | level, flat | |
| 2 | TECHNOLOGY | ten years | |
| 3 | STIMULATE | rush of activity in business | |
| 4 | SIMULTANEOUSLY | lacking variety, boring | |
| 5 | CENSOR | joins two companies together | |
| 6 | MONOTONOUS | occurring at the same time | |
| 7 | HORIZONTAL | upright | |
| 8 | VERTICAL | to encourage activity, to spur on | |
| 9 | DECADE | technical skills or practical application of | |
| 10 | MERGER | to ban material considered unsuitable | |

*5. Use your dictionary to find the meanings of other difficult words and write them into your Word Copy.*

*6. For pairs: Role play an interview in one of the following situations, between a journalist and*

*a. a student who witnessed a traffic accident or robbery etc. b. the mother or father of a student accused of cheating at an exam, or shoplifting etc.*

*c. a student who won £1,000,000 on the Lotto.*

*7. Be a Real Reporter. Find a real-life news item which has occurred in your locality (street, town, village, townland). Get all the details and write it up in newspaper style. Think up an appropriate headline. Can you get a photograph to go with it?*

*8. Groups. Find out what you can about the National and Provincial papers in Ireland today. Display your information on a wall-chart. Each group could take responsibility for finding out about one particular type of newspaper—daily, Sunday, weekly, evening, etc. Some individuals could write short articles on their research, for publication in your class newspaper.*

*If you are unsure about your spelling, then check the SPELLING GUIDE. Re-write, when necessary.*

# Radio

*The latest technology : Compere operated Studio; RTE*

## SOME ACTIVITIES ( for group discussion)

If you have a favourite radio station, say why you like it?

Do you have a favourite D.J.?

What is your favourite music programme? Why?

Write out the lyric of any song you like.

How many different types of radio programme are available every week—news, current affairs, farming, etc., etc. Study an RTE Guide to find out and list the different types of programme.

## R E P O R T   B A C K

**HOMEWORK:** Listen to any radio programme, other than a music programme. Prepare to describe it to the class: which type, what it was about, names of presenters, people interviewed, music played etc. A brief outline will do.

## A U R A L

Listen to a radio drama in class. Be prepared to name the main characters; outline the plot; say what it was about (the theme); recall any very dramatic episode.

> **GROUP PROJECTS:  a)** record a short radio drama.
> (You might like to try one from the Drama Section).
> **b)** Listen to a Radio News Bulletin
> Notice:  The attention-catching signature tune
> The dramatic headlines
> The urgent speech
> Convert one of your written news items into radio news
> and record it.

# Correct Writing

HOMOPHONES

These are words which are pronounced alike but are
different in meaning or spelling.  Example:  here; hear (hear
has an ear in it!).  Can you find simple ways of explaining
the different uses of the following:

| | |
|---|---|
| two; too | its; it's |
| there; their; they're | son; sun |
| no; know | none; nun |
| whose; who's | some; sum |
| your; you're | loan; lone |
| weigh; way | road; rode; rowed |
| eight; ate | altar; alter |
| weight; wait | miner; minor |
| reign; rain | cellar; seller |
| vein; vain | prey; pray |
| piece; peace | soul; sole |
| route; root | would; wood |
| flower; flour | course; coarse |
| pour; pore | seen; scene |
| sell; cell | sent; cent;  scent |
| practise; practice | not;  knot |
| write; right | |

Can you think of others which cause confusion?
What about:

      of; off

      quiet; quite

      were; where

      to; too; two

Are the sounds of these different?

# Advertising

*A short story about advertising 'The Poppycrunch Kid'*
*by Adele Geras*

'OK, my darling, let me just explain what I want you to do, and then we'll rehearse it a couple of times before we try it on camera. Right?' Melanie nodded. Bill, the producer, was being nice to her. Much nicer than he was to everyone else in the studio. He shouted at them sometimes. Swore even, but he never shouted or swore at her, because she was the Poppycrunch Kid and Very important. Melanie pulled her skirt down and fluffed out her bunches. Were her ribbons still all right? Mum said she was a Star. It was hard to believe. Two weeks ago, she'd lined up with a whole lot of other little girls, and they'd chosen her out of all of them to be the Poppycrunch Kid. Some of the girls had been much prettier, too.

'But your little girl, Mrs White,' Bill had said to her mother and right in front of her, too, 'has such zest, such life, such—how shall I put it? Spice, that's the word, the right word—the others were all—d'you know what I mean?—flavourless. And you see, what the makers do want to promote more than anything, is an image of Brightness, Vigour and Intelligence ... the concept is one of Life, you see, rather than an unreal kind of prettiness. I'm sure Melanie will be Perfection Itself.'

Melanie didn't understand why the sight of her trampolining, skipping, sliding down a helter-skelter, leaping out of bed or doing a tap-dance, dressed always in a red T-shirt and a short white skirt, should make everyone stop buying their favourite cereal and turn to Poppycrunch instead. She wasn't going to eat it.

'But you must,' said Mrs White in desperation.

'Why?'

'It's called Brand Loyalty. They're paying you enough money. You might at least do them the favour of eating their cereal. I think it's lovely.'

'It's horrible. All hard. I could think up a few truthful slogans, like "Tear your gums on a Poppycrunch," or something.'

'But you're going to be famous, Melanie. Don't you want to be famous? Isn't that what you've always wanted? You've said so over and over again. "I want to be a star" you said.'

'It's not being a star—not advertising cereal. I want to be in a proper show, like Annie. I wish I'd got into Annie.'

'You were too tall. I keep telling you. And besides, millions more people see advertisements than ever walk into a theatre. Maybe someone'll spot you. You never know. Anyway, it's good exposure, you've got to say that for it.'

That was the only reason Melanie could think of for doing it. Someone, someone from Hollywood even, would see her trampolining or skipping or whatever, and decide, right there on the spot, that she was exactly what he needed for his very next film, and whisk her far away in a jet to be a real actress, a child star.

'Are you ready, Melanie?' Bill cooed.

'Yes.'

'Right. Let's start then.'

Melanie skipped towards the trampoline (red, with 'Poppy-crunch' written on it in white letters) leaped on to it and began to bounce, singing at the same time the silly little tune they'd given her to learn, and smiling widely enough to crack her face open:

Full of goodness
Full of fun

Poppycrunch

The chewy one!

Three things at once—it was harder to do than it looked, like patting your head with one hand while rubbing the other hand over your stomach in circles. Melanie had to do it four times before she'd got it just right. At last, Bill was satisfied.

'Great my love,' he said. 'Absolutely scrumptious. Now as soon as you've got your breath back, we'll film it . OK?'

'Yes,' said Melanie. The thought of doing it all over again on film made the butterflies start up in her stomach, just as though she were about to act in front of a real, live audience. It was silly. There was only Bill, and Christine, his assistant and some lighting men and sound men, and her mother in the corner of the studio, and of course, the cameras. Melanie had never though about the cameras before. They were like robots: huge square tall things on long metal legs that slid across the floor trailing thick black cables like snakes. You had to look at them quite hard to spot the men who were working them. The cameras had lenses for eyes sticking out towards you. Never, never looking at anything else except you. Melanie shivered.

'Now, Melanie, I don't want you to think about the cameras at all. Just forget about them. They're not there, all right? I want you to be quite, quite natural, my love and Reg and Ben here will do all the work—focus on you like mad, all the time. Give Melanie a little wave, lads, just to show her you're there.'

Arms came out of the sides of the camera and waved. It was as if the cameras themselves were waving at her.

'Right-o, my dears,' said Bill. 'If you're all ready I'm going to do my Cecil B. de Mille routine ... Roll'em!'

Melanie sang and smiled and trampolined. She sang and smiled and trampolined seven times. They had to do seven 'takes' before everything came out exactly as Bill wanted it.

'That's fantastic, Melanie. Really fantastic. It's not unknown for me to do a dozen takes. Great. It's going to look great. Come and see.'

Melanie went. It seemed like a lot of other advertisements to her. She was quite pleased with how high she'd managed to jump on the trampoline, but it was all over so quickly—a few seconds, that was all. Tomorrow they would do leaping out of bed. That shouldn't be so tiring. Suddenly Melanie felt exhausted, unable to think straight. The silly words and silly tune of the Poppycrunch jingle had got stuck in her head and wound round her other thoughts like thin strings of chewing-gum that wouldn't come off.

Full of goodness

Full of fun

Poppycrunch

The chewy one!

Round and round in her head.

That night, Melanie dreamed that Camera One was in her bedroom. Standing in the doorway and looking at her room. And there was a wind. It blew all round the room and sucked the furniture and the toys and all her dolls and clothes and the pictures from the walls till everything was whirling round and round in a spiral that started out huge and got smaller and smaller until at last it vanished right into the lens of the camera and then the walls weren't there any longer either, just a bed with her in it, and Camera One floating about in a bright, colourless space that went on and on for ever and never stopped.

'Christine,' said Melanie, 'do you think you could ask Bill something for me?'

'Of course poppet. Anything you like. What is it?'

'Well, it's a bit embarrassing ...'

'Go on, you can tell me. Can't you? You know I'll help.'

'Yes, I know, but it's so stupid.'

'Never mind, it's obviously worrying you, so go ahead and tell me. You'll feel better, honestly.'

'It's Camera One, I'm scared of it.'

'Scared of a camera?' Christine smiled. 'But why, love? What do you think it can do to you?'

'I don't know. I dreamed about it, that's all.'

'You're overwrought, my love. Don't worry. You're frightened because it's new to you. It's ... well ... it's a bit like stage fright, only different. Come and have a look. I'll get Reg to let you touch it and get to know it so you'll never be frightened of it again.'

Reg was understanding. 'It's only a kind of mechanical eye, love. That's all. Metal and glass and stuff that can see. It is a bit like magic, I grant you, because it's a clever old thing. Does a lot that your eyes and mine can't do—it can give back the pictures that it sees and show them all over again, but it's not magic, see. It's called Technology. Nothing to be scared of, honestly.'

'No, I suppose not,' said Melanie. 'I'm being stupid.'

'No, no love,' said Reg. 'It's not stupid. I'll tell you something. There are primitive tribes in the world, New Guinea and places like that, and they don't even like snapshots being taken of them. They reckon every time a photo gets taken, it steals away a bit of their soul. That's their superstition, see? Bet you've had a million snapshots taken of you since you were born, and you're none the worse for it, are you? Neither is anyone else. So don't worry, OK?'

'OK', said Melanie and went over to the beautiful bed that had been set out on the studio floor. I wish Reg hadn't told me that, she thought. About those people in New Guinea. I know it's only superstition, but I wish he hadn't told me, all the same.

'Action!' Bill shouted and Melanie bounded out of bed, grinning and singing:

Ready for work
Ready for play
Start every day
The Poppycrunch way

She did it ten times. It wasn't her fault. They had to find some way of getting the pillow into the picture with her. The famous Poppycrunch symbol was printed on the pillowslip, and of course, it had to be seen, or what was the point?

There were three more films to make. The helter-skelter was fun. A very short tune and not a lot of words:

Bite it
Munch it
Poppycrunch it!

Also, Melanie didn't care how many times she had to come sliding down till the timing was just perfect. She was getting used to filming, beginning to enjoy it, just as Bill and Christine and Reg had said she would. She sang the songs at home, all the time. At school, she showed her friends exactly what she had to do. She found it very hard to concentrate on her work, because her head was full of bouncy music and bright slogan words and they seemed to be pushing whatever it was she was supposed to be thinking about into some corner of her mind where she could never quite reach it. Miss Hathersage, her teacher, asked her one day:

'Melanie, dear, what are seven nines?'

Melanie's mind raced. Seven nines? What were nines? Full of goodness ... Nine whats? Sevens ... Full of fun ...

'I don't know, please, Miss.'

'Of course you know, dear. You did the nine times table last year. Now come on, dear, think.'

Melanie thought ... the chewy one. She closed her eyes ... white skirt flying ... jump as high as you can ... Poppycrunch ... ready for work ... ready for play ...

'I can't think, Miss, I'm sorry.' Melanie hung her head.

'Very well, then. Sarah, some people have let being on television go to their heads, I can see. What are seven nines?'

'Sixty-three, Miss Hathersage.'

'Quite right. Sixty-three. Do you remember now, Melanie?'

'Yes, Miss.' But I don't remember, Melanie thought. I don't and I must. Seven nines are sixty-three, sixty-three. Even as she thought it, she felt the numbers slipping away, losing their meaning, losing themselves over the precipices that seemed to lie at the very edges of her mind.

That night, Melanie dreamed that she was reading. Camera One was looking at her as she turned the pages of her book. She watched as the words flew off the page and drifted on to the floor, millions of tiny black letters, all over the rug. She tried to pick them up and put them back into the book in the right order, but they fell out of her hands, and crumbled like ash when she touched them.

'What's the matter, love?' said Christine. 'You're looking a bit pale today. Are you tired? I bet you are, you know. You've had to do all these films one on top of the other, and never a rest in between. Bill,' she raised her voice. 'I'm going to take Melanie back to Make-up. I think she needs a spot more rouge, don't you?'

Bill came and stood in front of Melanie, frowning.

'Yes, darling. Oh, and ask them at the same time to see if they can get rid of those shadows under her eyes. You've not been looking after yourself, love, now have you? You must, you know. That's what we're paying you for—to look healthy, full of life. Run along with Christine now and see what Make-up can do

for you'

Melanie lay in the make-up chair listening to Christine's voice which seemed to come from very far away.

'I don't think you're getting enough sleep, love. Honestly. Are you?'

'I start every day the Poppycrunch way ... ' Melanie whispered.

'Are you sleeping properly, Melanie?'

'I dream a lot,' Melanie said.

'Bad dreams?' Christine sounded concerned.

'No. Poppycrunch dreams. Just me and Camera One.'

'You dream about Camera One? I thought you'd got over all that. You don't seem nervous in front of the cameras at all. What do you dream?'

'I dream I'm singing and I don't know what comes next and then Camera One looks at me and I know ... I know what to do if it looks at me. It tells me what to say.'

'What does it tell you to say?'

'Words. Tunes.
Poppycrunch for you
Poppycrunch for me
Poppycrunch for breakfast
Poppycrunch for tea.'

'Those are today's words,' Christine sounded worried. 'I'll have a word with your Mum and Bill after the filming today. I reckon you need a damn good rest. You're just exhausted. Tell me,'she added as though something has just occurred to her, 'what do you do at home? For relaxation? Do you read any books?'

'No. I stopped. I used to like it, but then I stopped.'

'Why did you stop?'

Melanie looked up. 'Because I can't remember what the story's about any more. I can't hold the story in my head. It's as though,' Melanie hesitated, 'as though my head's full of deep, black water and everything that goes in

*A still from a T.V. advertisement for Club Orange*

it just sinks under the water and won't come up to the surface again.'

'Right,' said Christine. 'See if you can get through this afternoon's filming and then I'll have a word with them. It won't be long now.'

'Oh', Melanie's face lit up, 'you don't have to do that. Don't worry. I love it. I love the filming. I love Camera One. I know all the words. And all the tunes. And just what to do.' Melanie skipped all the way back to the studio, singing the Poppycrunch jingle for today. Christine followed more slowly. All hell was going to break loose when she told Bill. That was for sure.

'Christine, my beloved', said Bill, 'you have clearly taken leave of your senses. Let me go over what you've just said. Melanie White is exhausted and overwrought and you think we should scrap the whole of the last film. Is that right?'

'Yes', said Christine quietly. 'That's quite right.'

'Well, now, I'll answer you as calmly as I can because I don't want a row. I'll try and go over the points one by one so that you understand. First, the Poppycrunch commercials are the hottest thing I've done since the Sucka-mints Campaign, and you know how many prizes that won. Sales of Poppycrunch are up twenty per cent in the last two weeks. It follows, therefore, that the makers are not going to look kindly on someone jeopardising their profits. Second, this last film is the biggest and most important of all. It's much longer. It's got fifteen other kids in it besides Melanie, doing things in the background while she dances at the front, and each one of those kids has to be cossetted and looked after, not to mention paid. It has a ten-piece band that has to be cossetted and looked after as much as the kids and paid even more. We've booked studio time. We've rehearsed, and we've even paid through our noses to be allowed to use the tune of "Sweet Georgia Brown". So I ask you, how can I cancel? Go on. Tell me. I'm anxious to know.'

Christine said nothing. Bill went on:

'What do you think, Mrs White? Would you be in favour of cancelling? Do you think Melanie is exhausted and over-wrought?'

'Well', Mrs White considered. 'She is a bit tired, naturally. I mean, we all are, aren't we? I am myself and I just sit here and watch. But Melanie would be ever so put out if it was cancelled. I do know that. Eats, drinks and sleeps Poppycrunch, she does. Obsessed with it. Sings those tunes all day and every day. If her friends come over she teaches them all the words, tells them everything she has to do. They just play Poppycrunch games. Well, they don't come round much any more. I reckon they're fed up and I have said to her she ought to ease up a bit, but it's as if she can't. It's as if, I can't explain it really, as if there's no room left inside her for anything else.'

'Then don't you think we should stop it before it's too late?' Christine said. 'You're her mother. You can see. You've said yourself—she's obsessed.'

'Yes, but,' Mrs White looked down at her hands, embarrassed, 'I'm sure it'll be all right when all the filming's finished. It is only one more, after all, isn't it?'

'Right,' said Bill. 'Only one more. So that's decided. I'm really glad we were able to agree, Mrs White. It's going to be a corker, this last film. Wait and see.'

That night, Melanie dreamed again. Her mother, and her school friends and Bill and Christine were all standing in the television studio and one by one they went up and stood in front of Camera One. Each one of them went right up to the camera and said something and then they got smaller and smaller until they disappeared altogether. Then she went and stood right up close to Camera One and said 'I'm the Poppycrunch Kid' and then she got larger and larger until she took up all the space in the studio and Camera One kept looking at her and she kept growing and growing until she was all there was left in the whole world.

Melanie knew all the words, of course, but they were written up on a big board for the benefit of the fifteen little girls who had to jiggle up and down in the background while Melanie tapdanced at the front. The only words Melanie had to sing were: 'The Poppycrunch Kid'. She had to sing it six times and then the film ended with her singing the last three lines all on her own. This is the best of all, thought Melanie. A real band, not a tape, all those other children, and that tune, so much more zingy than the others.

'Here we go kids,' said Bill. 'Let's try it from the top.'

The saxophone played an introduction and the children dutifully began jigging about and singing as Melanie went into the dance routine:

'Who's that kid with the bouncy step?'
'The Poppycrunch Kid!'
(this was Melanie's line)
'Who's the girl who's full of pep?'
'The Poppycrunch Kid!'
'Who's got the other kids all sewn up?'
'The Poppycrunch Kid!'
'The Poppycrunch Kid!'
'You said it, you did!'
'Who's got the shiny eyes and hair?'
'The Poppycrunch Kid!'
'When fun happens, who's right there?'
'The Poppycrunch Kid'
'The cereal this kid eats
Is the kind with the built-in treats ...
Nuts and honey
For your money
Be a Poppycrunch Kid!'

It was much harder, Melanie decided, filming with all the others. So many things went wrong. Someone's hair ribbon coming undone, someone looking the wrong way, a wrong note from one of the band: any one of a thousand things could happen and did happen and they had to start again. Melanie didn't mind. She fixed her eyes on Camera One's magic eye, and felt as though just looking at it, she was falling and falling down into a place where there was nothing except light and music and tapping feet and words that circled in her brain and didn't puzzle her or worry her or make her think: words that comforted her, made her feel safe, magic words that were all she needed to say. Spells, incantations that were so powerful they could empty your head of every other thought ...

'Twenty takes,' said Bill. 'I'm finished. Completely and utterly finished, Christine, and that's the truth.'

'You're not the only one,' said Christine. 'Did you see Melanie?'

'She's a real trouper, that kid. I mean she even looked as if she were loving every minute of it all the way through.'

'She was', said Christine. 'It's not normal. How's she going to go back to ordinary life? I worry about it sometimes.'

'Don't be silly, love. It's not as though she's the first child ever to appear on a commercial. We've got another lot coming in tomorrow to audition for the crisps film, Lord help us.'

'No, but she was different.'

'Bloody good on camera, though', said Bill, 'and that's what counts in the end isn't it?'

'Oh yes', Christine agreed dully. 'The camera just loved her. You could see that.'

On the studio floor, Camera One stood amid its cables with a plastic cover over it to protect it from the dust. Its work was finished. Until tomorrow. Until the next child was chosen.

'Hello, dear,' said the doctor. 'And how are you today?'

*Shooting the Club Orange advertisement.*

'Full of goodness, full of fun', said Melanie.

'You're looking much better, I must say. Have you thought about what I asked you yesterday?'

Melanie nodded.

'Good girl. That's a good girl. Now. Tell me who you are. Tell me your name.'

'The Poppycrunch Kid.'

'No Melanie. That's not your name, is it? Your name is Melanie White. Believe me. Say it.'

'Melanie White.'

'There, doesn't that sound better? Are you going to play today, Melanie?'

'Ready for work, ready for play, start every day the Poppycrunch way.'

'You could play outside today. It's a beautiful day.'

'I'm full of pep ...'

'I'm glad to hear it. Your mother will be coming to see you today. That'll be nice, won't it? You love having visitors, don't you?'

'Bite it, munch it, Poppycrunch it ...'

'I'll see you tomorrow then, Melanie.' The doctor stood up. 'I'll look in after breakfast.'

'Poppycrunch for breakfast,' said Melanie and turned over to look at the wall.

I've got shiny eyes and hair and when fun happens I'm right there, but they took Camera One away. Maybe if I'm extra good, it'll come back. I'm the kid with the bouncy step. That man. He's the producer. But I've got the other kids all sewn up. They can't let anyone else be the Poppycrunch Kid. They put me here to see. To see if I really am the Poppycrunch Kid and if I'm not, then they'll choose someone else. But I'm the one—The Poppycrunch Kid, you said it, you did—when fun happens who's right there, the cereal this kid eats, is the one with the built-in treats, nuts and honey, bite it, munch it, Poppycrunch it.

She could hear them at visiting time.

'Look, Herbert', said the lady's voice. 'Isn't that the kid who was on the telly? You know, the Poppycereal stuff. I'm sure it's her.'

'Don't be silly', said Herbert. 'She was pretty—full of life. That kid looks half-dead to me.'

I'm not, she thought, I'm full of fun, full of goodness ... Poppycrunch for me ...

# THE STORY

*DISCUSSION*
*(for pairs or larger groups)*
*1. Discuss the main characters in the story. Give a brief description of each, basing your views on evidence from the story.*
*2. What happened to Melanie? Suggest possible reasons.*

# REPORT BACK

*3. Did the adults behave responsibly, in your view?*
*4. What do you think are the themes of the story?*

## REPORT BACK

*5. Do you think the author wants us to draw a moral from this story? If so, suggest one.*
*6. Did you think the dialogue was realistic (would people speak like that)? Discuss examples.*
*7. What was your own reaction to the story?*

## REPORT BACK

*8. Do you know the meanings of the following terms? producer; star; studio; lenses; a 'take'; commercial.*
*9. Use your dictionary to find the meanings of any difficult words and write them into your Word Copy.*
*10. Were there any descriptions which you thought particularly well done?*
*11. Write a happy ending for the story.*
*12. Read it again.*

# ADVERTISING: THE PURPOSE

## E X E R C I S E S

*1. What was the purpose of the commercial in the story? Discuss.*

*The main purposes of advertising are:*
*A. To persuade us to buy*
*B. To give information, about a product, service or job.*
*A small percentage of advertisements are neutral and convey information only but most advertisements both give information and try to persuade, at the same time.*

*2. Did the Poppycrunch commercial give us any information? If so, what? How did it try to persuade us? Discuss, in your groups.*
*3. Read through some of the advertisements in your newspaper or magazines. Notice the great range of products and the variety of advertisements, from great display ones to appointments, to classified advertisements. (Time limit: 10-15 minutes.) Then select one which you find very persuasive. Explain the reasons for your choice, to your group. Choose one from each group for Report Back.*
*4. Examine a few samples of classified advertisements and compose one about a house, a car, a school uniform, a fridge, or a bicycle for sale.*
*5. Examine a display advertisement and design one for: a soft drink or a new chocolate bar or a book or comic for young people or another cereal.*
*You must take great care that your advertisement says exactly what you want it to say. The writers of the following advertisements were very careless. You rewrite them so that they make better sense!*

### WANTED
Some additional female technicians at the fast-expanding Charles River Breeding Laboratory. No previous experience necessary.

*Advert in Massachusetts paper.*

American Electric Blanket for sale, new.
Owner leaving.
Rosepink colour.

*Advert in Sunday paper.*

Capital Pet Animal Hospital
Dogs called for, fleas removed and returned to you for $1.00.

*Advert in Washington Paper.*

Accommodation available. Will suit two working girls,
willing to share room or young respect-able working man.

*Wisbech Standard*

Cook wanted, March 1st. Comfortable room with radio;
two in family; only one who can be well recommended.

*Advert in Hereford paper*

**LOST**
Antique cameo ring, depicting Adam and Eve in Market Square Saturday night.

*Advert in Essex paper*

Girl wanted for petrol pump attendant.

*Advert in Oxford Mail*

## TARGET AUDIENCE

We meet many forms of advertising each day, from TV and radio advertisements (called commercials), newspaper and magazine advertisements, posters, notices on church door or shop window, to leaflets dropped through our letter-boxes.

Each advertisement is attempting to appeal to a particular category or type of person. The advertising company sets out deliberately to target a particular age group or people in a certain financial bracket or social class etc. Some advertisements are directed mainly towards women, some towards men, some towards young people. Advertisers even use the term Target Audience to describe the kind of people to whom the advertisement is directed.

### E X E R C I S E S

*1. What do you think was the target audience in the Poppycrunch commercial?*
*2. Examine your chosen newspaper advertisement again, or find another one and see if you can discover the target audience.*
*3. Study some TV advertisements and see if you can spot the target audience.*
*4. Bring in a selection of magazine advertisements and have a discussion about the target audience of some of them.*

"She wants a
shoe that fits."

"I want a shoe
that's stylish."

Buying new shoes for a daughter
can turn out to be a battle of wills.
  She's only interested in fashion (and
what her friends might think or say).
  You, her caring Mum, are more
concerned about the
fit of the shoe and
health of her
feet.

Princess

Fortunately, with Clarks there's no
conflict of interest.
  Our latest shoes for girls are
flatteringly stylish enough to
satisfy the most fashion-conscious
young lady.
  But, of course, they all have leather
or suede uppers
so young feet
can breathe.

Tanita

And, of course, they're available in
width fittings and whole and half sizes
so young feet can grow straight and
strong.
  And, of course, they'll be fitted by a
trained fitter who'll use a Clarks
footgauge plus a wealth of expertise to
ensure that vital,
correct fit.

Brosette

So with fashion and fit, you'll both be
very happy with her Clarks new shoes.
Let harmony reign.

# Clarks

# Why be at loggerheads when she could be in Clarks?

STYLES FEATURED: PRINCESS SIZES 9–3 FROM £20.99, TANITA SIZES 11–5½ FROM £19.99, BROSETTE SIZES 3–7½ FROM £26.99 AVAILABLE IN WIDTH FITTINGS
FROM CLARKS SPECIALISTS. ALSO FEATURED CLARKS 'SOFTLIFE' FOR WOMEN STYLE STELLA AT £32.99 PRICES CORRECT AT TIME OF GOING TO PRESS.

# A little earlier and the picture would have told a different story.

We know how worrying and distressing it can be for you, as a caring mother, to see your normally bright-eyed happy child suddenly red cheeked, restless and crying in pain. And all the usual comforting doesn't help.

So, especially with mothers of young children in mind, who want only the best for them, we've developed a pleasantly flavoured, liquid pain reliever called Medised.

Medised is a combination of Paracetamol and Promethazine; it soothes and relieves pain. Medised can be given day or night to children aged from three months. It quickly relieves painful conditions such as toothache, feverish cold, sore throat and general minor discomforts. Therefore Medised allows your child to sleep, and gives you peace of mind.

Medised is available without prescription from your Chemist who will be pleased to advise you.

## Eases children's pain to sleep

185

## CREATING AN IMAGE
### THE STORY AGAIN

### E X E R C I S E S

*1. Think again about Melanie. What sort of girl is she? Is she an ordinary young girl with ambitions and hopes for the future? Is she completely happy with the commercial? Is she convinced by it or is she more realistic? Is she completely confident always? Always full of life?*

*2. What sort of person is 'The Poppycrunch Kid' in the advertisement? Look at the detail of the story.*

*3. So could it be said that the story is about reality and fantasy? How? Are there two different examples of this idea?*

*4. Have you ever tried to create an image by appearing cool, tough, brainy, stupid, etc. Think about it.*

**A.** Advertisers often use Pictures or Images to create an illusion, a fantasy world. These frequently suggest that a product is more exciting or better than it actually is. What pictures or images did the commercial use to suggest health or vitality? Was this real? It is important to examine an advertisement for: a) what it says; b) what it does not say; c) what it suggests.

Study the following advertisements. Look particularly at the picture or image. What does the advertisement actually say? Now what does it suggest, through the picture? Write two paragraphs on this.

# Take a deep breath and say–
# 'Thank you, Natural Gas'

At Bord Gáis Éireann, it's our job to bring Natural Gas to homes and industry. And this great natural resource has brought enormous benefits to both our environment and our economy.

As more and more industries change over to this clean pure energy, pollution levels decrease. The air we breathe is getting sweeter. Literally thousands and thousands of tons of sulphur dioxide have disappeared from our atmosphere.

Industry itself is beginning to clean up as lower energy costs help make companies more competitive in home and export markets. Saving the country a breathtaking £1.75 billion in foreign fuel bills to date.

Some things are looking better for the future. So breathe a little sigh of relief.

BORD GÁIS

# Agfa cine film:

## Setting the scene for a perfect take.

Many of the world's outstanding feature films are shot on Agfa film.

**Agfa products are already part of your everyday life…**

Starting with your morning paper – all over the world newspapers are produced using Agfa repro films…or in the office, when you run off a series of perfect copies on your Agfa copier…or when you step off an aircraft that's been inspected using Agfa X-ray film. And talking of X-rays, the last one you had may well have been made with Agfa film. When you're enjoying a record or a video cassette, chances are the recording was made on Agfa magnetic tape. At the cinema, the film you're seeing may have been shot on Agfa cine film. And how often have you proudly passed around your holiday snaps printed on Agfacolor paper?

All over Europe and throughout the world, you come across Agfa quality every day – the kind of quality you'll find in the new Agfacolor Maxi XRG 100 film shown here. If you'd like to get the whole Agfa story, just write to: Agfa-Gevaert Ltd., P.O. Box No. 368A, John F. Kennedy Drive, Naas Road, Dublin 12 or call us on: 01-50 67 33.

# A European name – a worldwide reputation

**B.** Advertisers also use words (called 'copy'). These can be whole paragraphs of persuasive writing or just slogans or catchy phrases. Just like newspaper headlines, slogans have a more immediate effect on the reader. And the advertisers hope they will remain longer in the memory—slogans such as: 'Whenever there's a snack gap—"Twix" fits!'. Often these slogans are put to music (jingles) such as: 'Let your fingers do the walking' or 'Yes Yes Yes with the EBS'.

# E X E R C I S E S

*1. What other advertising slogans or jingles can you remember? What does each one sell?*

*2. Bring in a collection of magazine advertisements without captions and show them around.*

*Compose slogans for them. Have a slogan competition for some particular advertisements.*

*3. If you have not already done so, design an advertising poster for your Newsletter.*

*4. Working in groups of three, compose an advertisement for a particular product, to appeal to a particular age group. (New crisps; a soft drink; a bicycle; a watch; a new skin cream; clothes; or any other)*

*5. Record some Radio Commercials.*

*\* You might like to read 'The TV Kid' by Betsy Byars. This is a short novel about an American boy, who is a TV addict and daydreams himself into the programmes, instead of doing his homework.*

## HAVE A DEBATE

Debating is a little different from the Public Speaking you have done so far. Debating, like advertising, is about convincing people that you are right.

### HINTS

**A.** Put forward well argued points.

**B.** Use examples or word pictures/images so that people can see clearly what you mean.

**C.** Speak in a confident tone of voice.

**D.** Some humour often wins an audience.

**E.** Be prepared to deal with objections.

Have a discussion on the format of your debate. Perhaps 3-minute speeches would be sufficient, where each speaker has 2 uninterrupted minutes but can be heckled during the last minute!

Some Possible Topics:

That advertising is a good idea.

That comics should be banned.

That television is a waste of time.

Other?

# Correct Writing
## ANSWERING ADVERTISEMENTS
## AND
## FILLING APPLICATION FORMS

## E X E R C I S E S

*1. Imagine that you have seen the following advertisement in the local paper. Write for an application form.*

# NIRVANA HOTEL TULLA

We have vacancies for

lounge-boys;

lift attendants;

junior waiters and

waitresses;

telephonists;

chambermaids and

car park attendants.

Write to the Assistant Manager for an application form, stating which position interests you.

**NOTE:** A business letter is just like a personal letter except -

**a.** you put in the title and address of the person to whom you are writing, at the left side.

**b.** you usually sign off as 'Yours faithfully'.

**c.** the style of language is usually formal rather than chatty.

**d.** you must decide what to say about yourself.

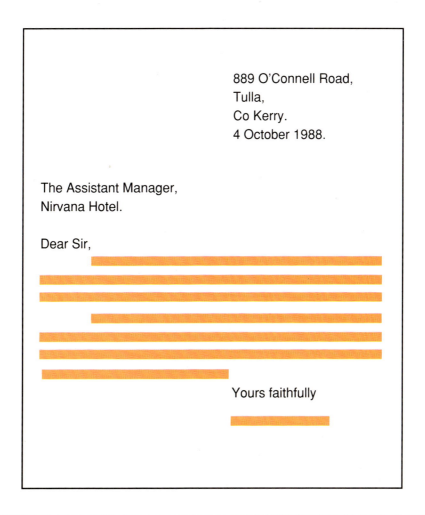

889 O'Connell Road,
Tulla,
Co Kerry.
4 October 1988.

The Assistant Manager,
Nirvana Hotel.

Dear Sir,

Yours faithfully

## E X E R C I S E

*2. Using the headings from the following application form, complete the various sections in your exercise copy. You may need more space than is provided here. Neatness is important.*

# APPLICATION FORM

**1.** Name (block capitals) — — — — — — — — — — — — — — — — — —

**2.** Address — — — — — — — — — — — — — — — — — — — — — —

— — — — — — — — — — — — — — — — — — — — — — — — — —

**3.** Date of Birth — — — — — — — — — — — — — — — — — — — —

**4.** If under 18, give name and address of parent or guardian — — — — — —

— — — — — — — — — — — — — — — — — — — — — — — — —

— — — — — — — — — — — — — — — — — — — — — — — — —

— — — — — — — — — — — — — — — — — — — — — — — — —

**5.** Post for which application is made — — — — — — — — — — — — —

**6.** Date when applicant could start work — — — — — — — — — — — —

**7.** Information on schooling (schools attended, with dates, certificates, if any, etc. — — — — — — — — — — — — — — — — — — — — — —

— — — — — — — — — — — — — — — — — — — — — — — —

— — — — — — — — — — — — — — — — — — — — — — — —

**8.** Hobbies or Interests — — — — — — — — — — — — — — — — —

— — — — — — — — — — — — — — — — — — — — — — — —

— — — — — — — — — — — — — — — — — — — — — — — —

**9.** Position of responsibility held, if any, in school or club — — — — — — —

— — — — — — — — — — — — — — — — — — — — — — — —

— — — — — — — — — — — — — — — — — — — — — — — —

**10.** Details of any other employment. Give name and address of employer and position held, with dates — — — — — — — — — — — — — — —

— — — — — — — — — — — — — — — — — — — — — — — —

— — — — — — — — — — — — — — — — — — — — — — — —

**11.** Serious illnesses, with dates — — — — — — — — — — — — — —

— — — — — — — — — — — — — — — — — — — — — — — —

**12.** Names and addresses of two people to whom we may apply for a reference — — — — — — — — — — — — — — — — — — — —

— — — — — — — — — — — — — — — — — — — — — — — —

# REVISION

## TEST YOURSELF

**1.** Can you remember what each of the following terms means?

THE MASS MEDIA
NEWS
A CLASSIFIED AD.
AN EDITORIAL
AN OBITUARY
A FEATURE
BROADSHEET
TABLOID
MASTHEAD
COLUMNS

HEADLINE
CAPTION
REPORTER
BULLETIN
A COMMERCIAL
TARGET AUDIENCE
'COPY'
SLOGANS
JINGLES
THE W QUESTIONS

**2.** Name three Irish local or provincial newspapers.

**3.** - When is an apostrophe used?

When do you use 'its' and when 'it's'?

Use the following words correctly in sentences: to; too; two; of; off; quite; quiet; were; where.

**4.** Write a letter to a local shop or store, applying for a summer job.

**5.** Design a display advertisement for a dictionary.

**6.** Have you got the following words in your Word Copy and can you remember what each means?

ELECTRONIC
INVENTION
ALLITERATION
ASSONANCE
PYRAMID
HOROSCOPE
LEGISLATION
DISPATCH
PRIMITIVE
REMARKABLE
MINSTREL
ASSEMBLED
EXPAND
REVENUE
INDUSTRY

FINANCIAL
INTRODUCTION
CONTINUOUS
CENTURY
UNIVERSAL
DESPERATION
FAMOUS
TRAMPOLINE
AN ASSISTANT
VANISHED
OVERWROUGHT
TO CONCENTRATE
PRECIPICES
EXHAUSTED
CANCELLED

# UNIT 4

## FICTION

THE WORK IN THIS SECTION
IS CENTRED AROUND THE
NOVEL 'FLIGHT OF THE DOVES'
*BY WALTER MACKEN*

# Focus On A Novel

There are many ways of approaching a novel. You might, for instance, just read the novel right through, for the sheer enjoyment of it. Or we could make the novel the focus of a considerable unit of work, as is done here. So, depending on time and circumstances, your teacher may wish you to use some or all of the questions, suggested work and readings contained here.

But at the very least you should have a separate copy, where you can note down your ideas on the characters as they emerge, chapter by chapter. You could also enter your reactions to the story or plot as it develops, or keep a diary as if you were one of the characters. You should make lists of new words and meanings at the back of this copy. These exercises presume that you now use your dictionary every day.

## CHAPTER 1

## COMPREHENSION

**1.** What is the relationship between Uncle Toby and the children? Is he really their uncle?

**2.** Describe the house as accurately as you can. Have a competition to see who can recall the most accurate and detailed descriptions.

**3.** Working in pairs compose an accurate description of the two missing children for an 'ALL OUT ALERT' on the 6 o'clock news. Write it and then read it aloud or record it.

## CHARACTER STUDY

**4.** Build up a character study of Uncle Toby, from the details in the first chapter. Comb the chapter again for references to him.

**(a)** PHYSICAL DESCRIPTIONS

**(b)** HIS ACTIONS—Look at what he does and decide what these actions suggest about him.

**(c)** WHAT HE SAYS—It might help to read his lines in an Uncle Toby tone of voice.

In this way build up a written character study of him. Leave lots of space in your copy so that you can add to it, chapter by chapter.

**5.** Keep an imaginary diary as Finn or Derval or Uncle Toby. Choose a character and plan to keep his or her diary throughout the novel. Try to keep your diary character true to the character in the novel.

# Correct Writing

MORE ABOUT NOUNS.

\* Words used to name everyday things are called COMMON NOUNS. For example: desk, school, road, house, office, teacher, pupil etc.

\* Words used to name specific people, places or things are call PROPER NOUNS. They are written with capital letters. For example: John, Limerick, Christmas, 'The Independent', the Dáil, Ireland, Mrs Williams, etc.

\* Words used to describe a collection of people or things are called COLLECTIVE NOUNS.

**For Example**
a pair of shoes
a pack of cards
a flock of birds
a school of whales

## E X E R C I S E

Have brainstorming sessions in your small groups to make lists of the more unusual collective nouns. Compile a class list and display it. For example a — of witches; a — of horses; a — of puppies etc. Have a collective noun quiz.

*\* Words used to name feelings, ideas, qualities, states, actions are ABSTRACT NOUNS. They are called abstract, as opposed to concrete, because they name feelings, ideas, etc., which you cannot touch or visualise in a concrete way. For example, honesty, happiness, knowledge, destruction, etc.*

**6.** Look at the opening section again, from 'Finn' to 'Derval'. Write out a list of all the nouns you can find and say whether each is common, proper, abstract or collective.

**7.** Study how dialogue is written in this chapter. Write the dialogue that might have occurred between Uncle Toby and a friend in 'The Red Dragon', later that evening.

**8.** Have a meaning and spelling competition based on the words in this chapter.

# ORAL

**9.** Describe exactly how you would prepare for a journey by boat or plane; or a walking or cycling trip; or a camping weekend. Plan it in precise detail. You can make notes but don't write out every word. Then relate it to the class. The class silently makes notes as you speak and then tries to spot errors in the order of instructions or the details of your plan.

**10.** Now read 'Empty House' by Gareth Owen. After a number of silent readings each student should be able to make a one-sentence statement beginning 'I noticed that ....' Have a class discussion on this poem. What are the speaker's feelings? Can you find a noun to describe them? What images do you like? etc.

## EMPTY HOUSE

There is nothing
Quite so dismal
As an empty house;
The door bell's clangour
Tears apart the silence
Rousing no one.
Nothing moves;
Not a sound
Save the chasing echoes
And the clock's hollow
Tock, tock
Measuring the emptiness;
Behind the frosted door
No friendly, welcome shadow looms,
No footsteps cross the floor.

The yellow key
Hides coldly in its hiding place
Behind the rusty carcass of the B.S.A.
Amongst old tins of paint;

Maps of oil stain the floor
And in the air the smell
Of dust and turps and sawdust
(Property of all garages).
Whistling softly,
I turn the key
And open the door slowly,
As if the emptiness
Was a stranger
I might find sitting
Silent in an armchair.

The house is strange,
Not mine any more,
Holding its breath,
Waiting; a house not real,
Not itself
But an accurate copy taken from life,
Familiar but lacking warmth.
The note from mother
Telling me not to let the fire go out
Scrawled on an envelope
Leans against the clock.
I wander through deserted rooms
Touching familiar objects;
Comforted by companionable flowers in a jar
And by the bulk of our white cat
Who dozes on whatever.

The coals have crumbled to ash;
The fire is out.
I lie, my feet up on a chair,
Reading my comic,
Wishing my mother could be home
To tell me not to put them there.

## CHAPTER 2

# DRAMA

**1.** Devise a short dramatic scene (involving the whole class) set in a railway or bus station.

Take roles as paper sellers, food vendors, ticket collectors and other officials, cleaners, travellers in small groups, etc. Decide who you are, your age, name, sex, occupation, nationality, etc.

Decide the layout of the station and take up positions.

At a given signal the station comes to life. Have a conversation, in your chosen role. If you have a tape of station noises (taken from radio, television or real life) play it for atmosphere. Do people talk loudly or quietly? Is it peaceful or bustling?

Play out the scene for 5 or 10 minutes. Do people meet? You might introduce a focus action such as someone jumping the ticket queue and explaining why. Be imaginative.

**2.** Then get together in groups of three or five and brainstorm one another for lists of words on the sights, sounds, feelings, etc. you might experience in a station.

**3.** Write a little poem about a railway station or a conversation you might have in one.

**4.** Do you think many of the people in the station scene in Chapter 2 are Irish? Look at the dialogue again.

**5.** There is a high level of dramatic excitement in this chapter. Where would you locate the climax? Perhaps there are more than one?

## CHARACTER STUDY

**6.** Make written notes for a character study of Finn. Examine his actions, thoughts, words, as you did with Uncle Toby. Leave space for further additions.

**7.** Attempt a character study of Derval. What are the difficulties? Record her thoughts as you imagine they might have been.

## GOOD WRITING

**8.** Examine a passage of descriptive writing such as his attempt to portray the ship at sea: 'Now he suddenly felt cold ... the broken waves', page 24. Notice the simile: 'The regular beat of the engines was like the beating of a person's heart.' Notice the adjectives in 'white water' and 'broken waves'.

Have you ever been on a boat or a train or a plane? What do you remember about it? Plan a description of it and then relate it to the class.

**9.** Have a vocabulary and spelling competition based on the chapter.

**10.** Do you know any good poems about the sea? Find one. Or play a recording of 'Orinoco Flow' from the 'Watermark' album by Enya.

## CHAPTER 3

## CHARACTER STUDY

**1.** What evidence in this chapter suggests that Mr Purdon is not quite honest?

**2.** Add to your character study of Uncle Toby.

## DIALOGUE

**3.** In your groups invent interviews between the detective and Finn's friends at school or neighbours on the road.

## WRITING

**4.** Compose a letter the lawyers might have sent to Mr Purdon.

## CHAPTER 4

## GIVING DIRECTIONS

**1.** Study the map underneath and plot a journey from Dun Laoghaire Car Ferry Terminal to 'the road west' mentioned in the chapter. Write down accurate directions for a traveller. Work in pairs and have someone check your directions for accuracy.

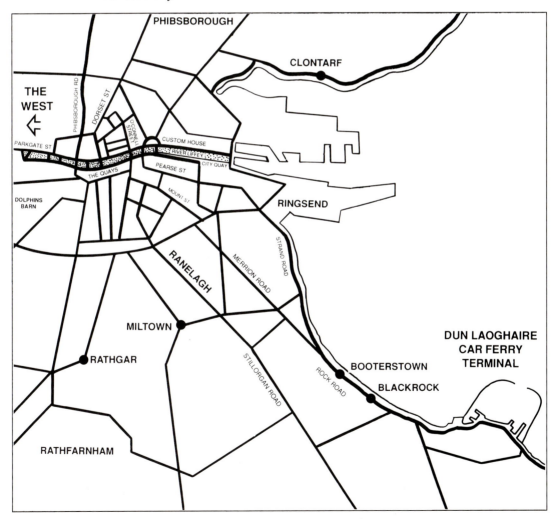

**2.** Study the train timetable underneath.

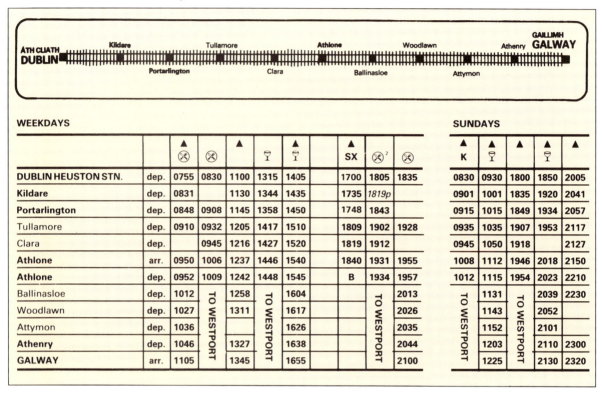

**WEEKDAYS**

**SUNDAYS**

| | | ▲ ⊗ | ⊗ | ▲ | ☕ | ▲ ☕ | | ▲ SX | ⊗² | ⊗ | ▲ K | ▲ ☕ | ▲ | ▲ ☕ | ▲ |
|---|---|---|---|---|---|---|---|---|---|---|---|---|---|---|---|
| **DUBLIN HEUSTON STN.** | dep. | 0755 | 0830 | 1100 | 1315 | 1405 | | 1700 | 1805 | 1835 | 0830 | 0930 | 1800 | 1850 | 2005 |
| **Kildare** | dep. | 0831 | | 1130 | 1344 | 1435 | | 1735 | *1819p* | | 0901 | 1001 | 1835 | 1920 | 2041 |
| **Portarlington** | dep. | 0848 | 0908 | 1145 | 1358 | 1450 | | 1748 | 1843 | | 0915 | 1015 | 1849 | 1934 | 2057 |
| Tullamore | dep. | 0910 | 0932 | 1205 | 1417 | 1510 | | 1809 | 1902 | 1928 | 0935 | 1035 | 1907 | 1953 | 2117 |
| Clara | dep. | | 0945 | 1216 | 1427 | 1520 | | 1819 | 1912 | | 0945 | 1050 | 1918 | | 2127 |
| **Athlone** | arr. | 0950 | 1006 | 1237 | 1446 | 1540 | | 1840 | 1931 | 1955 | 1008 | 1112 | 1946 | 2018 | 2150 |
| **Athlone** | dep. | 0952 | 1009 | 1242 | 1448 | 1545 | | B | 1934 | 1957 | 1012 | 1115 | 1954 | 2023 | 2210 |
| Ballinasloe | dep. | 1012 | TO WESTPORT | 1258 | TO WESTPORT | 1604 | | TO WESTPORT | | 2013 | TO WESTPORT | 1131 | TO WESTPORT | 2039 | 2230 |
| Woodlawn | dep. | 1027 | | 1311 | | 1617 | | | | 2026 | | 1143 | | 2052 | |
| Attymon | dep. | 1036 | | | | 1626 | | | | 2035 | | 1152 | | 2101 | |
| **Athenry** | dep. | 1046 | | 1327 | | 1638 | | | | 2044 | | 1203 | | 2110 | 2300 |
| **GALWAY** | arr. | 1105 | | 1345 | | 1655 | | | | 2100 | | 1225 | | 2130 | 2320 |

**a)** If they arrived in Heuston station at 12.30, what is the earliest time they could arrive in Galway by train?

**b)** Could they have a meal on that train?

**c)** If they only had money enough for the fare to Athlone, what train would they take and at what time would they arrive?

**d)** At what time is the next train for Ballinasloe?

## CHARACTER STUDY

**3.** What does the milk bottle episode tell us about Finn? Add to your character study.

**4.** Make character study notes on Poll's mother and father. To help you decide, study their descriptions, what they say, what they do and what others say about them. Decide what each of these things tells you about the kind of person each is.

**5.** Write a diary extract of Derval's thoughts.

## DESCRIPTIVE WRITING

6. Remembering about the use of adjectives and similes, write a colourful description of the inside of a church or street you know well.

7. Read this poem by T.S. Eliot. What images best describe the winter evening? Why?

### PRELUDES

The winter evening settles down
With smells of steaks in passageways.
Six o'clock.
The burnt-out ends of smoky days.
And now a gusty shower wraps
The grimy scraps
Of withered leaves about his feet
And newspapers from vacant lots;
The showers beat
On broken blinds and chimney pots,
And at the corner of the street
A lonely cab-horse steams and stamps
And then the lighting of the lamps.

*T.S. Eliot*

## CREATIVE WRITING

**8.** "'Why don't you play in the park?'", Finn asked. "Ah, that's private," said Poll. "The gates is locked. They don't like young people ...'"

Write a story abut this park.

## ORAL AND AURAL

**9.** Read aloud Brendan Behan's 'The Confirmation Suit', which is about tenement life in Dublin fifty years ago.

## CHAPTER 5

## WORD POWER

**1.** Have a vocabulary and spelling competition based on Chapters 3, 4 and 5.

## CHAPTER 6

*Compose a story or a poem or a piece of drama based on this.*

## CHARACTER STUDY

**1.** Write notes on the character of Mickser, basing your ideas on his description, actions, sayings, thoughts, etc.

## DESCRIPTIVE WRITING

**2.** Write three descriptive paragraphs on the activities of a traffic policemen.

**3.** Describe the scene from a window of a bus, car or train, the first time you went into the country or the city. Or describe your first view of a strange country you visited on holiday. Remember to write in paragraphs.

## GIVING DETAILED INSTRUCTIONS

**4.** Write detailed instructions for a Martian, explaining how it could do the weekend shopping in a supermarket.

**5.** Describe in detail how you would fill a car with a gallon of petrol, if you were a garage attendant.

## WORD POWER

**6.** Use you dictionary to look up any difficult words, as usual.

Then have a competition to see who can find the greatest number of synonyms for twenty or so specified words.

## DEBATE/DISCUSSION

**7.** Have a discussion or debate on the attitudes of city people to country people or vice versa.

## CHAPTER 7

## GOOD WRITING

**1.** Look again at the climax of the episode, page 58. '"Walk out of the town the way west," said Mickser urgently .... Finn looked desperately for a doorway ...' Notice how the use of adverbs increases the sense of drama.

The use of strong verbs also carries the sense of excitement and activity. For example: 'He started the van again and roared away.'

Write a description of a chase or a narrow escape, paying particular attention to the verbs and adverbs.

## Correct Writing

### More about verbs

As we have seen already verbs are action words. The _tense_ of the verb indicates **when** the action takes place: Present, Past, Future, Conditional.

Present Tense: _I play_ badminton for the school.
Past Tense: I _played_ a match yesterday and won.
Future Tense: I _will play_ in the final next week.
Conditional Tense: I'm sure I _could play_ for Ireland if I had more time to practise!

The _Person_ indicates who is doing the action.

|  | Singular | Plural |
|---|---|---|
| 1st Person | I play | We play |
| 2nd Person | You play | You (plural) play |
| 3rd Person | He/She/It plays | They play |

**FORMS** of the Verb:

The INFINITIVE is the simplest form of the verb—to play; to see; to laugh; to be; to run; to sing, etc.

The PRESENT PARTICIPLE is made by adding -ing to the infinitive—playing; seeing; laughing, etc.

The PAST PARTICIPLE is generally formed by adding -d or -ed to the infinitive.

FOR EXAMPLE, 'I have played against her before,' or 'I have laughed at that joke before,' muttered the daring boy to the shocked teacher.

(Simple trick: Put 'I have' before the verb and it must then form the past participle.)

**Regular** verbs form the past tense and past participle simply by adding -d or -ed. But there are many Irregular Verbs and you just have to learn the different forms. Here are some examples:

| Present | Past | Past Participle |
| --- | --- | --- |
| Arise | Arose | Arisen |
| Bleed | Bled | Bled |
| Catch | Caught | Caught |
| Draw | Drew | Drawn |
| Eat | Ate | Eaten |
| Fall | Fell | Fallen |
| Go | Went | Gone |
| Hide | Hid | Hidden |
| Know | Knew | Known |
| Lie | Lay | Lain |
| Mistake | Mistook | Mistaken |
| Prove | Proved | Proven |
| Quit | Quit | Quit |
| Rise | Rose | Risen |
| See | Saw | Seen |
| Sing | Sang | Sung |
| Slay | Slew | Slain |
| Swear | Swore | Sworn |
| Teach | Taught | Taught |
| Think | Thought | Thought |
| Wake | Woke | Woken |
| Write | Wrote | Written |

\* Make a list of as may irregular verbs as you can think of, under each letter of the alphabet. Have a competition for this.

## DIALOGUE/DRAMA

**2.** In groups of three, play out an interview between the police and Mickser. Whoever plays Mickser should try to keep close to what the character in the novel might say. Spend 5-7 minutes rehearsing this and then put on your dialogue for the class.

**3.** Working in groups of seven to ten develop a courtroom drama based on Mickser's case. Perform it for the class.

## SPELLING

**4. Dropping e before a suffix.**
Do you remember the rule?
Words that end in e usually ...................
Consult the SPELLING GUIDE p.159 - 162

**EXAMPLE:** p.57 'He stopped reversing and drove the van into another lane.'
REVERSE - REVERSING

| | | |
|---|---|---|
| Love | - | Loving |
| Have | - | Having |
| Crime | - | Criminal |

But there are exceptions:

| | | |
|---|---|---|
| Die | - | Dying |
| Lie | - | Lying |
| Tie | - | Tying |
| Canoe | - | Canoeing |
| Peace | - | Peaceable |
| Notice | - | Noticeable |
| Courage | - | Courageous |
| Outrage | - | Outrageous |

Make two lists, one where -e is dropped and one where it is retained.

## CHAPTER 8

# MEDIA

**1.** Working in groups of three, plan, design layout and write the front page of a newspaper which carries the story of the Doves. You can handwrite it neatly on an A3 size page or bigger. Or get it typed up for A4 size. You will need to do a lot of rewriting and proof-reading before the final copy. Post them up on the wall or notice board. Decide which one you would buy and why.

**2.** Design and write a REWARD NOTICE which might appear in the same paper. Decide which is the most effective and why.

**3.** Working in pairs, with 10 minutes to prepare, do a radio or television interview with Uncle Toby. Have a competition for the best interview. Then have a class discussion on what makes a good interview.

# CREATIVE WRITING

**4.** Re-read the end of the chapter: 'Then he took Derval's hand and walked into the field ...'

Write a different ending to this chapter. This poem of Hilaire Belloc's might give you some ideas. Try to find an unexpected ending.

### SARAH BYNG
### WHO COULD NOT READ AND WAS TOSSED
### INTO A THORNY HEDGE BY A BULL

Some years ago you heard me sing
My doubts on Alexander Byng.
His sister Sarah now inspires
My jaded Muse, my falling fires.
Of Sarah Byng the tale is told
How when the child was twelve years old
She could not read or write a line.

Her sister Jane, though barely nine,
Could spout the Catechism through
And parts of Matthew Arnold too,
While little Bill who came between
Was quite unnaturally keen

On 'Athalie', by Jean Racine.

But not so Sarah!  Not so Sal!
She was a most uncultured girl
Who didn't care a pinch of snuff
For any literary stuff
And gave the classics all a miss.
Observe the consequence of this!
As she was walking home one day,
Upon the fields across her way
A gate, securely padlocked, stood,
And by its side a piece of wood
On which was painted plain and full,

BEWARE THE VERY
FURIOUS BULL.

Alas!  The young illiterate
Went blindly forward to her fate,
And ignorantly climbed the gate!
Now happily the Bull that day
Was rather in the mood for play
Than goring people through and through
As Bulls so very often do;
He tossed her lightly with his horns
Into a prickly hedge of thorns,
And stood by laughing while she strode
And pushed and struggled to the road.

The lesson was not lost upon
The child, who since has always gone
A long way round to keep away
From signs, whatever they may say,
And leaves a padlocked gate alone.
Moreover she has wisely grown
Confirmed in her instinctive guess
That literature breeds distress.

## WORD POWER

**5.** Have a vocabulary and spelling competition based on Chapters 7 and 8.

## CHAPTER 9

## DISCUSSION

**1.** Is Michael a good detective? Why? Swap ideas about your favourite detective or mystery stories.

## SPELLING

**2.** Towards the end of the chapter (on page 72) you will find the words SLEEPING and PLANNING, obviously made from SLEEP and PLAN. Why is the final letter doubled in one new word and not in the other?

Do you remember the rule? Words of one syllable ending in a single consonant which is preceded by a single vowel usually ................................

So  STOP  -  STOPPED

      RUN  -  RUNNER

      PLAN  -  PLANNING

      WHIP  -  WHIPPED

Make a list of similar examples in everyday use. But notice:

**a)**

    RANT  -  RANTING (two consonants)

    SMILE  -  SMILED (ends in a vowel)

    SAIL  -  SAILING (preceded by 2 vowels)

    SHIP  -  SHIPMENT (suffix does not begin

                with a vowel)

**b)** Words of more than one syllable also double the final consonant if the last syllable of the word is stressed or accented.

**Example**:

    BEGIN  -  BEGINNING

    COMMIT  -  COMMITTED

    PERMIT  -  PERMITTED

    FORGET  -  FORGETTING

Make a list of similar examples.

**Notice:**

LIMIT      LIMITED

(last syllable unstressed)

OPEN      OPENED

FASTEN      FASTENED

But there are exceptions:

TRAVEL      TRAVELLED

## MEDIA

**3.** Before going 'on holiday' Michael may have picked up some brochures. Read this introduction to a Bord Failte guide. Pick out the phrases or images which you think might persuade someone to visit the region. Explain your choice. Examine what the adjectives suggest.

*Introducing*

# WESTMEATH

Situated in the centre of Ireland, Westmeath has scenery and attractions that are different; it has no majestic mountain ranges nor alluring sea-side resorts but it offers calm and tranquil scenery that, once tasted, will keep beckoning the traveller to come back for more.

The principal tourist attraction of Westmeath is its lakes, the county is a veritable angler's paradise. Within 10 km of Mullingar are four large lakes, Loughs Owel, Ennell, Derravaragh and Lene; further north on the Cavan border is beautiful Lough Sheelin, but there is a large number of smaller lakes, Loughs Iron, Bane, Kinale, Annalla. The series of lakes provide excellent trout fishing and also bream, tench, rudd and pike. North of Athlone the Shannon expands into Lough Ree, used by the Vikings one thousand years ago to gain access to the heart of the country but nowadays becoming very popular for cruising and sailing; it also has excellent coarse fishing. The lake is studded with small islands with intriguing names, Hare Island, Inchbofin; on many of these are the remains of early Christian and medieval churches.

## Geology

The landscape indeed is unique; the northern part of the county is drumlin country, a rolling undulating land with numerous low grassy hills, none of which exceed 180m. There is a wonderful view from the summits. The little hills look down on numerous lakes, whose shores are clothed with deciduous trees and multi-flowered undergrowth. The central and southern parts of the county are flatter, again with numerous lakes and a hitherto unappreciated attraction—bogs. These large tracts of peat are, as yet, untouched by modern technology, and, if you want to experience a feeling of peace and inner healing, take a walk into the heart of one of these; perhaps Glynwood bog, 4.8 km east of Athlone or Hall bog, 1.6 km from Moate; then just stand still on the carpet of sphagnum moss and bog-cotton and listen to the sounds of silence; the only disturbance of your peace will be the music of the grasshopper or the song of a lark overhead.

*The Catstone near Mullingar*

**4.** Read the following excerpts from the same brochure. Use your dictionary to find meanings of any difficult words. Then choose a section or two and examine the use of adjectives. What do they add to the piece?

### Lough Derravaragh

The most majestic of the Westmeath lakes 8.04 km long. It affords good fishing for trout, pike and perch and its steep wooded shores set against a background of rolling grassland gives a view to be remembered. The lake is associated with the most tragic of all Irish legendary romances—the Children of Lir; changed into swans by a jealous step-mother, they spent 300 years on its dark waters. Nine km further on is the village of Castlepollard.

### Castlepollard

An ideal centre from which to explore or fish the north Westmeath or south Cavan lakes. It is well laid out with an expansive triangular green, surrounded by buildings of 19th century architectural style. Tullynally Castle, seat of the Earls of Longford and home of the literary Pakenham family, is just 2 km from the town. The castle has a spectacular facade of turrets and towers; the demesne features some fine woodland and walled gardens and is

*Tullyvally Castle,County Westmeath.*

open to visitors. There is a picturesque forest walk 2 km from the town of Mullingar road. Five km east of Castlepollard is the historic village of Fore.

## Fore

Nestles cosily in the bosom of the surrounding hills. It is the most historic site of the Christian period in Westmeath. St. Fechin, a native of Sligo, founded a monastery here in 630 A.D., which grew into a community of 300 monks. Nothing now remains of the earliest and loosely scattered buildings in which they lived but the remains of 10th century and later buildings are impressive.

St. Fechin's Church, situated in the western graveyard, dates from the 10th century and is the oldest structure in Fore. It probably marks the site of the original monastery founded by the saint. An unusual feature is the massive cross-inscribed lintel stone. Originally the church consisted of a rectangular nave, but about 1200 A.D. a chancel was added. Inside the church is a baptismal font of about 1200 A.D., the remains of an altar and fragments of gravestones.

The Benedictine Priory was founded early in the 13th century by the De Lacy family. It is an imposing structure, the square towers and loop-hole windows resemble a castle rather than an abbey. It is the only Irish Benedictine foundation of which remains survive to any extent. The choir of the church, the kitchen and some other walls in the domestic quarters were built shortly after the foundation and some cross-decorated tombstones preserved in the building are also 13th century.

The Town Walls were erected in the middle of the 15th century to protect the Benedictine priory from attacks by marauding clans; two town gates of these walls remain.

According to local tradition there are seven wonders in Fore; why not investigate some of them? They are:

1) water which will not boil,

2) wood which will not burn,

3) water flowing uphill,

4) the abbey built on a quaking sod,

5) a mill without a race,

6) miraculous emplacement of the large lintel stone above the door.

7) St. Fechin's fingermarks on the lintel stone.

Now return to Castlepollard and take the road to Finea.

## Finea

A picturesque village on the River Inny, between Loughs Sheelin and Kinale. In the centre of the village there is a memorial to Myles "Slasher" O'Reilly, who defended the town bridge in 1646, during the confederate wars. On the shore of Lough Sheelin is Ross Castle where O'Reilly slept on the eve of the battle. Sheelin is probably the best known brown trout lake in the midlands; it is a lake to be enjoyed by all the family, you can picnic, swim or just enjoy the scenery. If you are interested in craft work visit nearby Mountnugent. There is an attractive drive along the southern shoreline and further on at Mullaghmeen you can enjoy a forest walk. Continue on to Oldcastle.

The Anchorite Cell is a tower on the Castlepollard road, dating from the 15th century. It got its name from a hermit, named Patrick Beglan, who lived in it for many years prior to his death in 1616.

## PROJECT

**5.** Research and write up local myths, legends or stories which might be used to promote the character of your native townland, street, village, parish or town.

Find out about local amenities and write a few paragraphs promoting them. Write letters for brochures.

Examine some holiday brochures and discuss how the photographs as well as the words try to persuade you.

Finally compose your own brochure for the area.

## CHAPTER 10

**1.** In your own words summarise the main events as they happened in this chapter.

## SPELLING

**2.** 'Finn didn't know how many miles they had travelled but the pack on his back seemed to get heavier and heavier.'

HEAVY - HEAVIER

Do you remember the rule?—When a word ends in a consonant and y....

**Example**

PARTY    ·-·     PARTIES

BEAUTY    -    BEAUTIFUL

EMPTY    -    EMPTINESS

EASY    -    EASILY

SPY    -    SPYING

TRY    -    TRYING

DRY    -    DRYING

FRY    -    FRYING

**3.** Are there any words in this chapter which you frequently misspell?  Make a list.

## CHAPTER 11

**1.** Read 'The Donkey' by G.K. Chesterton.  Discuss, with your teacher, the meanings of the words and images.  How does the donkey feel about himself?  What is your favourite image from the poem?

**THE DONKEY**

When fishes flew and forests walked,
And figs grew upon thorn,
Some moment when the moon was blood
Then surely I was born;

With monstrous head and sickening cry
And ears like errant wings,
The devil's walking parody
On all four-footed things.

The tattered outlaw of the earth,
Of ancient crooked will;
Starve, scourge, deride me:  I am dumb,
I keep my secret still.

Fools!  For I also had my hour;
One far fierce hour and sweet:
There was a shout about my ears,
And palms before my feet.

*G.K. Chesterton*

**2.** You might like to read 'Timoney's Ass', a short story by Liam O'Flaherty, to be found in 'The Pedlar's Revenge and Other Stories' published by Wolfhound.

## SPELLING

**3.** 'It was very cheer<u>ful</u>. It lighted the place up, and when the warmth started to come from it, even the donkey came over to graze near it.'

Rule: When ALL, FILL, FULL, SKILL, TILL and WILL are used as part of a new word they usually drop one -1.

So we get:

| | | |
|---|---|---|
| ALMOST | FULFIL | AWFUL |
| ALTHOUGH | UNTIL | SKILFUL |
| ALWAYS | | BEAUTIFUL |
| | | WILFUL |

Can you add to the list?

**4.** Have a vocabulary and spelling competition based on the chapter.

## CHAPTER 12

**1.** Read this poem 'The Tinker's Wife' by Patrick Kavanagh and find the meanings of any difficult words. The poet uses two similes to describe the woman. What do these suggest about her?

## TINKER'S WIFE

I saw her amid the dunghill debris
Looking for things
Such as an old pair of shoes or gaiters.
She was a young woman,
A tinker's wife.
Her face had streaks of care
Like wires across it,
But she was supple
As a young goat
On a windy hill.

She searched on the dunghill debris,
Tripping gingerly
Over tin canisters
And sharp-broken
Dinner plates.

**2.** The following is an excerpt from 'Nan: The Life of an Irish Travelling Woman',written for her by Sharon Gmelch. Read it and have a class discussion on it.

• NOTE: Nan had stolen a little piglet from a farmyard nearby.

Me mother called me over, 'Come here, Nan.'

'What?' I said.

'You took the little pig. Give it to me and I'll hand it back to the man.'

I started roaring then, 'I'm not giving me pig! I'm not giving me pig!'

'What's this about the pig?' said me father.

'Nan has it.' Me mother had to tell him then.

'Nan, did you take him?' me father said. 'I'll give you a beating you'll never forget.'

The farmer looked at me and he felt sorry then. 'Oh,' he said, 'I understand now. Come here and show me.'

'I won't show you,' I roared and I took off running through the fields. Me father sent me brother Willie out after me, and he caught me and held me. On comes me father then with his army belt and three straps he give me of this belt, right across the legs and I tore with briars and all.

'Show me where the pig is, ' he said.

'All right, I'll show you,' I said. 'Don't touch me no more.' And I took them to the pig. I had the pig in a lovely little hole with straw.

When the farmer seen it, he got sorry. 'Don't beat her anymore, John.'

Me father got sorry too. 'How much is the pig,' he said. A pig was only cheap that time.

'I'd give her the pig, John, but it won't live. The pig is too young. It'd die with her,' the farmer said.

'It wouldn't,' I said. 'It et the bread and me mother's can of buttermilk.'

'Oh no!' yelled me mother. 'I never washed the can. I'm going to kill you altogether now.'

I did get kilt the next morning. Me father was like that. He wouldn't beat you right away

217

if you done anything bad. He'd be real sneaky. He'd smile and let you go to bed, then at six in the morning he'd let you have it. I never forgot that beating and I never will. I was nine years old.

I think it was a week after, me father was out cleaning chimneys in a cottage and he was telling this woman about what I'd done with the pig. Travellers always talked when they'd be doing anything. 'I'll give you something for her now,' the woman said. 'A bantam.' So on comes me father home.

'Nan, I got you a lovely little pet,' he said.

'What'd you get me?'

'A little bantam. You forget about that dirty old pig. You'd never have reared him. We couldn't look after it in the house in winter because he'd have growing too big.'

I hadn't thought of that; I thought that time the pig would always keep small.

Well, I was pleased with this little bantam. It was a beauty and ever so small. Every day I'd go out into the fields where there'd be young oats and tear the tops off the oats and throw them in to the little hen. And she started to lay eggs, and the little eggs was so small.

One day me father said, 'An old friend of ours has come to camp with us.' She was a first cousin of me father—a widow woman with a bad leg—he always took her out for a couple weeks in the summer.

'It couldn't be that you're rearing bantams!' she said as soon as she saw me pet.

'A little bantam is no harm,' said me mother, 'it's Nan's pet.' But Travelling People that time didn't like the idea of bantams. They thought if a bantam crowed at night, after twelve o'clock, that something would go wrong. And that if a hen crowed, there'd be trouble.

So after that, me brother Joe told me, 'Nan you'd better watch your bantam or they'll do away with her.'

We were staying out by Gaybrook. It was a big wood, a lovely place but lonesome at night. And what happened, Sharon? Up gets me bantam about one o'clock in the morning and starts crowing. Only the way I cried meself sick saved her: they had to let me keep her.

'We'll leave it,' said me mother. 'If I done away with that bantam, Nan would go mad.' But she blessed herself a hundred times that day.

In the afternoon, they yoked up the pony and cart—me brother John, me father, me mother, and our friend. 'Come on,' said John. 'I'll bring you to the fair.' There was a fair in Mullingar. Me brother had a great trotting mare, very fast, and he loved to get a good drive with his mare. So they climbed into the cart and away with them all into Mullingar. None of us children used to be allowed into fairs. Me father never liked the idea of bringing children into town.

Well, they got their few bottles of stout and they were coming on home at night on this big lonely road. They were going along singing when the wind came up strong and something hopped out of the ditch—a newspaper or a white bit of cloth on a dark road. And didn't the pony freckin' [get frightened] and away goes the pony in a runaway. The next thing, the harness broke and the pony run right out from under the cart, and they were all thrown out on the side of the road. Me brother's arm was broke. The old woman—the poor crayture—her face and her arms was all scraped. And the rest of them had bruises all over them. They were miles from Mullingar and they couldn't catch the pony. But for the luck of God, a man passed them going home. I believe the moans and curses coming out of them were terrible. And he gathered them up and brought them back to Mullingar hospital and got them dressed.

We were sitting up waiting for them, wondering what had kept them. 'They got drunk or they met friends,' we said and we were happy enough and went to bed and didn't bother with it anymore. Near morning here they come all in bandages, and John with his arm in plaster. The very minute they landed, we got up and made them a cup of tea. Then they all went and lay down for an hour.

But when they got up: 'Where's that bantam? Where's that bantam? It's not lucky. It's not right to keep a bantam hen that's crowing. Nan can cry anyway she likes this time, she's not lucky, with the red hair on her. She and her bantam are crying bad luck at us.' A red-haired girl they used to count as unlucky. They didn't pass any heed about boys, but if a girl had red hair, it was bad luck. 'She's not lucky, that red one. She's crying us away, her and her pets,' they said.

Well, when I heard about me bantam, I said to meself, I hope to God me bantam won't move. There was a tree up overhead, a big white thorn bush. We had a fire under it, and the little bantam was roosting in the top of the bushes.

'Where's that bantam?' said me father. He had his sweeping stick—the one with the big metal screw on the top—in his hand. Oh, I said to meself, me poor little bantam is dead if he gets a clout of that. I didn't know what to do and I started crying.

They looked everywhere, up and down, and couldn't find the bantam. But the very next morning the poor little thing started crowing. 'There it is,' said me mother. 'There's the unlucky bantam. Get it quick! It's a devil. Get it away from us.' Me father went up with the stick and broke the little bantam's head.

'He's dead now. He's dead!' I cried, catching it be the legs. And I pult it in the bushes and tried to hide it. The poor little thing crawled and crawled for about an hour after. But they had killed it. Every pet I used to get, there was something wrong with it.

I was always unlucky.

## DISCUSSION

a) From your reading of this extract, what kind of girl do you think Nan was? She did steal the pig but ...

What were your feelings towards her when you finished reading?

c) How many examples of unusual phrases or odd ways of saying things can you find?

c) On the evidence of the extract do you think the travellers had a very tough life? Explain. Is there any evidence that they enjoyed themselves at all?

d) What else did you learn about travellers, from this extract.

## DESCRIPTIVE WRITING

**3.** Study the details used to describe Powder (pages 95, 96). His hair, beard, teeth and eyes are all mentioned. The description is quite simple yet memorable.

## WRITING DIALOGUE

**4.** Re-read the conversation between Powder and Finn.

NOTICE: The variety of ways you can structure a question. Example: 'You have come for?' instead of 'Have you come for?'

Reactions are included as well as the dialogue. Example: 'Powder grunted. He was picking his teeth with a match.'

One feels the questions are leading up to something, so there is a certain tension about it all.

Now write a conversation between a travelling young person and a member of the settled community, in any situation you like to imagine.

## CHAPTER 13

**1.** When you have read the chapter and worked on the vocabulary, get into groups of three or five and brainstorm one another for words you might use to describe the sounds, sights, feelings, etc. of a busy town. Then write a description of a visit to a town. Think in paragraphs.

**2.** Study how the dramatic confrontation is written (page 103).

NOTICE: The use of strong verbs to carry the sense of action. Example: ' ... he was shouting ... we'll drive you out ... he was swinging his arms ... waving his big arms ...', etc.

Short sentences and phrases give the effect of breathless excitement. Example: "Out now!", he was shouting. "Away from here now. We are sick of you. A bunch of thieves. Dirty locusts ...", etc.

## STORY

**3.** Read this short story about Apartheid.

# TWO CHILDREN

*Fay Goldie*

Grandma had said, 'Put on your shady hat, darling. I want you to take Umfaan round to the new house. You'll find the broom behind the kitchen door. He must sweep the house right through—every room, and the verandah, too. Grandpa did explain it all to him before he went to work, so he should know what he has to do.'

'Why can't the girl take Umfaan round? Why should I have to?'

'Because I ask you to, darling. It won't take you long. Just give him the broom and leave him to get on with things. Now fetch your shady hat, Fay, there's a dear child.'

With mutiny in her heart, and without a backward glance at the Zulu child who followed her, the little girl set off for the large, empty house where her family would live when they arrived from Durban the following week.

She kicked up clouds of red dust with the toes of her black patent-leather shoes, because she had been told repeatedly to pick up her feet when she wore her best shoes. And she led the way down the middle of the wide wagon road because it was forbidden.

Only by performing such small acts of rebellion could she endure the boredom and loneliness of the endless days and weeks spent with her grandparents, waiting for her family to arrive.

Behind her lagged Umfaan, keeping at a respectful distance, for if his short period of service in the dorp had taught him little else, it had instilled an appreciation of the white person's superiority into his nine-year-old mind, and of his corresponding inferiority as an unimportant member of another race.

The sun blazed down from the bleached blue sky, and the air was acrid with the smell of parched veld, of fires and pepper trees.

As he shuffled along Umfaan imagined what the boys of his kraal would be doing that day, and his bare toes dug into the powdered red earth in the bitterness of his aloneness.

They would have driven the sheep and cattle up into the hills very early in the morning. As the heat of the day increased they would discard the old military jackets, sacks or tattered shirts that clothed them, and pursue their games with the sun beating down strongly on their bodies.

They would play warriors with shields and weapons made of sticks, and their battle cries would be shouted back at them from the mouth of the high black cave where they sheltered from sudden storms, or played at being Bushmen. He could picture it all so clearly: M'futa, with his round belly and slow legs, standing on a high anthill directing the campaign, Sezulu leaping like a springbok, egging his side on with great shouts. Sezulu's was the strongest voice among all the children of the district. Umfaan's little brother, Jegejela, would undoubtedly get cracked over the head early in the battle, his howls adding to the glorious din.

They would abandon their game presently as the sun mounted higher in the sky. They would throw away their weapons and race down the hill to plunge into the river, swimming like frogs and splashing until the water was brown with mud, and the women screamed at them from the fields to end their fooling or there would be no clean water for drinking or for washing.

The little girls would sometimes join them in the water, dumping the babies they carried on their hips onto the veld, and making even more noise, with their high-pitched screams, than the boys made. Not that this happened very often, for usually the girls were busy in the mealie-fields with the women, or engaged in work at the kraals.

Umfaan began to sing softly, to force his spirits up.

How his father had lied to him when he told him what a good time he would have working for the white people in the dorp.

It was not that he minded changing his name to 'Umfaan' or 'Jim'. He could tolerate the tight white uniform with the red bands that had been bought for a much smaller boy. And the daily shower. He could stand the long hours of stupid work without complaint—washing piles of clean dishes, sweeping spotless floors, polishing steps that were already so glassy that one could slide on them—if one dared!—as a snake slides on a very smooth stone.

Oh, yes, he could bear all that.

And yet he was seriously churning over and over in his bewildered mind the thought of running away, back to his kraal.

He knew that the police might catch him before he had gone very far, and beat him or lock him up. Even if he succeeded in evading the police and his boss, there would undoubtedly be a beating awaiting him at his father's kraal, for the three half-crowns he was to earn at the end of each month were needed to help pay his father's taxes, and to buy food for his father's wives and numerous children.

No, it was not his work that troubled him. It was not that. He had never been afraid of work.

In truth it was his kia that frightened him to the point of death each night, that made his new life unbearable. Sleeping quite alone in a tiny corrugated iron room at the far end of the long, dark garden. All his life he had shared the floor of his mother's hut with a huddle of brothers and sisters. All his life he had known their constant companionship, their chatter, quarrels and games.

Now, for the first time in his life, he was alone. Alone in a strange town, without freedom or friends, or a clear understanding of what was required of him.

His mistress did not speak Zulu, nor could he understand her language, for he had never before been in contact with English-speaking people. To overcome the difficulty, his mistress would talk very quietly in her incomprehensible tongue to Umfaan, making what efforts she could to convey her meaning by complicated gestures and actions. She thought him slow and stupid, and sometimes very wilful, when he misinterpreted her meaning.

Fortunately, the boss knew a smattering of Zulu, and he would correct and direct him at the beginning and the end of each interminable day.

As for the only child of the house, he was forbidden to approach her. In any case she treated him as all little white girls must treat Bantu children—as though they only existed as servants to obey orders, to fetch and carry for

them, and to follow meekly at a respectful distance.

They did not see them as children, like themselves. That was clear.

The children turned the corner and Fay suddenly broke into a run. She flung herself at the white gate that led to the back entrance of the new house, and clung to the top rail, swinging herself violently to and fro to the accompaniment of creaking hinges, with a loud bang as the gate hit the brick border, and another bang as it struck the gate-post.

Umfaan's eyes shone, and he grasped the sagging wire fence with both hands and held on to prevent himself from rushing forward to share the rapture of swinging on the gate with the white child.

He knew that he dared not do such a thing, no matter how great the temptation.

There had been an old wooden gate leading into the paddock where the district dipping tank was built, back at his kraal. It was a crude affair made of wattle poles, a few old nails, and some wire. And it invariably collapsed under the strain of the weight of one small child, as often as not dragging its post from the ground as it fell.

There would follow feverish activity on the part of the horde of children who had dared ride the forbidden gate, while they vainly tried to repair it before they were caught. Usually a whipping would close the incident with yells.

But this gate was an entirely different matter.

It was strong, high and white, and it swung free and wide, and crashed as hard as anyone could reasonably wish into the border of bricks, and back against its clasp.

The little girl jumped from the gate as it swung out, landing on her hands and knees. She shot a glance over her shoulder at Umfaan, and saw his face break in a wide white grin. Her pale, thin face burned with an angry colour, and she scrambled to her feet, choking with shame, and raced down the garden path towards the back door.

'Come on!' she cried, without looking back. 'Come on!'

Umfaan watched her white frock switch round the corner of the red brick house. He glanced hastily up the road and down to make sure it was deserted. Then, with his heart beating hard against his ribs, he pulled the gate back to its post, stepped up onto the bar, and pushed himself off as hard as he could. Creak—BANG! He lowered one foot to the ground and swung back. Just one more ride. Just one more. Creak—BANG!

'Get off that gate—I'll tell on you!' Fay shouted, peering round the side of the house.

How dared he ride on her gate? she thought furiously and with a giddy feeling of fear. He had been caught on her swing on the very afternoon he had started work for her grand-mother. She remembered how shocked and indignant her grandma had been. The swing had been scrubbed, and Grandpa had given Umfaan a proper talking to, and had boxed his ears.

Mrs Ridley, who lived next door, had seen him, and had come right over to report what was going on in the back garden.

If it were wrong for Umfaan to use her swing, then it must be very wrong indeed for him to swing on her gate, Fay reasoned. For she was forbidden to do so herself.

She raced indoors and pressed her face against the kitchen window, staring out into the wilderness that was the orchard. The trees there were to climb!

It would be a good idea to pick her special tree before her sisters and brothers arrived, she decided, and dabs-I it for her own.

Which one should she have? One of those great bushy naartje trees? What about that peach tree with the lovely twisted branches? It would be easy to climb, and there was a branch shaped like an arm-chair right at the top. She could feel how it would rock in the wind.

There were oak trees down by the garden wall, with the birds' nests in their branches, and the acorns you could use for dolls' cups. It was going to be a difficult choice.

There was a greengage tree directly outside the kitchen window, too. It was beauty. She pressed her nose flatter still, and craned up to see. Yes, two strong branches led right out over the roof. One could easily climb on to the roof from the tree, and whoever dabs-I'd that tree, would dabs-I the roof as well.

But it was too near the house. Mother would be sure to see her climbing in her socks, or her good clothes. Better choose one farther away.

Umfaan's voice broke into her little world.

'What do you want?' she asked, turning reluctantly.

He spoke again in Zulu, and smiled at her. His eyes were dancing with mischief, and he leant on the broom that was so much taller than he.

'I don't know what you say. Oh, why can't you speak English?' Fay snapped, embar-rassed. 'You've got to sweep every room.' She waved her arms to try and convey her meaning, as she had seen Grandma do. 'Every room. When you've finished you can come home by yourself. I'm going now.'

She made to go, but Umfaan stood directly in her path. He pointed out of the window and his voice was excited.

Fear suddenly swooped down on the white child. Why had Mother never allowed them to learn any Zulu words? Because what they talked about wasn't fit for white children to understand, Mother had explained. Umfaan must be saying something dreadful to her. He was so excited, and his eyes were as unveiled and intimate as a white boy's: as her brother's, or any of the other little white boys who played robbers and police with them at home.

She made to dash past, but Umfaan put a hand on her arm. She knocked it off and screamed, fear beating about her with dark wings.

No African had ever before touched her—except Zulu women like Nanny, and Sarah the house girl, of course. It was something that couldn't happen. She made another effort to escape, but the boy grabbed her frock, and his eyes were scared and angry and not like any African's eyes she had ever seen before.

'Let me go—you beast—YOU BEAST!' she screamed.

With a tug she was free of him and had rushed from the house. Her sobs were shaking her body to pieces. She had never known such terror and rage and disgust. A black boy had caught her by the arm. A black boy had grabbed her frock!

She ran as though pursued. And at the very back of her mind, through all the fear and the anger, a tiny thought was flashing like a blinking red light—'This will wake things up!' But it was not as clear as that. It was more like a tiny comforting glow flickering through her black terror.

Grandma was sitting on the front step drowsing over the paper when Fay tore open the gate and flung herself up the path and into her grandmother's arms.

'Good gracious, child! Whatever is the matter?'

Her grandmother's voice was strained, her hands hard on the child's shoulders.

'Darling—you MUST tell me. What is it that's frightened you so? A snake -?'

'Umfaan,' Fay sobbed, gasping for breath. 'He—touched me! He grabbed hold of my dress! Oh, Granny—he wouldn't let me go!'

'My God!' her voice was a whisper. She held the child tightly to her. 'Oh, my poor child! My poor, darling child!' she moaned.

Mrs Ridley appeared at the fence.

'Whatever is it, Mrs Ellis?' she called. 'I saw Fay careering past our place as though she'd gone mad. Whatever is it?'

'Come over at once. I need you,' Grandmother said.

And Fay knew that it was even more dreadful than she had thought. She knew that Umfaan had done something far, far worse than using her swing or the gate.

'For such a thing to happen!' Mrs Ridley exclaimed, hearing the story. 'Mrs Ellis, that child should be put to bed at once. The shock will make her ill if we're not careful. She's such a sensitive child, so highly strung. Get her to bed right away. I'll run up myself and fetch Mr Ellis and Sergeant McNab.'

'Oh—the police! Do you think we should? After all, a thing like this—the publicity—we mustn't do -'

'Your husband will know what to do, my dear. I'll be right back with him.'

Fay was in bed sobbing quietly when her grandfather arrived with the sergeant of police and Mrs Ridley. She was exhausted with emotion, and her throat ached from crying, but she must keep it up for a little longer, for she felt in a vague way that it was expected of her.

Within an hour or two the dorp was alight with news of the affair. Umfaan had been caught making off across the veld in the direction of his father's kraal, and was now safely locked up in jail. Grandmother was suffering from shock, and the doctor had examined Fay and declared that she must be kept quiet, and allowed to sleep for as long as possible. He made her swallow a bitter white pill.

Umfaan was brought to justice.

He was scared half out of his wits, and had only a very hazy and imperfect understanding of the nature of his crime.

He had wanted to play with the white girl. He had wanted her to go into the garden with him, to climb trees and steal some of the fruit that weighed the branches so heavily. He hadn't wanted to hurt her. He had only wanted to play with another child.

Fay wore a new white organdie frock with a pink sash, and her very best hat with the clusters of pink rosebuds on it.

There was half-a-crown in her white kid purse, given her by her grandfather for promising to 'be a brave little girl, and tell the magistrate exactly what happened'.

She would get the half-crown changed into thirty pennies later on and drop them into her red money box.

They stood her on a table shaped like a horse-shoe, and she knew she was a heroine in spite of being shaken and afraid. What if the magistrate should ask her if she had swung on the gate? She hoped that wouldn't be found out and held against her.

The courthouse was packed to the doors. Several farmers had ridden into town especially to attend the case and to see that the little black bastard got what he deserved. Feeling was high.

Umfaan stood in the dock with only his small, frightened face visible over the black wooden partition. Behind him stood a European policeman and two large African police 'boys', and he saw only hatred and anger on the faces that swam around him.

What would the white child say? What would the magistrate do to him? He stood frozen with fear.

He still didn't know what it was all about when they lifted the little girl from the table and his mistress took her into her arms and wept.

He didn't know what it was all about when the policeman jabbed him in the back and he was led away through the side entrance, with a great noise in his head, and his heart was like a cold stone inside him.

He was to be beaten! Wah-meh! He was to be beaten. And he was to be locked up in jail for how long? For three months? He was to be beaten and locked up.

'Six strokes,' Fay heard, and knew that it must be a nightmare. 'Six strokes, and three months' hard labour.'

And suddenly she saw Umfaan for the first time. She knew that he was a little boy. That he could feel pain and fear and could know loneliness just as she could. He had touched her arm. He had caught her dress. He had wanted to play with her. But he couldn't speak her language and tell her so. And, even if he had been able to ...

Six strokes and three months' hard labour.

She wanted to behave like a wild cat. She wanted to scream and fight and throw herself at the policemen who were taking Umfaan away to be punished. Instead, she fainted.

And she didn't open her eyes when she found herself lying on her bed, because Mrs Ridley was saying:

'Physical punishment's the only thing they understand.' And her hand gently massaged the child's arm in the direction of her heart. 'I may be sentimental, my dear Mrs Ellis, and you must forgive me, but I don't quite like the idea of that Umfaan being locked up with hardened criminals for three months. I'm afraid he'll come out more of a menace than he's going in. A child can learn so much in three months—especially the naturally vicious type.'

And Grandmother's anxious voice had whispered.

'Hush! We mustn't ever mention this again. I want this poor child to forget the whole terrible business. She mustn't ever be reminded of it. My poor little girl!'

The white child's parents, brothers and sisters, arrived from the city to comfort and protect her from the possibility of further outrages. The incident was never mentioned again in the family in her hearing.

They quite believed the child had forgotten that it had ever happened ...

## GROUP WORK

(a) In your groups build up character studies of Fay and Umfaan, from the details of the story. Make notes and report back to the whole group.

(b) Work in pairs. One should write the diary of Fay and the other of Umfaan, as they might have recorded these events. Swap diaries and discuss them.

# PROJECT

*4. Go to your local library and find out more about APARTHEID or THE LIVES OF ITINERANTS IN IRELAND. Make notes.*

*5. Then have a class debate on some aspect of the topics. You could stage it like a television discussion programme, with presenter, panel of experts, opposing factions, audience etc.*

## CHAPTER 14

## CHARACTER STUDY

**1.** Make notes on the character of Moses, as seen over the last three chapters. As usual examine his description, what he says, what he does etc.

## WORD POWER

**2.** Have a vocabulary and spelling competition based on Chapters 13 and 14.

## CHAPTER 15

## DIALECT

**1.** Study the local dialect of the conversation between the man in the van and Finn. What phrases strike you as odd or different from the way you speak?

**2.** Working in pairs and using local dialect, plan and write a conversation between two people.

## CREATIVE WRITING.

**3.** Write a short story beginning: 'Who was the man? He didn't look like the police...'

**4.** Work on your diary of Finn or Derval or Uncle Toby.

## CHAPTER 16

**1.** 'He looked at the two children crouched against the wall. He held out his hand. "Don't be frightened," he said. "I'm your friend."' (page 122)

What reasons did Finn have for disbelieving this?

## CREATIVE WRITING

**2.** 'He stepped on to the flags and looked over the top.' What would Finn see from the top of the old ruined castle? Write a haiku or other little poem about this. Perhaps Seamus Heaney's poem 'Railway Children' might give you some ideas.

### THE RAILWAY CHILDREN

When we climbed the slopes of the cutting
We were eye-level with the white cups
Of the telegraph poles and the sizzling wires.

Like lovely freehand they curved for miles
East and miles west beyond us, sagging
Under their burden of swallows.

We were small and thought we knew nothing
Worth knowing. We thought words travelled the wires
In the shiny pouches of raindrops,

Each one seeded full with the light
Of the sky, the gleam of the lines, and ourselves
So infinitesimally scaled

We could stream thought the eye of a needle.

*Seamus Heaney*

228

**3.** 'I made a mistake,' he thought. 'I should never have come into this beckoning castle. We should have taken to the fields. We could have hidden ourselves behind the walls or in the briars ... If you listened you might hear the laughter of men, and the clashing of shields and swords. See helmets glinting in the sunlight ...' Imagine the life of the castle hundreds of years before and write a story about it.

## CHAPTER 17

**1.** What do we find out about Nicko?
**2.** Add to your character study of Finn.
**3.** How many new words did you learn from this chapter?

## CHAPTER 18

## CHARACTER STUDY

**1.** In your group investigate:
**(a)** What we learn about Finn from this chapter;
**(b)** What we learn about Derval.
Report back.

## CREATIVE WRITING

**2.** Study the last paragraph of the chapter.
NOTICE: Sometimes you can create a sense of excitement by piling up phrases.
**3.** 'They sat on the grass. It was like living in an opaque world, a beautiful white world that made you light-headed ...'

Suppose that, when the mist clears, Finn and Derval find themselves in a different century. Now continue the story.

Remember to make good descriptions, using adjectives, adverbs, similes, etc. Use some of your new vocabulary, learned from the novel.

## Correct Writing

'They sat on the grass.' The word 'on' is a Preposition here. A preposition shows us the relationship between two things or their relative positions. Other prepositions are: in, under, over, above, behind, around, before, through, from, to, etc. Read the first four paragraphs of this chapter again and pick out the prepositions.

## CHAPTER 19

## CHARACTER STUDY

**1.** Compose a character study of Granny O'Flaherty. Study her description, actions, words, etc. But also notice the TONE of voice she uses. What tone is suggested by the words? Read the dialogue dramatically and so work out the tone. Practise saying it in different ways.

## CHAPTER 20

**1.** At what points exactly and why did the reporters become frantic with excitement? Does this indicate anything about news reports? Discuss this.

**2.** Add to your character study of Granny O'Flaherty.

**3.** Have a spelling and vocabulary competition based on the last two chapters.

## CHAPTER 21 AND 22

## MEDIA

**1.** Working in pairs, role-play Uncle Toby being interviewed by a reporter. The reporter should prepare very searching questions and Uncle Toby should try to maintain his tone of sorrow and generosity in the face of this hard questioning.

**2.** Working in groups of 3 or 5, compose the front page of the local paper, after this incident. Your page might include interviews with various people involved, a description of the scene, likely local news, etc.

**3.** Then do a front page report for an English or American newspaper!

## WRITING

**4.** Write an entry in Uncle Toby's diary as he goes back to Wales on the boat.

**5.** Compose five descriptive paragraphs about a visit to the beach.

# DISCUSSION

**6.** Read this poem 'The Sea' by James Reeves. Read it quietly a number of times and then discuss it in your groups.

## THE SEA

The sea is a hungry dog,
Giant and grey.
He rolls on the beach all day.
With his clashing teeth and shaggy jaws
Hour upon hour he gnaws
The rumbling, tumbling stones,
And 'Bones, bones, bones, bones'
The giant sea-dog moans,
Licking his greasy paws.

And when the night wind roars
And the moon rocks in the stormy cloud,
He bounds to his feet and snuffs and sniffs,
Shaking his wet sides over the cliffs,
And howls and hollos long and loud.

But on quiet days in May or June,
When even the grasses on the dune
Play no more their reedy tune,
With his head between his paws
He lies on the sandy shores,
So quiet, so quiet, he scarcely snores.

*James Reeves*

He compares the sea to a great big dog. This kind of comparison is called a metaphor. Do you think it is a good comparison? Why or why not? Discuss this.

The poet tries to communicate the sounds of the sea. What words do this best and why?

Each group should prepare a dramatic reading or recitation. Try to convey the different moods of the sea.

# THINKING ABOUT THE NOVEL

*Think about the PLOT of this novel. Was it a simple plot or a complex one? Was it dramatic? Where? How?*

*What were the most interesting characters? Why? Were they all realistic? Were they credible (i.e. was it possible to believe in them as real people)? Discuss.*

*What do you think were the main themes or ideas the novel dealt with?*
*Would cruelty to children be one?*
*Was the book trying to make a point about families?*
*Would 'being responsible' be one of the themes?*
*What was it saying about people in general?*
*What other themes?*
*Discuss in your groups.*

*Hold a 'Novel Trial'. 'This book has been accused of being uninteresting, etc.' (Make up a specific charge.) Have a judge, prosecuting counsel, defence counsel, jury, witnesses, etc. Hold the trial.*

*Have you read any other adventure books or stories? Prepare a brief report on one and tell the class about it.*

# APPENDIX A
## FINDING AND USING BOOKS

# USING THE LIBRARY

## LIBRARIES

A library can be anything from a shelf of books, comics and annuals in your bedroom or a box of books in your classroom, to the more sophisticated school, college or public library. Some will be better equipped than others but all libraries will welcome you as a reader and member. So find out the opening hours of your school library (if you are lucky enough to have one) and have a browse through the shelves. Perhaps the teacher could arrange for your entire class to visit the local public library. Most libraries now have whole sections given over to Children and Young Adult Readers. Don't be afraid to ask for help from the assistants. You should certainly be able to find a book suitable to your interests and reading ability.

## FINDING A BOOK

To find a particular book you need to know the AUTHOR and TITLE or SUBJECT. You then look it up in the CATA-LOGUE, which has an AUTHOR INDEX and a SUBJECT INDEX, both arranged alphabetically. The catalogue may be on CARDS or on MICROFICHE.

## FACT OR FICTION

The books in all libraries are divided into two main kinds —FACT and FICTION.

FICTION—These are books in which the stories have been made up by the author. They are usually about adventures, mysteries, romance etc. The characters are imaginary.

Fiction books are arranged on he shelves in Alphabetical Order of the AUTHORS' SURNAMES.

FACT—Books on fact, also called Non-Fiction, are about the real world; people, places and events; animals, plants, discoveries, games, etc.

Books on FACT are arranged or classified by Subject and they are placed on the shelves according to Numbers. This is called the DEWEY DECIMAL CLASSIFICATION SYSTEM. Numbers stand for subject areas, in the following way:

| | | | |
|---|---|---|---|
| **000** | **General Works** | 570 | Anthropology & biology |
| 020 | Library science | 580 | Botany |
| 030 | General encyclopaedias | 590 | Zoology |
| 070 | Journalism | **600** | **Technology (Applied science)** |
| 100 | Philosophy | 610 | Medical science |
| 150 | Psychology | 620 | Engineering |
| 160 | Logic | 630 | Agriculture, food production |
| 170 | Ethics | 640 | Home economics, housecraft |
| 180 | Ancient & medieval philosophy | 650 | Business & business methods |
| 190 | Modern Western philosophy | 660 | Chemical technology |
| **200** | **Religion** | 670 | Manufactures |
| 210 | Natural theology | 680 | Other manufactures |
| 220 | Bible | 690 | Building |
| 230 | Christian doctrine | **700** | **The Arts** |
| 140 | Devotional & practical theology | 710 | Town & country planning |
| 260 | Work of Christian church | 720 | Architecture |
| 270 | Christian church history | 730 | Sculpture |
| 280 | Christian churches & sects | 740 | Drawing, decorative arts, design |
| 290 | Other religions | 750 | Painting |
| **300** | **Social Sciences** | 760 | Prints & print making |
| 320 | Political science | 770 | Photography |
| 330 | Economics | 780 | Music |
| 340 | Law | 790 | Recreations, hobbies |
| 350 | Public administration | **800** | **Literature** |
| 360 | Social welfare | 810 | American literature |
| 370 | Education | 820 | English literature |
| 380 | Public utilities: communication | 830 | Germanic literature |
| 390 | Customs & folklore | 840 | French literature |
| **400** | **Language** | 850 | Italian literature |
| 420 | English language | 860 | Spanish & Portuguese literature |
| 430 | Germanic languages | 870 | Latin literature |
| 440 | French language | 880 | Greek literature |
| 450 | Italian language | 890 | Other literatures |
| 460 | Spanish & Portuguese | **900** | **History, Geography, Biography** |
| 470 | Latin | 910 | Geography, travels, description |
| 480 | Greek | 920 | Biography |
| 490 | Other languages | 930 | Ancient history |
| **500** | **Pure Science** | 940 | History of Europe |
| 510 | Mathematics | 950 | History of Asia |
| 520 | Astronomy | 960 | History of Africa |
| 530 | Physics | 970 | History of North America |
| 540 | Chemistry | 980 | History of South America |
| 550 | Earth sciences | 990 | History of other regions |
| 560 | Paleontology | | |

If you have difficulties ask the Librarian.

## FICTION OR NON-FICTION !
### Study the following list of titles:

a. Write 'Fiction' or 'Non-Fiction' in the space provided.

b. If Non-Fiction, can you also fill in the reference number under which you will find the book? If it is not clear, find out from the librarian.

| | |
|---|---|
| Charlie and the Chocolate Factory | |
| Using the Computer | |
| The Trouble with Donovan Croft | |
| The Silver Sword | |
| Coal | |
| The Hobbit | |
| The Story of Cinema | |
| The Secret Garden | |
| The TV Kid | |
| Nigeria in the Nineteenth Century | |
| Silas Rat | |
| Bob Geldof, by Charlotte Gray | |
| The Adventures of Tom Sawyer | |
| Understanding the New Testament | |
| The Pan Dictionary of Synonyms | |
| Run with the Wind | |
| The New School Curriculum | |
| Greek Sculpture | |
| The Plays of Shakespeare | |
| Business Methods | |

## USING A NON-FICTION BOOK

During the year you may have to do many projects for which you will need to look up references or sections in specialist books. The following steps will help to narrow down your search.

**1.** First scan the CONTENTS PAGE, which gives you the chapter headings. You may get some idea of which chapter is likely to contain the information you want.

**2.** Use the INDEX, at the back, which is arranged in alphabetical order. This should give you an exact page fix.

**3.** SKIM through the page in question, looking for the word or name you are interested in. Then read it carefully and make notes.

**4.** Sometimes you will find a GLOSSARY (list) of names or terms at the back. This might help.

Here is an example of CONTENTS PAGE and INDEX from Paddy Crosbie's memoir of growing up in Dublin in the 1920s. It is entitled 'Your Dinner's Poured Out!' How would you find out about his school days?

**a.** Read the 'Contents' page. Which pages are most likely to contain information about his school days?

**b.** Look at the 'Index'. Does that help you find more detailed references to school? If you don't find an entry under 's' for school, then start at the beginning and list all the references likely to have information about school.

# CONTENTS

# Index

# TAKING NOTES 1

You could not possibly remember everything you are taught during the year, unless you take notes to help your memory. Notes should be:

BRIEF
CLEAR
IN YOUR OWN WORDS

## The First Paper-makers

One of the most important functions of our everyday lives is the ability to communicate—that is, to pass on information to others. In very ancient times people could only communicate by talking to each other face to face. A great and important change in human history came about when men first learned to write.

At first they wrote on stones, bones, leaves—anything suitable that nature provided in their primitive world. Many of the materials available were not very easy to use. They withered away, had rough and uneven surfaces, were heavy to carry, or bulky to store. Then around 2,200 BC the Ancient Egyptians discovered that a reed called 'papyrus' could be used to make a writing surface.

Although the use of papyrus spread far and wide outside Egypt, animal hides were often used for writing. The skins of calves, goats and sheep were washed, stretched on frames, and coated with chalk and lime paste, which helped to remove grease and hair. After drying they were rubbed with a stone to smooth the surface. The finished material was called 'parchment', and was used all over Europe from about 170 BC onwards. Fine quality parchment was quite valuable, so it was treated with great care and was often used more than once.

These early writing materials served an immensely important purpose in the cultural development of mankind, but they did not have very practical qualities. It is to the Chinese that we owe the invention of what can truly be called paper, and it happened as long ago as 250 BC.

The first known paper-maker, T'sai Lun, is thought to have used waste products—old rags, pieces of hemp-rope, and old fishing nets. The raw materials were boiled in water and wood ash. Then they were beaten, so that the fibres broke apart to make a mushy pulp, which looked rather like porridge. By passing the pulp through a flat, mesh strainer—like a kitchen sieve—the paper-makers drained out the water, leaving the matted fibres behind. When dried out, the flattened fibres became the first ever sheets of paper.

They made an ideal writing surface—cheap, easy to use, and light to store and carry.

Paper has been made in the same way ever since—by pulping plant fibres, then removing the water—but over the centuries the machines have become more and more complicated.

*Chinese woodcuts showing four stages of paper-making.*

2. *Read the following extract from Paddy Crosbie's autobiography 'Your Dinner's Poured Out', and make notes of the main points.*

*It might be better to rearrange some of the ideas in this one. For example, you could try this running order:*
*historical details of the school*
*his first entry to the school at 6 $^3/_4$*
*his experiences in the First School with Br. Cass*
*the yard and buildings*
*the Christian Brothers and the Irish language*

### The School Around the Corner

I arrived at the Christian Brothers' School, North Brunswick Street, on August 23rd, 1920. The old school was, and still is, a solid building. In 1920 there was only one main building, with a science room and a manual room at the rear. The school has always been called Brunner.

The main building began its life in February, 1869, ten years before the apparitions at Knock. The walls are of Wicklow granite and I believe this old building will be standing, when all the new ones at present surrounding it, have fallen. There were four very large rooms, each of which was given the title of School. A boy commenced in First School and finished upstairs in Fourth School.

When I arrived from Stanhope Street Convent at the age of six and three-quarters, Brother Curley was examining the newcomers in the Second Reader. I passed with flying colours because I had most of the lessons off by heart from watching and listening to my brother Mossy. Brother Curley had succeeded Brother Redmond, who had earned a great name for saintliness.

When Brunner opened its doors first in February 1869, according to the annals, practically all of the boys who turned up to be enrolled were barefooted. They were an unruly lot, as none had ever been to school before. Beside the school was a site, lately vacated by the Medical School, and when the boys were let out to play, they made their way to this site, where, within a large shed, they found human bones. One of the Brothers was horrified to find his new pupils playing hurling with the skulls and bones. He quickly took command and the bones were interred in a safe place.

The cost of the original building was £4,000. The Brothers were made welcome in the district, and lived for a while in Prussia Street, before removing to the corner of Charleville Road on the North Circular Road. The present monastery is on the other side of the N.C. Road at No. 242.

The desks in First School were long wooden affairs and very shaky. One shake from a boy at one end put blots on twelve copies. The inkwells were filled with a home-made black concoction, and the ink was used for more purposes than writing. There was no formal teaching done, as we know it now, simply because the room was too crowded. There were three monitors and one brother. His name was Brother Cass, and he had succeeded a Brother Morrissy. The monitors were 'five bob a week' ex-pupils, whose job it was to examine the boys in home tasks. The tasks were allotted each afternoon for home-work, and these were examined the following morning. The names of the monitors in First School in 1920 were Lawless, Caffrey and Fitzsimons. We had no fully qualified lay teachers. A failure at lessons meant a chalk-mark on the desk in front of the boy who had failed. For every chalk-mark a scholar received one 'biff' from the brother, but we always managed to lighten our troubles by rubbing out some of the marks before his tour began. Brother Cass used a leather, which we all preferred to the sticks used by the monitors when the brother left the room.

The schoolyard was a very small one—too small for almost six hundred boys. There was no lighting or heating in the rooms, although there was a stove for the latter purpose—a stove which was never used. There were no cloakrooms so coats and caps were hung on hooks on three walls of each room. Along the fourth wall, which was a wood-plus-glass partition affair, there was a rostrum for the Brother and a large altar to the Blessed Virgin with presses beneath. Every time the clock struck the classes stood and recited a Hail Mary and in the month of May the wooden structure of the altar was covered and decorated with blue and white paper. The boys brought in flowers and candles, and there was great rivalry between the classrooms, as to which altar was the best.

The lavatories in the schoolyard were dry ones, but were flushed periodically by a mysterious someone, whom we never saw. Later on in 1924 Brother Murray had the old toilets knocked down and a line of twelve new flush ones plus a wash-hand basin and urinals built on a new extension of the schoolyard. Civilization had arrived.

Long before the British left Ireland the Christian Brothers were teaching Irish. The Brothers used a huge chart of pictures for conversation lessons, and their 'Aids to Irish Composition' was a book which gave wonderful help in problems of grammar. I doubt that it will ever be bettered. Regarding the chart, I can recall every figure and scene on it.

As I entered the school in 1920, I little dreamed that I was destined to spend almost fifty-seven years of my life within its confines, or that my own name was to be wedded to that of the school that was to become 'The School Around the Corner'.

**3.** *What is the difference between BIOGRAPHY and AUTOBIOGRAPHY?*

# TAKING NOTES 2

You might use a 'spider diagram' to help you remember. This usually displays the main idea in the centre and then ties on the less important points, like a spider's web. For example, if you had to find out about the poet Patrick Kavanagh, you might record your notes like this:

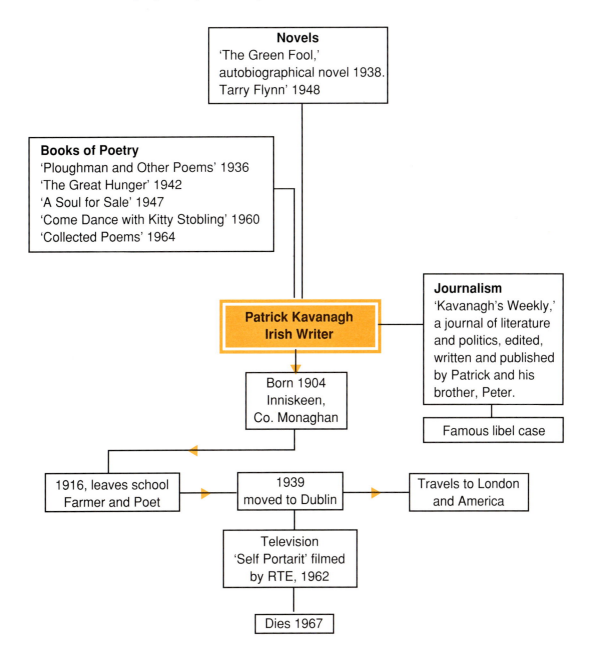

**Novels**
'The Green Fool,'
autobiographical novel 1938.
Tarry Flynn' 1948

**Books of Poetry**
'Ploughman and Other Poems' 1936
'The Great Hunger' 1942
'A Soul for Sale' 1947
'Come Dance with Kitty Stobling' 1960
'Collected Poems' 1964

**Patrick Kavanagh
Irish Writer**

**Journalism**
'Kavanagh's Weekly,'
a journal of literature
and politics, edited,
written and published
by Patrick and his
brother, Peter.

Born 1904
Inniskeen,
Co. Monaghan

Famous libel case

1916, leaves school
Farmer and Poet

1939
moved to Dublin

Travels to London
and America

Television
'Self Portarit' filmed
by RTE, 1962

Dies 1967

He * had married well, too. In 1557 his bride was Mary Arden, daughter of his father's old landlord, who had died the year before. It was a good match; as Robert's favourite, Mary had inherited substantial money and some farmland in Wilmcote. The first two children, both girls, died as babies. In April 1564, Mary gave birth to her third child, a son named William. The exact date of his birth, like so much else about his life, is disputed. He was certainly baptized at Holy Trinity Church on 26 April, as the Parish Register tells us. Tradition says he was born on 23 April, which, by a happy coincidence, is also the Day of St George, the patron saint of England.

William was fortunate to survive. In the 1564 Burial Register, there is an ominous note on 11 July: 'Here begins the plague'. Bubonic plague swept the country in devastating waves: in this outbreak, 200 people died in Stratford before the end of the year. Luckily it did not reach the Shakespeares' house and William lived on. Other children followed: Gilbert (who was to become a London haberdasher), Joan (the longest lived), Anne and Richard, who died young, and Edmund, who grew up to be a London actor like his brother.

There are no documents to tell us how William spent his boyhood, but we can make intelligent guesses about certain points. He probably had a fairly privileged life as son of an important citizen. For a time, John continued to prosper, his career reaching its height in 1568 when he became High Bailiff (or Mayor) of Stratford, and applied, unsuccessfully at this time, to the Heralds' College in London for the coat-of-arms of a gentleman. No doubt he and his son enjoyed the ceremonial connected with his position; wearing his scarlet, furred robe, he was escorted to official functions, fairs or markets by buff-uniformed sergeants, carrying maces.

The many references to the Bible or the Prayer Book in the plays tell us that the Church was an important part of William's upbringing, as it was for all Elizabethans. The government compelled church attendance, determined to re-establish the Protestant faith after the Catholic revival under Queen Mary I.

Shakespeare's first contact with plays probably came at the Guildhall, regularly visited by touring acting companies from 1568 onwards. One of his father's duties was to grant licences to such visiting groups, and one of his privileges was to sit with his family in the front row at performances. The plays themselves were mostly moralities, simple dramas: 'godly, learned and fruitful', containing some religious message, but also enlivened by 'pleasant mirth and pastime' and vivid special effects that would impress an imaginative boy.

*Now read about Shakespeare's education and record the main points in spider diagram form.*

Shakespeare's formal education, after 'Petty School' where he learned his letters, was certainly at Stratford Grammar School, although there is no written record of his attendance there. Its recently opened schoolroom above the Guildhall was only a quarter of a mile from Henley Street. Highly qualified masters gave the New King's School a good reputation but its regime was harsh. Boys endured a long, tedious day from 6 am to 5 pm, with a 2 hour midday break. This schooling went on 6 days a week, with rare holidays when a boy might enjoy 'his home and sporting place', No wonder a boy carved a protest in Latin on one of the school desks: 'Nothing comes from working hard'. Lines in the plays seem to show Shakespeare's distaste for school:

... The whining schoolboy with his satchel
And shining morning face, creeping like snail
Unwillingly to school.
(*As You Like It*, II, vii)
Love goes toward love as schoolboys from their books,
But love from love, toward school with heavy looks.
(*Romeo and Juliet*, II,ii)

*William Shakespeare's school.*

*William Shakespeare 1564 - 1616.*

The curriculum was still based almost entirely on Latin. The pupil began with Lily's Latin Grammar, a 200-page pamphlet that he learned by heart, before moving on to simple texts. Much of the work was spoken rather than written; in the picture of Sir Hugh Evans teaching William in *The Merry Wives of Windsor*, Shakespeare gives us a comic version of the teaching style. In the upper forms, pupils were forbidden to speak English at school, as everything had to be done in Latin. Senior boys composed Latin speeches and studied Roman poets: Ovid's *Metamorphoses* re-

mained Shakespeare's lifelong favourite. Work was demanding and the boy William learned much more than the 'small Latin' that Ben Jonson attributed to him.

Shakespeare may not have completed his school course. In 1576, a sudden change came in John Shakespeare's fortunes. Possibly he had some accident or illness that reduced his activity, or he suffered some religious persecution, in that he may have returned to Catholicism, while living in a fiercely Protestant society. He began to miss Council meetings, although he was kindly treated by his fellows, and then he ran into debt, and sold some of his land to obtain cash.

Shakespeare's first biographer of 1709, Nicholas Rowe, claimed that it was these misfortunes 'the narrowness of his circumstances and the want of his assistance at home'—that made John remove William from school to help him in the shop. Certainly, references to leather craft in the plays show an expert knowledge. A story, collected by John Aubrey in the seventeenth century, shows him working for his father:

*'I have been told heretofore by some of the neighbours, that when he was a boy he exercised his father's trade, but when he killed a calf he would do it in high style, and make a speech'.*

(John Aubrey, *Brief Lives*, 1681)

# Correct Writing

## COMMA

Just as paragraphs are used to break up a piece of writing into units of sense, so commas are used to separate words and phrases in the sentence, in order to make it easy to understand quickly. The comma suggests a slight pause or hesitation.

**1.** Commas are used to separate a list of words, except for the last two on the list which are joined by 'and', 'or' etc. Example: 'The drama teacher asked the student to bring in: buckets, mops, tea-towels, soap, tape recorders and leotards.'

**2.** Commas are used to separate phrases. Example: 'The boy charged in the door, clumped down between the rows, threw himself into his seat and reluctantly dragged out a book.'

**3.** Commas are used to mark off a phrase in the middle of a sentence. Example: 'The student, who was a Black Belt in karate, merely looked disdainfully at the angry teacher', or : 'John, with a voice like that, you could become a professional fog-horn!'

**4.** Use after an adverbial or adjectival opening to a sentence. Example: 'Gloriously, the music came to a triumphal if sudden ending'. 'Marginally, the government is showing a small lead in the opinion polls.' or 'Disgusted, I picked up a dozen discarded sweet papers as I came into the classroom.'

**Note:** Don't over-use this type of sentence.

Use also after words like 'however', 'notwithstanding', 'nevertheless', etc. at the start of sentences:

Nevertheless, I will give you another chance to spell 'nevertheless'.

**5.** Use after words like 'Yes', 'No', 'Thank you':

No, I didn't do that question.

Thank you, I really needed that money.

*Don't* use commas instead of full stops:

**X** She came to school late, the teacher gave her a punishment exercise.

√ She came to school late.  The teacher gave her a punishment exercise.

## COLON

A colon is used before a list or before direct speech.
Example:  The requirements for your English class tomorrow are the following:  copy, pen, dictionary and a clear head.

She stood at the top of the room and shouted:  'You have disgraced yourselves, again!'

## SEMI-COLON

The semi-colon is a bit like a comma.  You might find it particularly useful to break up lists of phrases which already have commas in them.

Example:  The night before her first cookery class Carmencita packed everything neatly into her bag:  baking tins; packets of salt, pepper, flour and oregano; a tube of tomato puree already half used; two tea towels, neatly ironed by her mother; and a tin opener.

# Using a Dictionary

Look at the page from the Oxford Senior Dictionary which is printed on the next page (p.563 scatty—school)

Notice the following:

All the words are in alphabetical order. If all the words begin with the same letter, as they do here, then the alphabetical order of the second, third, fourth, etc. letter decides where a word fits on the page.

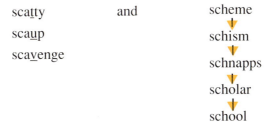

Use the GUIDE WORDS as a quick way to find the right page. These are the first and last words of any page and they are printed at the top, as here SCATTY—SCHOOL. If the word you want comes between these then you will find it on this page. For example, SCENE will be found between SCA ... and SCH ...

There is a pronunciation guide after most words. This shows the number of syllables in the word. (A syllable is a unit of sound: 'school' has only one sound unit but 'scenario' (scen-ar-i-o) has four.) The heavy dark type indicates which one is stressed in pronunciation.

The guide also helps with pronunciation which is not obvious from the spelling. For example, the c in 'scenic' is silent—(seen-ik)—and the c in 'sceptical' in pronounced like a k—(skep-tic-al).

Many non-student dictionaries now use the International Phonetic Alphabet as a guide to pronunciation. This might be quite confusing for a young student, so ask your teacher for help.

> **scenario** /sɪˈnɑːrɪəʊ/ *n.* (*pl.* **scenarios**) script or synopsis of film, play, etc.; imagined sequence of future events. [It. f. L (foll.)]

*Extract from 'Oxford Dictionary of Current English'*

points whose coordinates are the pairs of values corresponding to various particular instances.

**scatty** *adj.* (scattier, scattiest) (*slang*) scatter-brained, crazy.

**scaup** (*pr.* skawp) *n.* a kind of diving duck of northern coasts.

**scavenge** *v.* **1.** (of an animal) to search for decaying flesh as food. **2.** to search for usable objects or material among rubbish or discarded things. **scavenger** *n.*

**scenario** (sin-**ar**-i-oh) *n.* (*pl.* scenarios) **1.** the outline or script of a film, with details of the scenes. **2.** a detailed summary of the action of a play, with notes on scenery and special effects. **3.** an imagined sequence of future events. ¶ This word does not mean *scene* or *scenery*.

**scene** *n.* **1.** the place of an actual or fictional event; *the scene of the crime*, where it happened. **2.** a piece of continuous action in a play or film, a subdivision of an act. **3.** an incident thought of as resembling this. **4.** a dramatic outburst of temper or emotion, a stormy interview, *made a scene*. **5.** stage scenery. **6.** a landscape or view as seen by a spectator, *the rural scene before us*. **7.** (*slang*) an area of action, a way of life. ☐ **be on the scene**, to be present.

**scene-shifter** *n.* a person who moves the scenery on a theatre stage.

**scenery** *n.* **1.** the general appearance of a landscape. **2.** picturesque features of a landscape. **3.** structures used on a theatre stage to represent features in the scene of the action.

**scenic** (**seen**-ik) *adj.* having fine natural scenery. **scenic railway**, a miniature railway running through artificial picturesque scenery as an amusement at a fair.

**scent** *n.* **1.** the characteristic pleasant smell of something. **2.** a sweet-smelling liquid made from essence of flowers or aromatic chemicals. **3.** the trail left by an animal and perceptible to hounds' sense of smell, indications that can be followed similarly, *followed* or *lost the scent*; *on the scent of talent*. **4.** an animal's sense of smell, *dogs hunt by scent*. **scent** *v.* **1.** to discover by sense of smell, *the dog scented a rat*. **2.** to begin to suspect the presence or existence of, *she scented trouble*. **3.** to put scent on (a thing), to make fragrant. **scented** *adj.*

**sceptic** (**skep**-tik) *n.* a sceptical person, one who doubts the truth of religious doctrines.

**sceptical** (**skep**-tik-ăl) *adj.* inclined to disbelieve things, doubting or questioning the truth of claims or statements etc. **sceptically** *adv.*

**scepticism** (**skep**-ti-sizm) *n.* a sceptical attitude of mind.

**sceptre** (**sep**-ter) *n.* a staff carried by a king or queen as a symbol of sovereignty.

**schedule** (**shed**-yool) *n.* a programme or timetable of planned events or of work. — *v.* to include in a schedule, to appoint for a certain time, *the train is scheduled to stop at Milan*. ☐ **on schedule**, punctual according to the timetable.

**schematic** (skee-**mat**-ik) *adj.* in the form of a diagram or chart. **schematically** *adv.*

**scheme** (*pr.* skeem) *n.* **1.** a plan of work or action. **2.** a secret or underhand plan, *a scheme to defraud people*. **3.** an orderly planned arrangement, *a colour scheme*. — *v.* to make plans, to plan in a secret or underhand way. — **schemer** *n.*

**scherzo** (**skairts**-oh) *n.* (*pl.* scherzos) a lively vigorous musical composition or independent passage in a longer work.

**schism** (*pr.* sizm) *n.* division into opposing groups because of a difference in belief or opinion, especially in a religious body.

**schismatic** (siz-**mat**-ik) *adj.* of schism. — *n.* a person who takes part in a schism.

**schist** (*pr.* shist) *n.* a kind of coarse rock made up of elongated crystals of different minerals, which splits easily into thin plates.

**schizoid** (**skits**-oid) *adj.* resembling or suffering from schizophrenia. —*n.* a schizoid person.

**schizophrenia** (skits-ō-**freen**-i-ă) *n.* a mental disorder in which a person becomes unable to act or reason in a rational way, often with delusions and withdrawal from social relationships.

**schizophrenic** (skits-ō-**fren**-ik) *adj.* of or suffering from schizophrenia. —*n.* a schizophrenic person.

**schnapps** (*pr.* shnaps) *n.* a kind of strong gin.

**schnitzel** (**shnits**-ĕl) *n.* a fried veal cutlet.

**scholar** *n.* **1.** a person with great learning in a particular subject. **2.** a person who is skilled in academic work. **3.** a person who holds a scholarship. **scholarly** *adj.*

**scholarship** *n.* **1.** a grant of money towards education, usually gained by means of a competitive examination. **2.** great learning in a particular subject. **3.** the methods and achievements characteristic of scholars and academic work.

**scholastic** (skŏl-**ast**-ik) *adj.* of schools or education, academic.

**school**[1] *n.* a shoal, e.g. of fish or whales.

**school**[2] *n.* **1.** an institution for educating children or for giving instruction. **2.** its buildings. **3.** its pupils. **4.** the time during which teaching is done there, *school ends at 4.30 p.m.* **5.** the process of being educated in a

*Extract from 'Oxford Senior Dictionary'*

The dictionary also shows how you can use the word in its different forms.

Example: sceptic n.
sceptical adj.
sceptically adv.

n. = noun
adj. = adjective
adv. = adverb

It may also indicate if the word is SLANG (i.e., has special meaning in a certain locality only) or if it is for INFORMAL or COLLOQUIAL use (i.e., used in everyday speech but not when writing or speaking formally).

Consult the Introduction to help you interpret the symbols in a particular dictionary.

If you can't spell a word, then you must make some guesses at the first syllable and try under these.

# E X E R C I S E S

*1. Compose a number of paragraphs on the subject 'LIFE IN OUR SCHOOL', correctly using as many as you can of the words on the printed dictionary page!*
*2. Have a spelling competition based on the page.*
*3. Use your dictionary to find the meanings of the following words:*

| | |
|---|---|
| ALMANAC | ENCODE |
| ANNOTATE | LEXICON |
| APOCRYPHAL | SCAN |
| CENSOR | TRANSCRIBE |
| COHERENT | VERIFIABLE |

*Find out whether they are verbs, nouns, adjectives etc. and use each one correctly, in a sentence.*
*4. Make a list or glossary of amusing, clever or colourful slang words or phrases you have heard. (Use only those passed by the censor!)*
*Here are some from Paddy Crosbie's 'Your Dinner's Poured Out'.*

## PHRASES

*He'd talk the teeth off a saw.*
*He's gone for his tea (anyone killed or after dying).*
*Don't be acting the maggot (messing).*
*As scarce as hobby horse manure.*
*That fellow'll be late for his own funeral (slow).*
*Sure it was like throwin' apples into an orchard (doing something stupid).*

## SLANG WORDS

| | |
|---|---|
| AYTIN HOUSE | restaurant |
| BEAVER | a beard |
| BOWSY | a scoundrel |
| BIFF | a slap in school |
| BRONICAL | bronchial |
| CHANEY | broken bit of delf |
| CHISLER | a young boy |
| TO COG | to copy |
| DECKO | a look |
| DICKIED OUT | dressed up |
| DOORSTEPS | thick slices of bread |
| JOW OFF | buzz off |
| MOSEY | a stroll |
| MOT | woman or girlfriend |
| ON THE JARE | mitching |
| ROZZER | a policeman |
| AN OUL' WAN | a woman |
| A YOUNG WAN | a girl |
| WING | a penny |

**5.** *Script a conversation between two people, using colloquial speech.*
**6.** *Write a letter to your aunt, uncle, cousin or a penpal, describing your visit to the local library. Check mistakes, revise it and then post it!*

# HAVE FUN WITH WORD GAMES AND X-WORDS.

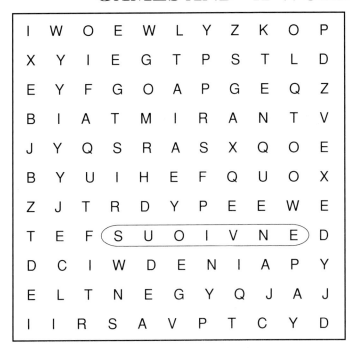

```
I  W  O  E  W  L  Y  Z  K  O  P
X  Y  I  E  G  T  P  S  T  L  D
E  Y  F  G  O  A  P  G  E  Q  Z
B  I  A  T  M  I  R  A  N  T  V
J  Y  Q  S  R  A  S  X  Q  O  E
B  Y  U  I  H  E  F  Q  U  O  X
Z  J  T  R  D  Y  P  E  E  W  E
T  E  F  S  U  O  I  V  N  E  D
D  C  I  W  D  E  N  I  A  P  Y
E  L  T  N  E  G  Y  Q  J  A  J
I  I  R  S  A  V  P  T  C  Y  D
```

**Find The Adjectives**

ENVIOUS

GAY

GENTLE

PAINED

PLEASED

RAGE

SHY

SPIRITED

VEXED

WEEPY

**Write Something**

DIARY

EPIC

ESSAY

LINES

NEWS

PROSE

SPEECH

STORY

THESIS

VERSE

```
F  K  Y  P  L  L  I  L  G  C  F
F  H  A  G  S  S  P  S  S  S  B
E  T  S  B  P  D  E  R  I  K  U
U  N  S  E  I  N  B  S  O  U  G
U  E  E  A  I  E  E  F  M  S  R
Q  C  R  L  S  H  N  S  T  Y  E
H  Y  P  R  T  F  Z  T  L  U  F
H  Z  E  B  C  A  L  O  V  Q  U
V  V  R  I  Z  O  T  R  V  Z  Z
Q  F  P  V  T  L  Y  Y  C  S  A
G  E  Q  H  X  S  F  S  W  E  N
```

## ACROSS

**1.** Protected by insurance (7)
**5.** Injure with hot liquid (5)
**8.** Rodent (3)
**9.** Being away (7)
**10.** Room at top of house (5)
**11.** Disc of light round saint's head (4)
**12.** Non-acceptance (7)
**14.** Intellectual ability (6)
**16.** Cropped up (6)
**19.** Hearing distance (7)
**21.** Cut with scythe or machine (4)
**24.** Grim (5)
**25.** Cause to turn another faith, etc (7)
**26.** Largest existing animal of deer kind(3)
**27.** Shadowy (5)
**28.** One of logs on which railway rails rest (7)

## DOWN

**1.** Crustacean with ten legs (4)
**2.** Prospect (5)
**3.** Stop for want of winding (3,4)
**4.** Gloomy (6)
**5.** Body of assistants required to carry on institution, etc (5)
**6.** Painters (7)
**7.** Young swimming bird (8)
**13.** Haunted (8)
**15.** Stuffy (7)
**17.** Tale with incidents remote from everyday life (7)
**18.** Stores ready for drawing on (6)
**20.** Sweet viscid fluid produced by bees (5)
**22.** Unmannerly child (5)
**23.** Agitate (4)

**ACROSS**

**1.** Female prison guard (8)
**7.** Scottish family group (4)
**8.** Volume, what vessel will hold (8)
**9.** Take, receive (6)
**10.** Slip by, pass on (6)
**11.** Hearing organ (3)
**12.** Mark left by coffee, etc (5)
**14.** Retains (5)
**16.** Energy, vigour (3)
**18.** Old-time ballroom dance (6)
**20.** Astonished (6)
**22.** Bright-red pot-plant (8)
**23.** Stop up, seal (4)
**24.** Properly constructed (4-4)

**DOWN**

**1.** Savage Scottish tabby (7)
**2.** Open prairie (5)
**3.** Read out (6)
**4.** Evening meal (6)
**5.** Locations (5)
**6.** Rub roughly (6)
**13.** Frozen region of Earth (3-3)
**15.** Introductory performance (7)
**16.** Travelling bag, suitcase (6)
**17.** Breast-fed animal (6)
**19.** Odds that get your money back (5)
**21.** First letter of Greek alphabet (5)

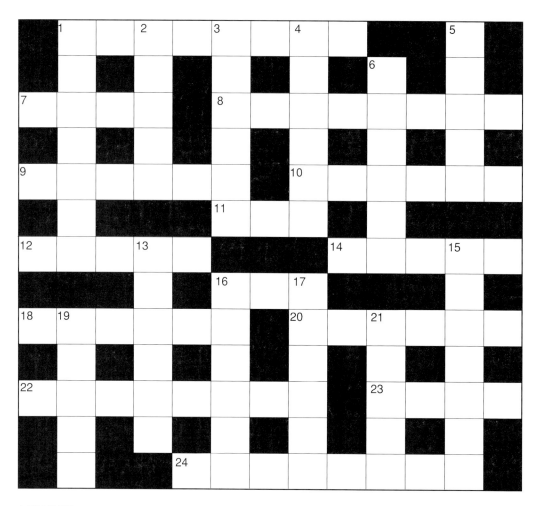

**ACROSS**

**1.** Finished, entire (8)
**7.** School principal (4)
**8.** Military township (8)
**9.** Theatre dancing (6)
**10.** Get aboard a ship (6)
**11.** Have a meal (3)
**12.** Discourage (5)
**14.** Bird's standing-place (5)
**16.** Cry chokingly (3)
**18.** Continental system of measurement, now ours too! (6)
**20.** Rogue (6)
**22.** Set apart for religious purpose (8)
**23.** Part of a house (4)
**24.** Sniffer, instrument for searching (8)

**DOWN**

**1.** Dispose of body in fire (7)
**2.** Photographer's pose-girl (5)
**3.** Pope's ambassador (6)
**4.** What you aim at (6)
**5.** Storey, part of a building (5)
**6.** Sprightly, alert (6)
**13.** Pincer-armed insect (6)
**15.** Uproar, loud outcry (7)
**16.** Rub roughly (6)
**17.** Gentle wind, zephyr (6)
**19.** Happening (5)
**21.** Small fry, tiny fish (5)

## ACROSS

**1.** Suspended by rope (6,2)
**5.** Additional quantity (4)
**8.** Monk's hood (4)
**9.** Not guilty (8)
**10.** Bind up wound (7)
**12** Shouter (5)
**13.** American (6)
**15.** Struggled (6)
**17.** Clear off (5)
**18.** Gun (7)
**22.** Bring to neat finish (5,3)
**23.** Earth (4)
**24.** Lord (4)
**25.** Short-distance runner (8)

## DOWN

**1.** Invalid quarters on ship (4-3)
**2.** Mountain Ash (5)
**3.** Leaving (5)
**4.** Pale red (4)
**6.** Beginning (7)
**7.** Go in (5)
**11.** At right angles to ship's length (5)
**12.** Company of singers (5)
**14.** Bring up (7)
**16.** Drinking-glass (7)
**17.** Leather fastening (5)
**19.** Deduce (5)
**20.** Approximately (5)
**21.** Spin a coin (4)

# FICTION

At the end of this section you will find a list of titles I think you would enjoy reading. I recommend that you club together and buy a small selection of interesting books which you can keep in your own classroom and borrow whenever you wish. So for the price of one book, you can read up to twenty or thirty! Have a class discussion on this. Perhaps other people have interesting books to recommend or can loan books for the year. You will need to organise a system of borrowing.

But whether you use this system or the school or public library, you should keep a record of the books you read during the year. It would be best to keep a separate copy for this. You could also include reports on some of the films you watched or the music you enjoyed. Your teacher may let you submit this copy as part of your term assessment.

YOUR CULTURE RECORD!—Perhaps the first entry in this should be a description or profile of you, the reader. This would help your librarian or teacher to recommend books for you.

---

NAME ......................................................................

ADDRESS ................................................................

..............................................................................

..............................................................................

SCHOOL ..................................................................

CLASS ....................................................................

AGE .......................................................................

DO YOU FIND READING:

ENJOYABLE    ☐

HARD WORK    ☐

BORING    ☐

---

LIST SOME OF THE BOOKS OR MAGAZINES YOU HAVE ENJOYED:

(Author and title, if possible)

.....................................................................................................................

.....................................................................................................................

.....................................................................................................................

.....................................................................................................................

.....................................................................................................................

DO YOU HAVE FAVOURITE AUTHORS?

.....................................................................................................................

.....................................................................................................................

.....................................................................................................................

.....................................................................................................................

.....................................................................................................................

LIST YOUR HOBBIES AND INTERESTS:

.....................................................................................................................

.....................................................................................................................

.....................................................................................................................

.....................................................................................................................

.....................................................................................................................

.....................................................................................................................

WHAT KIND OF BOOK DO YOU PREFER:  adventure, detective, family

story, animal story, school story, science fiction, romance, non-fiction, other?

Write two or three paragraphs or pages about the kinds of books you enjoy.

.....................................................................................................................

.....................................................................................................................

.....................................................................................................................

.....................................................................................................................

READING RECORD: It might look something like this.
Add other sections, if you wish.

AUTHOR .................................................................................................................

TITLE ....................................................................................................................

CATEGORY ...........................................................................................................

NO. OF PAGES .....................................................................................................

BRIEF OUTLINE OF PLOT AND CHARACTERS:

.................................................................................................................................

.................................................................................................................................

.................................................................................................................................

YOUR OWN REACTION TO THE BOOK:

(You could write this in the style of advertising blurb for the back cover)

.................................................................................................................................

.................................................................................................................................

.................................................................................................................................

STAR RATING: such as   XXXXX  =  brilliant          or some uniform
                        XXXX   =  very good          system agreed
                        XXX    =  good               by the class.
                        XX     =  O.K.
                        X      =  poor or boring

DESCRIBE AN EXCITING EVENT IN THE BOOK:

.................................................................................................................................

.................................................................................................................................

.................................................................................................................................

.................................................................................................................................

.................................................................................................................................

.................................................................................................................................

.................................................................................................................................

.................................................................................................................................

# OTHER BOOK ACTIVITIES

AUTHOR PROFILE - comprises a brief profile of your favourite author. You can include a list of his/her books, brief life story, photograph with caption, advertising blurb for the back cover etc. Here are some pages from Chris Powling's profile of ROALD DAHL, published by Puffin.

**Contents**

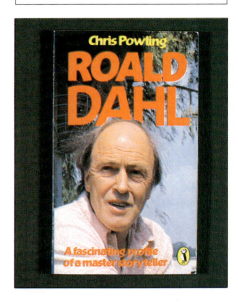

**Roald Dahl's Books**

**For Adults**

| | |
|---|---|
| Over to You | 1945 |
| Someone Like You | 1948 |
| Sometime Never | 1948 |
| Kiss Kiss | 1959 |
| Switch Bitch | 1965 |
| My Uncle Oswald | 1979 |
| The Best of Roald Dahl | 1983 |
| Boy: Tales of Childhood | 1984 |

**For Children**

| | |
|---|---|
| The Gremlins | 1944 |
| James and the Giant Peach | 1961 |
| Charlie and the Chocolate Factory | 1964 |
| The Magic Finger | 1966 |
| Fantastic Mr Fox | 1970 |
| Charlie and the Great Glass Elevator | 1973 |
| Danny The Champion of the World | 1975 |
| The Wonderful Story of Henry Sugar | 1977 |
| The Enormous Crocodile | 1978 |
| The Twits | 1980 |
| George's Marvellous Medicine | 1981 |
| Revolting Rhymes | 1982 |
| The BFG | 1982 |
| Dirty Beasts | 1983 |
| The Witches | 1983 |

SLOGANS - Make up slogans to promote books and reading or to sell particular books.

BOOK QUIZ - Have a class quiz on authors, titles, characters, names, places etc. about books.

TOP TEN - Compile a chart of the most popular books enjoyed by the class. Revise it every few weeks as new books are discovered and rated.

BOOK TRAIL - Choose a book which was highly rated by someone in your class and badly rated by someone else. The book will then have to be read by at least two 'lawyers' and say six 'jurors'. Have a trial to decide the book's rating, with prosecuting and defending lawyers etc. You will need to prepare for this week in advance. You could plan for two or three 'cases' in the same session, so that all class members are involved.

## SOME NOVELS AND BOOKS YOU MAY ENJOY

Among this lot you will surely find a couple of novels to read during the year. Enjoy them.

### THE FIRST DOZEN

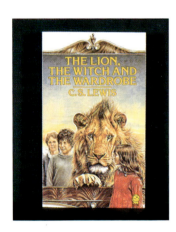

**1. The Lion, The Witch and The Wardrobe**

*by C.S. Lewis*

During the war years, when Peter, Susan, Edmund and Lucy are packed off for safety to live with an old professor and his housekeeper in the heart of the country, strange things begin to happen to them. They find themselves on the run from the White Witch, in the freezing forests of Narnia. Worst of all Edmund has been deceived by her and plots to betray them all.

This is a really gripping story, set in a world of witches, unusual creatures and strange powers.

If you enjoy this you might like to read the rest of the NARNIA stories.

■ ■ ■ ■ ■ ■ ■ ■ ■ ■ ■ ■ ■

**2. Why The Whales Came** *by Michael Morpurgo*

This is an exciting adventure set on the island of Islay, off Scotland. Life on the island seems ordinary enough, with fishing, school, playing on the hidden beaches, salvaging wreckage etc. But why are Daniel and Gracie forbidden to go near the strange old man who leaves messages on the sand for them? What is the frightening secret of the small, abandoned island in the bay? And will there be terrible butchery once again when the unusual singing whales beach themselves in the cove? The story builds to a gripping finish.

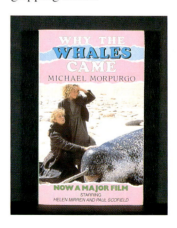

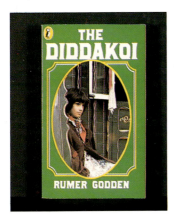

### 3. The Diddakoi *by Rumer Godden*

Kizzy is a diddakoi, a half-gypsy, who lived with her grandmother in a caravan at the edge of a village. She is bullied and tormented at school and made to feel different. But when her gran dies, things get even worse ...

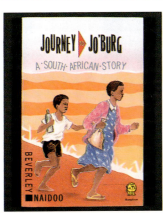

### 4. Journey To Jo'burg *by Beverly Naidoo*

Do you know anything about APARTHEID? Have you seen any films or read anything about it?

This story is from South Africa. Naledi, Tiro and their baby sister Dineo are being looked after by their granny because their mother must live and work in Johannesburg, which is 300 miles away! Dineo becomes very ill and they must get word to their mother. So they set out to walk there! But this is a very dangerous journey for a young girl and boy, particularly if they are black ...

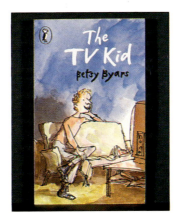

### 5. The T.V. Kid *by Betsy Byars*

Are you forever getting into trouble for watching television when you should be doing your homework? If so you have a lot in common with Lennie in this story, who likes to dream technicolour adventures all day. Until suddenly he is not in a dream anymore but in a real-life adventure, more horrible than he ever imagined! A frightening and funny story.

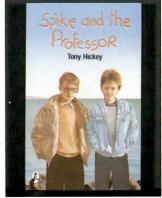

### 6. Spike and The Professor *by Tony Hickey*

Two Dublin boys, nick-named 'Spike' and 'The Professor', are desperate to raise some money for a day trip to Cork. When their sandwich stall doesn't make them millionaires overnight, they 'borrow' a dog to enter in the local 'Scruffs' dog show. But the dog has a will of his own!

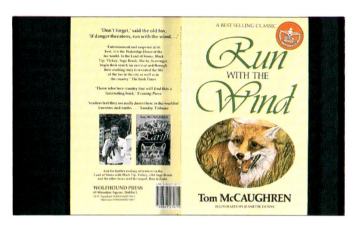

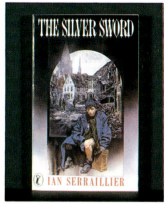

## 7. Run With The Wind *by Tom McCaughren*

There is drama in the animal world, among the foxes of Glensinna, Gleann an t-Sionnaig Bhain, the Valley of the White Fox. This is a lovely story where you share the excitement, the hopes, fears and fight for survival of the wild foxes.

If you enjoy this you might like to read the other books in this series.

■ ■ ■ ■ ■ ■ ■ ■ ■ ■ ■ ■ ■ ■ ■ ■ ■ ■ ■ ■ ■ ■ ■ ■ ■ ■

## 8. Silas Rat *by Dermot O'Donovan*

This is an animal tale with a difference! In this story we follow the daft adventures of Slick and his rat pack as they pit their wits against the owner of the local castle, Abigail Hennessy (known as Abigail the Awful); Julius Seizer, the cat; a crocodile named Murphy and many others. When Slick is killed, young Silas takes over but not before he has had a holiday in Egypt and meets such interesting characters as the Egyptian rat-catcher Buddak Farulak and his camel, Gamel; not to mention the President, Yusef Ben Razorblade. He manages to survive cobras, camels and old lady tourists and returns home to assault the castle once more.

**WARNING:** If you don't keep this book safely hidden, your parents will 'nick' it.

## 9. The Silver Sword *by Ian Serraillier*

What had happened to Joseph's family that night over a year ago, when the NAZI storm troopers called at the schoolhouse? Was what Mrs Krause said true? Had they taken his wife away? Had they returned and blown up the house with the children in it?

This is the story of a Polish family scattered and separated in war-torn Europe: mother and father Balicki; Ruth aged thirteen; Edek, eleven; and Bronia, three. The young people team up with Jan, a clever young thief, and some others as they search across the continent for their parents.

■ ■ ■ ■ ■ ■ ■ ■ ■ ■ ■

*P.S. If you enjoy this you might like to try 'Silas Rat And The Nuclear Tail', by the same author.*

266

*The Silver Sword cont/d..*

This novel is based on a true story. You might like to read: 'When Hitler Stole Pink Rabbit', by Judith Kerr or 'I am David' by Anne Holm - books about similar situations.

■ ■ ■ ■ ■ ■ ■ ■ ■ ■ ■ ■ ■

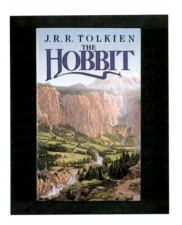

**10. The Hobbit** *by J.R.R. Tolkien*

'If you care for journeys there and back, out of the comfortable Western world, over the edge of the Wild and home again, and can take an interest in a humble hero (blessed with a little wisdom and a little courage and considerable good luck), here is the record of such a journey and such a traveller. The period is the ancient time between the age of Faerie and the dominion of men, when the famous forest of Mirkwood was still standing, and the mountains were full of danger. In following the path of this humble adventurer, you will learn by the way (as he did) - if you do not already know all about these things - much about trolls, goblins, dwarfs and elves, and get some glimpses into the history and politics of a neglected but important period.

For Mr Bilbo Baggins visited various notable persons; conversed with the dragon, Smaug the Magnificent; and was present, rather unwillingly, at the Battle of the Five Armies. This is all the more remarkable, since he was a hobbit...'

This book is a must, if you have not read it already - guaranteed to make you risk skipping your homework!

■ ■ ■ ■ ■ ■ ■ ■ ■ ■ ■ ■ ■

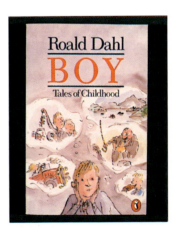

**11.Boy** *by Roald Dahl*

Roald Dahl tells the story of his own schooldays. As you'd expect it is a more remarkable story than yours or yours or mine - full of odd teachers, terrifying matrons, brutal moments, hilarious pranks and glorious holidays in Norway.

■ ■ ■ ■ ■ ■ ■ ■ ■ ■ ■ ■ ■

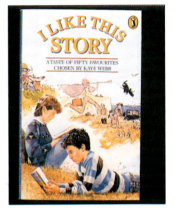

**12. I Like This Story** *compiled by Kaye Webb*

How about a look at fifty novels for the price of one? This has extracts from fifty books, old and modern, well-known and new, funny and sad. If you enjoy an extract you might like to go and read that book. Taste before you buy!

■ ■ ■ ■ ■ ■ ■ ■ ■ ■ ■ ■ ■

# THE SECOND DOZEN

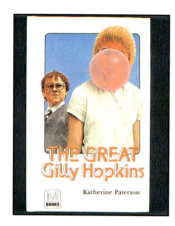

## 1. The Great Gilly Hopkins

*by Katherine Paterson*

'Gilly Hopkins has been in one foster home after another. The only things she seems to have learned from the experience are that you have to be tough to survive and that the first rule of life is always to be in charge. Make life as difficult as possible for everyone else, is Gilly's philosophy.'

But she reckons without Maime Trotter, a very large foster mother; William Ernest, who also lives there; and blind Mr Randolph, who lives next door. This most unlikely collection of people produces the most hilarious results. Is there a softer side to the gum-chewing, fist-flying Gilly? This is a sad but funny story.

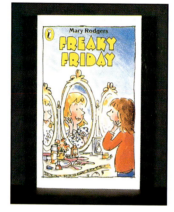

## 2. Freaky Friday *by Mary Rodgers*

What would you do if you woke up one morning to find you had turned into your mother? How would you deal with the pimply teen-ager from next door who has fallen in love with you; a parent-teacher meeting; a dinner party for six; and the boozy cleaning lady who says your daughter's (i.e., your) bedroom is a pig sty?

## 3. The Haunting *by Margaret Mahy*

This is an eerie story about a boy, Barney, who is being haunted. The ghost of his Great Uncle Cole is trying to get in touch with him. When he goes to visit his dead mother's family there is a very odd atmosphere in the house. And why do these relations all come, one by one, to visit him next day? What is the family secret or curse?

## 4. Bike Hunt *by Hugh Galt*

'A story of thieves and kidnappers. The characters: there's Niall. Almost thirteen, very keen on racing bikes. The focus of much attention from the girls, but he's not aware of it yet.

And Paudge, his friend. Tubby, and a little less grown up than Niall. Sometimes a bit confused, he has his own problems to cope with, but he tags along with Niall, and contributes in his own muddled way to the hunt.

Then there's Katy. Superintelligent and an electronics expert. She leads the hunt. She is growing up too, and has her eye on Niall.

There are the twins. Coy and superficial, they too set their sights on Niall. But can their tricks match up to Katy's brains?

Wasserman, the German industrialist. He's kidnapped by an armed gang ... but not for long!

Gaskin and his armed accomplices. Tough and ruthless, they are very angry at Wasserman's escape and desperate to find him.

PJ, and the bike thieves. They get caught up in the kidnap situation ...'

■ ■ ■ ■ ■ ■ ■ ■ ■ ■ ■

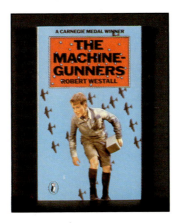

## 5. The Machine Gunners
### by Robert Westall

'Chas McGill had a second-best collection of war souvenirs in Garmouth, and he desperately wanted it to be the best. His chance came when he found the crashed German Heinkel, with a machine gun and all its ammunition intact. All he had to do was to remove it from the plane ...

The police, the Home Guard, in fact everybody in authority in Garmouth, knew the gun had been stolen. They were pretty sure the boys had it, but where? And did the boys realise that it could blow a hole through a wall at a quarter of a mile? It was essential to track it down before the boys killed themselves or anybody else. And all the time other things kept disappearing too: cement, a telescope, tin hats, fire buckets, stirrup pumps, even an Anderson shelter!'

What on earth were they up to?

■ ■ ■ ■ ■ ■ ■ ■ ■ ■ ■

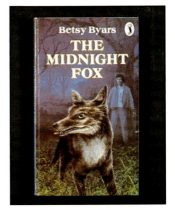

## 6. The Midnight Fox by Betsy Byars

Tom is packed off to his uncle's farm, somewhere in the USA, while his parents are on holiday in Europe. At first he hates the idea but then he discovers the den of a black fox, deep in the wood. He really enjoys watching her play with her cub. He tells no one.

But then some eggs disappear from the farmyard, then a chicken and finally the great turkey. So his uncle sets out to hunt the black fox and brings Tom along, unaware of his secret.

The story has a very dramatic ending.

■ ■ ■ ■ ■ ■ ■ ■ ■ ■ ■

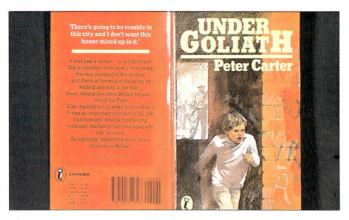

## 7. Under Goliath *by Peter Carter*

This is a dramatic disturbing story of the troubles in Belfast. If features two boys, one Catholic, the other Protestant - both interested in music. And it tells the story of their hatred and bigotry which gradually changes into friendship.

But then the troubles start ...

You might also like to try 'The Twelfth of July' by Joan Lingard.

■ ■ ■ ■ ■ ■ ■ ■ ■ ■ ■ ■ ■

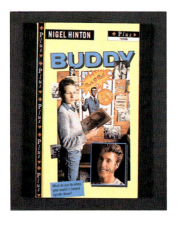

## 8. Buddy *by Nigel Hinton*

How would you feel if your dad came to the parent-teacher meeting dressed in his Teddy Boy gear - drain-pipe trousers, drape jacket, crepe-soled shoes and fluorescent green socks?

And this is not all that Buddy has to cope with - his dad is unemployed and may be involved in shady deals, his mother has left home and he is persuaded by his friends, Charmian and Julius, to investigate the unusual comings and goings at a great old house, down the road.

■ ■ ■ ■ ■ ■ ■ ■ ■ ■ ■ ■ ■

## 9. A Wizard of Earthsea *by Ursula Le Guin*

'The island of Gont, a single mountain that lifts its peak a mile above the storm-racked Northeast Sea, is a land famous for wizards. From the towns in its high valley and the ports on its dark narrow bays many a Gontishman has gone forth to serve the Lords of the Archipelago in their cities as wizard or mage, or, looking for adventure, to wander working magic from isle to isle of all Earthsea.

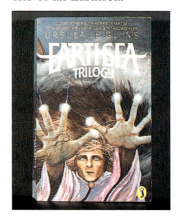

Of these some say the greatest, and surely the greatest voyager, was the man call Sparrowhawk, who in his day became both dragon-lord and Archmage. His life is told of in the *Deed of Ged* and in many songs, but this is a tale of the time before his fame, before the songs were made'.

This is the story of the early life of Ged, who was later to become the most powerful wizard of his time. It tells of his early training, his foolish boast which lets loose a dark spirit into the world and the dangerous journey he then has to undertake. Magic!

If you like this, then there are two other books in the trilogy.

■ ■ ■ ■ ■ ■ ■ ■ ■ ■ ■ ■

parents in an ordinary village, in ordinary Cornwall. But very little is as it seems and they get caught up in a gripping adventure with strange frightening people and a struggle of good and evil that goes back to the time of King Arthur. Who wins?

If you enjoy this, then the next book in the series is "The Dark Is Rising'.

■ ■ ■ ■ ■ ■ ■ ■ ■ ■ ■ ■

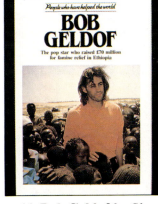

**11. Bob Geldof** *by Charlotte Gray*

[in the 'People Who Have Helped the World' series, published by Wolfhound Press]

It retells, with the aid of great colour photographs, the story of the popstar who raised 70 million for famine relief in Ethiopia.

There are also books on Mother Teresa of Calcutta and Martin Luther King in this series.

■ ■ ■ ■ ■ ■ ■ ■ ■ ■ ■ ■

**10. Over Sea, Under Stone** *by Susan Cooper*

Simon, Jane and Barney might be ordinary young people on holiday with their

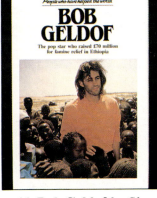

**12. Going Solo** *by Roald Dahl*

This is the second volume of his autobiography - full of extraordinary experiences, from a deadly encounter with a black mamba snake to crash-landing in the desert, during the war. A good read.

■ ■ ■ ■ ■ ■ ■ ■ ■ ■ ■ ■

# APPENDIX B
## SHORT STORIES

# SHORT STORIES

# 'A Crow Fight'

*Liam O'Flaherty*

There were twenty crows' nests in an oak tree that overlooked a mountain road. There were young birds in all the nests. It was in the middle of May, and the tree was green with leaves. All day the old crows filled the air for a long distance with the raucous sound of their voices.

There was a nest built on a low branch some distance down from the other nests. So that the people who passed threw stones at it. Very many tourists passed that way going to the mountains, because the road led from Dublin to the mountains. One day a party of three young men were passing, and they threw stones. Two of the young men threw two stones apiece, and then wiped their hands in their handkerchiefs and went away. They said: 'Let's go on. That's hard work on a hot day like this.' But the third young man was an American tourist, and he said: 'No, by Golly, I'm going to stay until I show you fellahs how to knock down that nest.'

He gave a little peasant boy sixpence to collect stones for him. After throwing stones for an hour or so, the American put a small stone through the bottom of the nest, and it fell to the ground. The American laughed, and went away to the publichouse farther up the road, where his Irish friends had retired to wait for him. He took no notice of the small crow that had fallen to the ground with the nest. The peasant boy also went away at a run to buy sweets for his sixpence without taking any notice of the little crow.

The little crow had no feathers on his body. Things like soft fluffy bristles grew all over him. He had fallen in a clump of long grass by the roadside and he was quite unhurt. But he was very terrified. With his mouth open and his bare wings stretched out, he worked his neck from side to side as if he was trying to unscrew it from his body. The straw from the broken nest lay all around him on the green long grass and on the white limestone road.

The old crows had fled when the stone-throwing began. They watched the affair from a high tree one hundred yards away from the nesting tree. They had grown quite used to the stone-throwing, and they were not in the least annoyed. They 'cawed' and they sharpened their beaks while they waited. But when they saw the nest falling they raised a wild and prolonged and raucous 'caw'. They flapped their wings and made a movement as if they had suddenly become intoxicated and were falling off their perches.

The mother of the young crow that had fallen flew into the air and turned a somersault three times with rage and sorrow. It was more through rage than sorrow, because she was a very old crow, and things had been going badly with her for the past month. Her mate had run away with a young female crow and gone to nest in an ash tree on the other side of the hill beyond the torrent. Two of her young ones had died on the day they came out of their shells. They died through exposure, since she had to leave them uncovered while she sought food. And now the third and last one had fallen to the ground, and she was without a nest even.

She flew back to the nesting tree, uttering harsh cries. She landed on the topmost branch and looked around. There was nobody in sight. A rabbit had already run out on to the road. He was looking about him, sitting on his thighs with his ears cocked. The old mother crow swooped down and landed in the middle of the road. She thrust out her chest, blinked her eyes, reached out her head sideways, listening. She 'cawed' gently. An answering mumble came from the long grass by the roadside where the young crow lay. The old mother crow immediately darted over. When she saw the young one, sprawled on its belly and with its distended mouth raised in the habitual manner to receive food, the old mother crow became overcome with emotion and she broke out into a series of thunderous and melancholy 'caws'. She jumped and ran about the road and flapped her wings like one gone mad.

The other crows gathered about. Some flitted on idle wings. Others sat on the fences that bound the road on either side. Now and again some would walk over sedately, reach out their necks and peer at the youngster that had been unnested. There was a terrific din.

Then the old mother crow flew up into the tree and darted about from branch to branch as if she were seeking something. Then she flew back to the road. She seized her young one in her beak and in her claws. With a sudden swoop she arose and landed in the fork of the lowest branch of the tree. The other crows followed her, 'cawing', urging her on as it were. She rested for several minutes in the fork of the branch, fondling the young one. The young crow was terrified once more by the fresh experience, and it held its mouth open, as if it were expecting something to attack it.

Then the mother lifted it again in her claws and flew upwards with a mighty effort. She landed on the second branch from the top. There were four nests there, made along the branch, supported by the twigs that grew thickly on either side of the branch, like the prongs of a comb. She planted her young one in a nest where there were two young crows ready to fly away. She attacked the two young crows furiously with beak and claw and drove them out of the nest. Then she spread herself out over the young one and waited for the attack from the parents of the young crows that she had expelled. The two young crows that had been expelled spread their wings and tried to soar. But their bodies were yet too heavy for their wings, and instead of rising they fell slantwise and landed clumsily on their breasts in the field, about one hundred yards away. There they lay, panting.

The two old crows rose screaming. They attacked the old mother crow with all their might. They showered blows on her back and head. They rooted at her with their claws and sent black feathers flying from her scratched back. She fought them as best she could in return. But principally she clung with all her might to the nest, determined to die rather than be ejected or expose her young one to death. The other crows gathered about the fighting ones. There was a terrific din.

The fight lasted fully a quarter of an hour, and then it stopped. The old mother crow was battered, but she still remained on the nest. The other two crows suddenly flew away to the field where their young ones had landed. For some time they strutted about 'cawing' to their young ones, sharpening their beaks and flapping their wings and making growling noises as if they threatened to go back again to the mother crow.

But they obviously thought better of it. Instead they set to teaching their young ones how to scratch the earth and drag out worms without cutting them with their beaks, and thus losing the better part of them.

# EXPLORING THE STORY

*1. Read the story. Use your dictionary to get out the meanings of any difficult words and write them into your Word Copy. Try to use some of these new words in your own writing.*

### 2. COMPREHENSION
*a) In what season of the year did this incident happen?*
*b) How many people were present when the nest fell?*
*c) Did the mother fly immediately to rescue the little crow? Explain.*
*d) Was this the first problem she had had this month? Explain.*
*e) While the mother was on the ground what were the other crows doing?*
*f) How did the two old crows react when she had taken over their nest?*
*g) What were the steps in this tragedy? List the main points, in your own words. It might be helpful to divide it up into scenes for a film. What is the key happening or idea in each scene?*

### 3. WRITING

*Examine paragraph four again. Notice how the writer makes this very memorable, with a few simple yet striking images:*

\* *'Things like soft fluffy bristles grew all over him.' This is a very accurate description, if you have ever seen a bird not yet fully fledged.*

\* *'He worked his neck from side to side as if he was trying to unscrew it from his body.' This unnatural image suggests the great terror of the bird.*

\* *'The straw...on the white limestone road.' There is something cold, hard, unwelcoming about the descriptive words 'white limestone'. There is great contrast with the softness of the straw nest he has just lost.*

*Choose any other paragraph and examine how the author creates colour and interest.*

**4.** *In your groups discuss what the story tries to tell us about the world of nature. Do we treat animals well? Report back to the class. Perhaps you might have a debate on some aspect of this.*

**5.** *After the discussion, plan and write five paragraphs on 'HOW MAN VIEWS THE OTHER ANIMALS'.*

### 6. READING

*If you enjoyed this story you might like to read some of Liam O'Flaherty's other animal stories, such as: 'All Things Come of Age', a tragic story of rabbits or 'Timoney's Ass'. Ask your teacher or librarian for guidance.*

**7.** *Other books about animals:*

*Richard Adams—'Watership Down'—rabbits.*

*Betsy Byars—'The Midnight Fox'.*

*Gerald Durrell—'My Family and Other Animals'.*

*(about his adventures as a young boy on the island of Corfu—highly recommended.)*

*William Horwood—'Duncton Wood'—moles.*

*Eugene McCabe—'Cyril, The Quest of an Orphaned Squirrel'.*

*Tom McCaughren—    'Run with the Wind'.*

*                   'Run to Earth'.*

*                   'Run Swift, Run Free, foxes'.*

*Gavin Marshall—'Ring of Bright Water'—otters.*

*T.H. White—'The Goshawk'.*

*Henry Williamson—'Tarka the Otter'.*

**8.** *a) Re-read the first three paragraphs of this story and list all the nouns, stating whether they are common, proper, abstract or collective.*

*b) Make a list of abstract nouns which you could use to describe the feelings, conditions etc. of each of the following: the young bird; the mother bird; the American; his Irish friends.*

# 'Feathered Visitors'

*———— Verney Naylor ————*

A few years ago a lady from the country wrote a letter to the editor of this newspaper asking where all the birds had gone, as there seemed to be very few left in her garden. I was tempted to write to the editor suggesting that many of them may have found their way to my own garden as I had no lack of bird visitors, either in quantity or variety.

I have been wondering since, why some gardens attract birds and others don't, and how we might encourage more of them to make their homes close to ours.

The birds in my garden give me immense pleasure, and I am fortunate that all the ordinary 'garden' birds are happy to spend time foraging for food in my town garden. Some are not quite so welcome, of course: the wood pigeons who devour my vegetables before I've had a chance to net them, the magpies who pull out my plant labels as fast as I can write them and the heron who decimated my goldfish population (and yet to watch this stately bird descend like a great jumbo jet gives me quite a thrill).

Then there are the rare visitors—the bullfinches who pass through about blossom time, without causing too much damage I'm relieved to say, and the cold, frightened woodcock I surprised one snowy January day when he was sheltering under some shrubs.

Ducks and swans fly over sometimes and I hear the call of the curlew, but these haven't actually alighted or, at least, not while I was watching.

A garden doesn't have to be large in order to attract birds but it seems to me that what it must have is 'cover'. This can be hedges, trees, large bushy shrubs or creepers on walls—so long as it's somewhere the birds can roost, hide from cats, shelter from the weather and build their nests.

If your garden consists largely of lawn, flower beds with bedding plants, and perhaps a few straggly bare roses—in fact, is rather open and flat, I suspect there won't be many birds, unless they just flit in and out for a quick meal of greenfly.

But take a derelict garden that is a jumble of overgrown trees and shrubs with walls covered in ivy, and it is probably teeming with birdlife. Now, I'm not suggesting that we all turn our garden into wildernesses—but if we want birds, we shouldn't be too tidy either.

A bird's main preoccupation is with feeding, so by providing lots of food we will also attract birds into the garden. I only 'feed' the

birds in severe frost or when the snow lies on the ground—the rest of the time I prefer to watch them feasting off the grubs and insects with which my garden abounds (I never use insecticides) or pecking at the rotting apples that I leave on the ground all winter, or gobbling up the varied harvest of berries and seeds.

Remember that water, too, is important both for drinking and bathing. If you do put up a bird table, make sure it is cat- and rat-proof.

*EXPLORING THE ARTICLE*

*1. Does the writer of the article have*

*a) very few*

*b) very many      birds in her garden?*

*2. The birds a) annoy her*

*b) worry her*

*c) please her*

*3. Which statement best shows the writer's attitude?*

*a) All birds are always welcome.*

*b) All birds, whether destructive or not, are a pleasure to watch.*

*c) Some birds are never welcome.*

*Explain.*

*4. In the context of the article, which is the odd one out: wood pigeon; magpie; swan; heron; bullfinch? Explain.*

*5. According to the writer, what are the important things a garden needs if it is to attract birds?*

*6. List the main points of the article in spider diagram form.*

*7. Write a letter, as if to the editor of a newspaper, describing an unusual bird or animal you have seen.*

*8. Which did you prefer—this article or the previous short story about birds? Why? Discuss this.*

*9. Can you make the plural of country; quantity; variety; heron; bullfinch; curlew; bush?*

*10. How many apostrophes can you find in the piece? Explain the reason for each one.*

# 'The Mile'

*George Layton*

What a rotten report. It was the worst report I'd ever had. I'd dreaded bringing it home for my mum to read. We were sitting at the kitchen table having our tea, but neither of us had touched anything. It was gammon and chips as well, with a pineapple ring. My favourite. We have gammon every Friday, because my Auntie Doreen works on the bacon counter at the Co-op, and she drops it in on her way home. I don't think she pays for it.

My mum was reading the report for the third time. She put it down on the table and stared at me. I didn't say anything. I just stared at my gammon and chips and pineapple ring. What could I say? My mum looked so disappointed. I really felt sorry for her. She was determined for me to do well at school, and get my 'O' Levels, then get my 'A' Levels, then go to university, then get my degree, and then get a good job with good prospects...

'I'm sorry, Mum...'

She picked up the report again, and started reading it for the fourth time.

'It's no good reading it again, Mum. It's not going to get any better.'

She slammed the report back on to the table.

'Don't you make cheeky remarks to me.

I'm not in the mood for it!'

I hadn't meant it to be cheeky, but I suppose it came out like that.

'I wouldn't say anything if I was you, after reading this report!'

I shrugged my shoulders.

'There's nothing much I can say, is there?'

'You can tell me what went wrong. You told me you worked hard this term!'

I had told her I'd worked hard, but I hadn't.

'I did work hard, Mum.'

'Not according to this.'

She waved the report under my nose.

'You're supposed to be taking your 'O' Levels next year. What do you think is going to happen then?'

I shrugged my shoulders again, and stared at my gammon and chips.

'I don't know.'

She put the report back on the table. I knew I hadn't done well in my exams because of everything that had happened this term, but I didn't think for one moment I'd come bottom in nearly everything. Even Norbert Lightowler had done better than me.

'You've come bottom in nearly everything. Listen to this.'

She picked up the report again.

'Maths—Inattentive and lazy.'

I knew what it said.

'I know what it says, Mum.'

She leaned across the table, and put her face close to mine.

'I know what it says too, and I don't like it.'

She didn't have to keep reading it.

'Well, stop reading it then.'

My mum just gave me a look.

'English Language—He is capricious and dilettante. What does that mean?'

I turned the pineapple ring over with my fork. Oh heck, was she going to go through every rotten subject?

'Come on—English language—Mr Melrose

says you're "capricious and dilettante". What does he mean?'

'I don't know!'

I hate Melrose. He's really sarcastic. He loves making a fool of you in front of other people. Well, he could stick his 'capricious and dilettante', and his rotten English Language, and his set books, and his horrible breath that nearly knocks you out when he stands over you.

'I don't know what he means.'

'Well, you should know. That's why you study English Language, to understand words like that. It means you mess about, and don't frame yourself.'

My mum kept reading every part of the report over and over again. It was all so pointless. It wasn't as if reading it over and over again was going to change anything. Mind you, I kept my mouth shut. I just sat there staring at my tea. I knew her when she was in this mood.

'What I can't understand is how come you did so well at Religious Instruction? You got seventy-five per cent.'

I couldn't understand that either.

'I like Bible stories, Mum.' She wasn't sure if I was cheeking her or not. I wasn't.

'Bible stories? It's all I can do to get you to come to St Cuthbert's one Sunday a month with me and your Auntie Doreen.'

That was true, but what my mum didn't know was that the only reason I went was because my Auntie Doreen slips me a few bob!

'And the only reason you go then is because your Auntie Doreen gives you pocket money.'

'Aw, that's not true, Mum.'

Blimey! My mum's got eyes everywhere.

She put the report back into the envelope. Hurray! The Spanish Inquisition was over. She took it out again. Trust me to speak too soon.

'I mean, you didn't even do well at sport,

280

did you? "Sport—He is not a natural athlete." Didn't you do anything right this term?'

I couldn't help smiling to myself. No, I'm not a natural athlete, but I'd done one thing right this term. I'd shown Arthur Boocock that he couldn't push me around any more. That's why everything else had gone wrong. That's why I was 'lazy and inattentive' at Maths, and 'capricious and dilettante' at English Language. That's why this last term had been so miserable, because of Arthur blooming Boocock.

He'd only come into our class this year because he'd been kept down. I didn't like him. He's a right bully, but because he's a bit older and is good at sport and running and things, everybody does what he says.

That's how Smokers' Corner started.

Arthur used to pinch his dad's cigarettes and bring them to school, and we'd smoke them at playtime in the shelter under the woodwork classroom. We called it Smokers' Corner.

It was daft really. I didn't even like smoking, it gives me headaches. But I joined in because all the others did. Well, I didn't want Arthur Boocock picking on me.

We took it in turns to stand guard. I liked it when it was my turn, it meant I didn't have to join in the smoking.

Smokers' Corner was at the top end of the playground, opposite the girls' school. That's how I first saw Janis. It was one playtime. I was on guard, when I saw these three girls staring at me from an upstairs window. They kept laughing and giggling. I didn't take much notice, which was a good job because I saw Melrose coming across the playground with Mr Rushton, the deputy head. I ran into the shelter and warned the lads.

'Arthur, Tony—Melrose and Rushton are coming!'

There was no way we could've been caught. We knew we could get everything away before Melrose or Rushton or anybody could reach us, even if they ran across the playground as fast as they could. We had a plan you see.

First, everybody put their cigarettes out, but not on the ground, with your fingers. It didn't half hurt if you didn't wet them enough. Then Arthur would open a little iron door that was in the wall next to the boiler house. Norbert had found it ages ago. It must've been there for years. Tony reckoned it was some sort of oven. Anyway, we'd empty our pockets and put all the cigarettes inside. All the time we'd be waving our hands about to get rid of the smoke, and Arthur would squirt the fresh-air spray he'd nicked from home. Then we'd shut the iron door and start playing football or tig.

Melrose never let on why he used to come storming across the playground. He never said anything, but we knew he was trying to catch the Smokers, and he knew we knew. All he'd do was give us all a look in turn, and march off. But on that day, the day those girls had been staring and giggling at me, he did say something.

'Watch it! All of you. I know what you're up to. Just watch it. Specially you, Boocock.'

We knew why Melrose picked on Arthur Boocock.

'You're running for the school on Saturday, Boocock. You'd better win or I'll want to know the reason why.'

Mr Melrose is in charge of athletics, and Arthur holds the school record for the mile. Melrose reckons he could run for Yorkshire one day if he trains hard enough.

I didn't like this smoking lark, it made me cough, gave me a headache, and I was sure we'd get caught one day.

'Hey, Arthur, we'd better pack it in. Melrose is going to catch us one of these days.'

Arthur wasn't bothered.

'Ah you! You're just scared, you're yeller!'

Yeah, I was blooming scared.

'I'm not. I just think he's going to catch us.'

Then Arthur did something that really shook me. He took his right hand out of his blazer pocket. For a minute I thought he was going to hit me, but he didn't. He put it to his mouth instead, and blew out some smoke. He's mad. He'd kept his cigarette in his hand in his pocket all the time. He's mad. I didn't say anything though. I was scared he'd thump me.

On my way home after school that day, I saw those girls. They were standing outside Wilkinson's sweetshop, and when they saw me they started giggling again. They're daft, girls. They're always giggling. One of them, the tallest, was ever so pretty though. The other two were all right, but not as pretty as the tall girl. It was the other two that were doing most of the giggling.

'Go on, Glenda, ask him.'

'No, you ask him.'

'No, you're the one who wants to know. You ask him.'

'Shurrup!'

The tall one looked as embarrassed as I felt. I could see her name written on her schoolbag: Janis Webster.

The other two were still laughing, and telling each other to ask me something. I could feel myself going red. I didn't like being stared at.

'Do you two want a photograph or summat?'

They giggled even more.

'No, thank you, we don't collect photos of monkeys, do we, Glenda?'

The one called Glenda stopped laughing and gave the other one a real dirty look.

'Don't be so rude, Christine.'

Then this Christine started teasing her friend Glenda.

'Ooh, just because you like him, Glenda Bradshaw, just because you fancy him.'

I started walking away. Blimey! If any of the lads came by and heard this going on, I'd never hear the end of it. The one called Christine started shouting after me.

'Hey, my friend Glenda thinks you're ever so nice. She wants to know if you want to go out with her.'

Blimey! Why did she have to shout so the whole street could hear? I looked round to make sure nobody like Arthur Boocock or Norbert or Tony were about. I didn't want them to hear these stupid lasses saying things like that. I mean, we didn't go out with girls, because...well...we just didn't.

I saw the pretty one, Janis, pulling Christine's arm. She was telling her to stop embarrassing me. She was nice that Janis, much nicer than the other two. I mean, if I was forced to go out with a girl, you know if somebody said, 'You will die tomorrow if you don't go out with a girl', then I wouldn't have minded going out with Janis Webster. She was really nice.

I often looked out for her after that, but when I saw her, she was always with the other two. The one time I did see her on her own, I was walking home with Tony and Norbert and I pretended I didn't know her, even though she smiled and said hello. Of course, I sometimes used to see her at playtime, when it was my turn to stand guard at Smokers' Corner. I liked being on guard twice as much now. As well as not having to smoke, it gave me a chance to see Janis. She was smashing. I couldn't get her out of my mind. I was always thinking about her, you know, having daydreams. I was forever 'rescuing' her.

One of my favourite rescues was where she was being bullied by about half-a-dozen lads, not hitting her or anything, just mucking about. And one of them was always Arthur Boocock. And I'd go up very quietly and say 'Are these lads bothering you?' And before she had time to answer, a fight would start, and I'd take them all on. All six at once, and it would end up with them pleading for mercy. And then Janis would put her hand on my arm and ask me to let them off...and I would. That was my favourite rescue.

That's how the trouble with Arthur Boocock started.

I'd been on guard one playtime, and had gone into one of my 'rescues'. It was the swimming-bath rescue. Janis would be swimming in the deep end, and she'd get into trouble, and I'd dive in and rescue her. I'd bring her to the side, put a towel round her, and then walk off without saying a word. Bit daft really, because I can't swim. Not a stroke. Mind you, I don't suppose I could beat up six lads on my own either, especially if one of them was Arthur Boocock. Anyway, I was just pulling Janis out of the deep end when I heard Melrose shouting his head off.

'Straight to the Headmaster's study. Go on, all three of you!'

I looked round, and I couldn't believe it. Melrose was inside Smokers' Corner. He'd caught Arthur, Tony and Norbert. He was giving Arthur a right crack over the head. How had he caught them? I'd been there all the time...standing guard...thinking about Janis...I just hadn't seen him coming...oh heck...

'I warned you, Boocock, all of you. Go and report to the Headmaster!'

As he was going past me, Arthur showed me his fist. I knew what that meant.

They all got the cane for smoking, and Melrose had it in for Arthur even though he was still doing well at his running. The more Melrose picked on Arthur, the worse it was for me, because Arthur kept beating me up.

That was the first thing he'd done after he'd got the cane—beaten me up. He reckoned I'd not warned them about Melrose on purpose.

'How come you didn't see him? He's blooming big enough.'

'I just didn't.'

I couldn't tell him that I'd been daydreaming about Janis Webster.

'He must've crept up behind me.'

Arthur hit me, right on my ear.

'How could he go behind you? You had your back to the wall. You did it on purpose, you yeller-belly!'

And he hit me again, on the same ear.

After that, Arthur hit me every time he saw me. Sometimes, he'd hit me in the stomach, sometimes on the back of my neck. Sometimes, he'd raise his fist and I'd think he was going to hit me, and he'd just walk away, laughing. Then he started taking my spending money. He'd say, 'Oh, you don't want that, do you?' and I'd say, 'No, you have it, Arthur.'

I was really scared of him. He made my life a misery. I dreaded going to school, and when I could, I'd stay at home by pretending to be poorly. I used to stick my fingers down my throat and make myself sick.

I suppose that's when I started to get behind with my school work, but anything was better than being bullied by that rotten Arthur Boocock. And when I did go to school, I'd try to stay in the classroom at playtime, or I'd make sure I was near the teacher who was on playground duty. Of course, Arthur thought it was all very funny, and he'd see if he could hit me without the teacher seeing, which he could.

Dinner time was the worst because we had an hour free before the bell went for school dinners, and no one was allowed to stay inside. It was a school rule. That was an hour for Arthur to bully me. I used to try and hide but he'd always find me.

By now it didn't seem to have anything to do with him being caught smoking and getting the cane. He just seemed to enjoy hitting me and tormenting me. So I stopped going to school dinners. I used to get some chips, or a Cornish pasty, and wander around. Sometimes I'd go into town and look at the shops, or else I'd go in the park and muck about. Anything to get away from school and Arthur Boocock.

That's how I met Archie.

There's a running track in the park, a proper one with white lines and everything, and one day I spent all dinner time watching this old bloke running round. That was Archie. I went back the next day and he was there again, running round and round, and I got talking to him.

'Hey, mister, how fast can you run a mile?'

I was holding a bag of crisps, and he came over and took one. He grinned at me.

'How fast can you run a mile?'

I'd never tried running a mile.

'I don't know, I've never tried.'

He grinned again.

'Well, now's your chance. Come on, get your jacket off.'

He was ever so fast and I found it hard to keep up with him, but he told me I'd done well. I used to run with Archie every day after that. He gave me an old track-suit top, and I'd change into my shorts and trainers and chase round the track after him. Archie said I was getting better and better.

'You'll be running for Yorkshire one of these days.'

I laughed and told him to stop teasing me. He gave me half an orange. He always did after running.

'Listen, lad, I'm serious. It's all a matter of training. Anybody can be good if they train hard enough. See you tomorrow.'

That's when I got the idea.

I decided to go in for the mile in the school sports at the end of term. You had to be picked for everything else, but anybody could enter the mile.

There were three weeks to the end of term, and in that three weeks I ran everywhere. I ran to school. I ran with Archie every dinner time.

I went back and ran on the track after school. Then I'd run home. If my mum wanted anything from the shops, I'd run there. I'd get up really early in the mornings and run before breakfast. I was always running. I got into tons of trouble at school for not doing my homework properly, but I didn't care. All I thought about was the mile.

I had daydreams about it. Always me and Arthur, neck and neck, and Janis would be cheering me on. Then I dropped Janis from my daydreams. She wasn't important any more. It was just me and Arthur against each other. I was sick of him and his bullying.

Arthur did well at sports day. He won the high jump and the long jump. He was picked for the half mile and the four-forty, and won them both. Then there was the announcement for the mile.

'Will all those competitors who wish to enter the open mile please report to Mr Melrose at the start.'

I hadn't let on to anybody that I was going to enter, so everybody was very surprised to see me when I went over in my shorts and trainers—especially Melrose. Arthur thought it was hilarious.

'Well, look who it is. Do you want me to give you half a mile start?'

I ignored him, and waited for Melrose to start the race. I surprised a lot of people that day, but nobody more than Arthur. I stuck to him like a shadow. When he went forward, I went forward. If he dropped back, I dropped back. This went on for about half the race. He kept giving me funny looks. He couldn't understand what was happening.

'You won't keep this up. Just watch.'

And he suddenly spurted forward. I followed him, and when he looked round to see how far ahead he was, he got a shock when he saw he wasn't.

It was just like my daydreams. Arthur and

me, neck and neck, the whole school cheering us on, both of us heading for the last bend. I looked at Arthur and saw the tears rolling down his cheeks. He was crying his eyes out. I knew at that moment I'd beaten him. I don't mean I knew I'd won the race. I wasn't bothered about that. I knew I'd beaten him, Arthur. I knew he'd never hit me again.

That's when I walked off the track. I didn't see any point in running the last two hundred yards. I suppose that's because I'm not a natural athlete...

"'Sport—He is not a natural athlete.' Didn't you do anything right this term?'

Blimey! My mum was still reading my report. I started to eat my gammon and chips. They'd gone cold.

## EXPLORING THE STORY

*1. In your own words, describe his mother's reactions when she reads the report.*
*2. What does the writer think of Mr Melrose?*
*3. What plan did the smokers use in order to avoid being caught?*
*4. Write three paragraphs describing the character of the boy who tells the story.*
*5. In your groups discuss what you liked and didn't like about this story.*

## REPORT BACK.

*[If you enjoyed this you will find more of George Layton's stories in The Fib and Other Stories, published by Collins Lions.]*
*6. What do you daydream about? Write one of your recent daydreams into your diary.*
*7. Read 'The Secret Life of Walter Mitty', by James Thurber, to be found in Exploring English.*
*8. In groups of three, role-play a scene where your Christmas report has just been received at home. Present the scene to the class.*
*9. Look again at a section of the story and study how dialogue is written.*
*Write a short conversation, which might have occurred between the author and Janis.*

# 'The Sniper'

*Liam O'Flaherty*

The long June twilight faded into night. Dublin lay enveloped in darkness, but for the dim light of the moon that shone through fleecy clouds, casting a pale light as of approaching dawn over the streets and the dark waters of the Liffey. Around the beleaguered Four Courts the heavy guns roared. Here and there through the city machine-guns and rifles broke the silence of the night, spasmodically, like dogs barking on lone farms. Republicans and Free Staters were waging civil war.

On a roof-top near O'Connell Bridge a Republican sniper lay watching. Beside him lay his rifle and over his shoulders were slung a pair of field-glasses. His face was the face of a student—thin and ascetic, but his eyes had the cold gleam of a fanatic. They were deep and thoughtful, the eyes of a man who is used to looking at death.

He was eating a sandwich hungrily. He had eaten nothing since morning. He had been too excited to eat. He finished the sandwich, and taking a flask of whiskey from his pocket, he took a short draught. Then he returned the flask to his pocket. He paused for a moment, considering whether he should risk a smoke. It was dangerous. The flash might be seen in the darkness and there were enemies watching.

He decided to take the risk. Placing a cigarette between his lips, he struck a match, inhaled the smoke hurriedly and put out the light. Almost immediately a bullet flattened itself against the parapet of the roof. The sniper took another whiff and put out the cigarette. Then he swore softly and crawled away to the left.

Cautiously he raised himself and peered over the parapet. There was a flash and a bullet whizzed over his head. He dropped immediately. He had seen the flash. It came from the opposite side of the street. He rolled over the roof to a chimney stack in the rear, and slowly drew himself up behind it, until his eyes were level with the top of the parapet. There was nothing to be seen—just the dim outline of the opposite house-top against the blue sky. His enemy was under cover.

Just then an armoured car came across the bridge and advanced slowly up the street. It stopped on the opposite side of the street fifty yards ahead. The sniper could hear the dull panting of the motor. His heart beat faster. It was an enemy car. He wanted to fire, but he knew it was useless. His bullets would never pierce the steel that covered the grey monster.

Then round the corner of a side street came an old woman, her head covered by a tattered shawl. She began to talk to the man in the turret of the car. She was pointing to the roof where the sniper lay. An informer. The turret opened. A man's head and shoulders appeared, looking towards the sniper. The sniper raised his rifle and fired. The head fell heavily on the turret wall. The woman darted towards the side street. The sniper fired again. The woman whirled round and fell with a shriek in the gutter. Suddenly from the opposite roof a shot rang out and the sniper dropped his rifle with a curse. The rifle clattered to the roof. The sniper thought the noise would wake the dead. He stooped to pick the rifle up. He couldn't lift it. His forearm was dead. 'Christ,'

he muttered, 'I'm hit.'

Dropping flat on to the roof, he crawled back to the parapet. With his left hand he felt the injured right forearm. The blood was oozing through the sleeve of his coat. There was no pain—just a deadened sensation, as if the arm had been cut off.

Quickly, he drew his knife from his pocket, opened it on the breastwork of the parapet and ripped open the sleeve. There was a small hole where the bullet had entered. On the other side there was no hole. The bullet had lodged in the bone. It must have fractured it. He bent the arm below the wound. The arm bent back easily. He ground his teeth to overcome the pain.

Then, taking out his field dressing, he ripped open the packet with his knife. He broke the neck of the iodine bottle and let the bitter fluid drip into the wound. A paroxysm of pain swept through him. He placed the cotton wadding over the wound and wrapped the dressing over it. He tied the end with his teeth.

Then he lay still against the parapet, and closing his eyes he made an effort of will to overcome the pain.

In the street beneath, all was still. The armoured car had retired speedily over the bridge, with the machine-gunner's head hanging lifeless over the turret. The woman's corpse lay still in the gutter.

The sniper lay for a long time nursing his wounded arm and planning escape. Morning must not find him wounded on the roof. The enemy on the opposite roof covered his escape. He must kill that enemy and he could not use his rifle. He had only a revolver to do it. Then he thought of a plan.

Taking off his cap, he placed it over the muzzle of his rifle. Then he pushed the rifle slowly upwards over the parapet, until the cap was visible from the opposite side of the street. Almost immediately there was a report, and a bullet pierced the centre of the cap. The sniper slanted the rifle forward. The cap slipped down into the street. Then catching the rifle in the middle, the sniper dropped his left hand over the roof and let his hand hang lifelessly. After a few moments he let the rifle drop to the street. Then he sank to the roof, dragging his hand with him.

Crawling quickly to the left, he peered up at the corner of the roof. His ruse had succeeded. The other sniper seeing the cap and rifle, thought that he had killed his man. He was now standing before a row of chimney pots, looking across with his head clearly silhouetted against the western sky.

The Republican sniper smiled and lifted his revolver above the edge of the parapet. The distance was about fifty yards—a hard shot in the dim light, and his right arm was paining him like a thousand devils. He took a steady aim. His hand trembled with eagerness. Pressing his lips together, he took a deep breath through his nostrils and fired. He was almost deafened with the report and his arm shook with the recoil.

When the smoke cleared, he peered across and uttered a cry of joy. His enemy had been hit. He was reeling over the parapet in his death agony. He struggled to keep his feet, but he was slowly falling forward, as if in a dream. The rifle fell from his grasp, hit the parapet, fell over, bounded off the pole of a barber's shop beneath and then clattered on to the pavement.

Then the dying man on the roof crumpled up and fell forward. The body turned over and over in space and hit the ground with a dull thud. He lay still.

The sniper looked at his enemy falling and he shuddered. The lust of battle died in him. He became bitten by remorse. The sweat stood out in beads on his forehead. Weakened by his wound and by the long summer day of fasting and watching on the roof, he revolted from the sight of the shattered mass of his dead enemy. His teeth chattered. He began to gibber to himself, cursing the war, cursing himself, cursing everybody.

He looked at the smoking revolver in his hand and with an oath he hurled it to the roof at his feet. The revolver went off with the concussion, and the bullet whizzed past the sniper's head. He was frightened back to his senses by the shock. His nerves steadied. The cloud of fear scattered from his mind and he laughed.

Taking the whiskey flask from his pocket, he emptied it at a draught. He felt reckless under the influence of the spirits. He decided to leave the roof and look for his company commander to report. Everywhere around was quiet. There was not much danger in going through the streets. He picked up his revolver and put it in his pocket. Then he crawled down through the sky-light to the house underneath.

When the sniper reached the laneway on the street level, he felt a sudden curiosity as to the identity of the enemy sniper whom he had killed. He decided that he was a good shot whoever he was. He wondered if he knew him. Perhaps he had been in his own company before the split in the army. He decided to risk going over to have a look at him. He peered around the corner into O'Connell Street. In the upper part of the street there was heavy firing, but around here all was quiet.

The sniper darted across the street. A machine-gun tore up the ground around him with a hail of bullets, but he escaped. He threw himself downwards beside the corpse. The machine-gun stopped.

Then the sniper turned over the dead body and looked into his brother's face.

*1. What sounds can be heard around the beleaguered Four Courts?*
*2. What detail suggests that the sniper is aware of his risky situation?*
*3. What metaphor is used to describe the armoured car? Do you think it is a good one? Explain.*
*4. In your own words describe exactly the steps of the sniper's plan.*
*5. What kind of man do you think he is - intelligent; determined; courageous; cruel; callous? Do we see two sides to him? Base your opinions on evidence in this story.*
*6. Is this a dramatic story? What would you consider to be the climax?*
*7. Re-read the paragraph beginning 'When the smoke cleared, he peered across ....' Write out the verbs in that paragraph and say what effect they create.*
*8. Pick out any ten adverbs which you think make the story more dramatic.*
*9. Rewrite a section of the story from the point of view of the other sniper.*
*10. What were your thoughts when you finished the story?*

# 'The Fun They Had'

### ———— *Isaac Asimov* ————

Margie even wrote about it that night in her diary. On the page headed May 17, 2157, she wrote, 'Today Tommy found a real book!'

It was a very old book. Margie's grandfather once said that when he was a little boy his grandfather told him that there was a time when all stories were printed on paper.

They turned the pages, which were yellow and crinkly, and it was awfully funny to read words that stood still instead of moving the way they were supposed to—on a screen, you know. And then, when they turned back to the page before, it had the same words on it that it had had when they read it the first time.

'Gee,' said Tommy, 'what a waste. When you're through with the book, you just throw it away, I guess. Our television screen must have had a million books on it and it's good for plenty more. I wouldn't throw it away.'

'Same with mine,' said Margie. She was eleven and hadn't seen as many telebooks as Tommy had. He was thirteen.

She said, 'Where did you find it?'

'In my house.' He pointed without looking, because he was busy reading. 'In the attic.'

'What's it about?'

'School.'

Margie was scornful. 'School? What's there to write about school? I hate school.'

Margie always hated school, but now she hated it more than ever. The mechanical teacher had been giving her test after test in geography and she had been doing worse and worse until her mother had shaken her head sorrowfully and sent for the County Inspector.

He was a round little man with a red face and a whole box of tools with dials and wires. He smiled at Margie and gave her an apple, then took the teacher apart. Margie had hoped he wouldn't know how to put it together again, but he knew how all right, and, after an hour or so, there it was again, large and black and ugly, with a big screen on which all the lessons were shown and the questions were asked. That wasn't so bad. The part Margie hated most was the slot where she had to put homework and test papers. She always had to write them out in a punch code they made her learn when she was six years old, and the mechanical teacher calculated the mark in no time.

The Inspector had smiled after he was finished and patted Margie's head. He said to her mother, 'It's not the little girl's fault, Mrs Jones. I think the geography sector was geared a little too quick. Those things happen sometimes. I've slowed it up to an average ten-year level. Actually, the over-all pattern of her progress is quite satisfactory.' And he patted Margie's head again.

Margie was disappointed. She had been hoping they would take the teacher away altogether. They had once taken Tommy's teacher away for nearly a month because the history sector had blanked out completely.

So she said to Tommy, 'Why would anyone write about school?'

Tommy looked at her with very superior eyes. 'Because it's not our kind of school, stupid. This is the old kind of school that they had hundreds and hundreds of years ago.' He added loftily, pronouncing the word carefully, 'Centuries ago.'

Margie was hurt. 'Well, I don't know the kind of school they had all that time ago.' She read the book over his shoulder for a while, then said, 'Anyway, they had a teacher.'

'Sure they had a teacher, but it wasn't a regular teacher. It was a man.'

'A man? How could a man be a teacher?'

'Well, he just told the boys and girls things and gave them homework and asked them questions.'

'A man isn't smart enough.'

'Sure he is. My father knows as much as my teacher.'

'He can't. A man can't know as much as a teacher.'

'He knows almost as much, I betcha.'

Margie wasn't prepared to dispute that. She said, 'I wouldn't want a strange man in my house to teach me.'

Tommy screamed with laughter. 'You don't know much, Margie. The teachers didn't live in the house. They had a special building and all the kids went there.'

'And all the kids learned the same thing?'

'Sure, if they were the same age.'

'But my mother says a teacher has to be adjusted to fit the mind of each boy and girl it teaches and that each kid has to be taught differently.'

'Just the same they didn't do it that way then. If you don't like it, you don't have to read the book.'

'I didn't say I didn't like it,' Margie said quickly. She wanted to read about those funny schools.

They weren't even half-finished when Margie's mother called, 'Margie! School!'

Margie looked up. 'Not yet, Mamma.'

'Now!' said Mrs Jones. 'And it's probably time for Tommy, too.'

Margie said to Tommy, 'Can I read the book some more with you after school?'

'Maybe,' he said nonchalantly. He walked away whistling, the dusty old book tucked beneath his arm.

Margie went into the schoolroom. It was right next to her bedroom, and the mechanical teacher was on and waiting for her. It was always on at the same time every day except Saturday and Sunday, because her mother said little girls learned better if they learned at regular hours.

The screen was lit up, and it said: 'Today's arithmetic lesson is on the addition of proper fractions. Please insert yesterday's homework in the proper slot.'

Margie did so with a sigh. She was thinking about the old schools they had when her grandfather's grandfather was a little boy. All the kids from the whole neighbourhood came, laughing and shouting in the schoolyard, sitting together in the schoolroom, going home together at the end of the day. They learned the same things, so they could help one another on the homework and talk about it.

And the teachers were people ....

The mechanical teacher was flashing on the screen: 'When we add the fractions 1/2 and 1/4—'

Margie was thinking about how the kids must have loved it in the old days. She was thinking about the fun they had.

FOR DISCUSSION OR DEBATE:

**1.** What are the advantages of this type of education over school as you know it?

**2.** What are the disadvantages?

**3.** Are there any similarities?

'The Illusionists', by Brian Friel

As this is quite a difficult story, perhaps your teacher might read it for you. Then, taking a section at a time, use your dictionary to find the meanings of the difficult words. Check with your teacher that you are using the most appropriate meaning, before you write them into your Word Copy. Now try to use some of these new words in your written exercises on the story.

# 'The Illusionists'

*Brian Friel*

The annual visit of M. L'Estrange to our school in the first week of March marked the end of winter and the beginning of spring. The bleak countryside around Beannafreaghan was cold-dead when he arrived and perhaps for a few weeks after he had gone, but when we heard the scrape of his handlebars against the school wall and saw his battered silk hat pass the classroom window, the terrible boredom of winter suddenly seemed to vanish, and we knew that good times were imminent.

We hadn't many visitors to Beannafreaghan Primary School where my father was principal and entire staff. Once a month Father Shiels, the manager, drove out the twisted five miles from the town, in one breath asked us were we good and told us to say our prayers, shook father's hand firmly, and scuttled away again as if there were someone chasing him. Occasionally an inspector would come, and father would show him the seeping walls and the cracked windows and the rotting floor, and the inspector would grunt sympathetically and nod his head sadly from side to side and leave without asking us anything. An odd time a salesman for books would come, but no one ever bought anything. And one morning a travelling theatre for schools, a great coloured caravan towed by a landrover, stopped at our gate, and a man with a beard and an English accent breezed in to the classroom. I distinctly overheard father telling him that unfortunately it would be impossible to put on a play that day because the recording unit of the BBC was coming that very afternoon to make choral and verse-speaking tapes. The whole story, of course, was a fabrication: there wasn't a note or a line of verse in any of us. The truth of the matter was that his twenty-five pupils could not afford to pay sixpence a head, not to talk of two-and-six, not even to see an international cast doing international plays.

I never knew which I liked better: to be playing in the school-yard at lunch-time, and look up, and suddenly see the tall figure of M. L'Estrange mounted on his bicycle and free-wheeling recklessly down the long hill that hid us from the town of Omagh; or to be in class, staring dreamily at an open book, and then to hear the scrape of his handlebars against the school wall. I think I preferred him to walk in on us when we were in the middle of lessons, to see the door opening, to hear his deep resonant voice boom out, 'Am I interrupting the progress of knowledge?' because then the delight was so acute that the mouth dropped open, and the eyes stared, and the heart raced, because there he was, M. L'Estrange, The Illusionist, back again to perform his magic on us. To us rustic children he was the most wonderful man in the world.

Father was stiffly polite to the manager and over-anxious with inspectors but he welcomed M. L'Estrange warmly and enthusiastically. Mother's attitude to the illusionist was at least consistent—she treated him quietly and with caution. But I could never understand father's attitude. There was no doubt that he was delighted to see him. He put his arm round his shoulder, and pumped his hand, and kept looking at us to find a match for his heartiness in our faces (perhaps he mistook our stillness for indifference). But as the afternoon went on, his exuberance quickly evaporated, and he became irritable again, and by the time M. L'Estrange left our house to cycle back to town—always late in the evening, and by then father and he were more than half-drunk— father had begun taunting him about being nothing more than a trick-of-the-loop man and scarcely better than a tramp. But when he first arrived you would think father had found a long-lost brother. He would exclaim, 'Look, children! Look who's here! M. L'Estrange! Back again!' As if there was any need to tell us to look. Because the moment he appeared in the doorway our quick, country eyes devoured him: the calm face; and the slender white hands; and the long silvery hair that had given a gloss to the collar of his frock-coat; and the black striped trousers, frayed at the bottom; and the soiled white scarf; and the glittering rings. And then, long before I had finished gazing at him, father would send me across the fields to the house to tell mother to have a meal ready for M. L'Estrange after the performance. This was a job I hated doing. Mother never shared my excitement—'Don't tell me that old trickster's here again!'—and by the time I got back the show was ready to begin. It was little consolation to me that, later in the evening when all the other pupils had dispersed, I would have M. L'Estrange all to myself in my own house. What happened was that invariably I missed the preparations: the clearing of father's table; M. L'Estrange putting on his black mask; the hanging of the curtain between the black-board and the fireplace; the arranging of the desks in three rows. The smallest children, frozen with delicious nervousness, sat in the front seats, the bigger ones sat in the middle, and the biggest along the back. Father stood at the door and smoked, his face relaxed and smooth with content.

Then M. L'Estrange would begin. He would stand in front of us for a few minutes, his hands joined at his chest as if he were praying, his lean, lined face raised and immobile, and stare at us with those soft, sad eyes of his. Mesmerized, we stared back at him, our throats drying with anticipation, giggles stirring and promptly dying in our stomachs. Suddenly he would crack his fingers and say 'Would someone please open a window at the back of the auditorium?' or 'Would it be possible to have a spot-light switched on?' in a voice so unexpectedly quiet and persuasive that instinctively we all moved to do his bidding, so great was our relief that he had spoken, so hypnotic was his power over us. From then on he had us in the palm of his hand.

Although I saw his tricks every year for five or six years I remember only two of them. In one he knotted a heavy rope to a back tooth, gave the rope a tug, and out came a heavy wooden molar, the size of a turnip. The other trick I remember was with a rabbit who had dull, weary eyes like mother's. He sat the rabbit on father's table, surrounded it with four sheets of cardboard, covered it with a black cloth, and to our horror collapsed the box with a great thump of his fists. Of course the rabbit had disappeared. With a tired smile he produced it from under his jacket.

We knew the show was over when M. L'Estrange walked over to where father stood, and led him by the hand to the middle of the classroom. Together they stood before us, both of them smiling and bowing (I was always embarrassed at father bowing, as if he had been part of the entertainment), while we clapped and cheered and whistled and stamped our feet. Then father made a speech of appreciation, thanked M. L'Estrange for 'including humble Beannafreaghan in his over-crowded itinerary,' reminded us to bring twopence each the next day—he paid the illusionist out of his own pocket, and during the following weeks badgered and cajoled his pupils to reimburse him—and gave us the rest of the afternoon off. It was then that I knew one of the few advantages of being the teacher's son: every year I was privileged to wheel M. L'Estrange's bicycle, with its precious box that held the rabbit and the giant tooth and the other sacred things securely sealed in a box attached to the carrier, from the school to our house. It was a quarter of a mile by road, and I was accompanied by a retinue of a dozen or more amateur illusionists who pantomimed around me, yanking out their teeth, and producing rabbits from schoolbags, and who offered me all the wealth of their pockets if I would allow them even to touch the rim of the mudguard.

M. L'Estrange's last visit to Beannafreaghan in the March of my tenth year is the one I remember most vividly because I had spent the whole doleful winter waiting for it. Father had decided that I was to be sent to a Jesuit boarding school in Dublin the following September (like so many of his grand plans this one fell through, too; when September came, mother got the Christian Brothers in the town to take me in as a day-pupil) and I had made up my mind that I would escape that terrible fate by getting M. L'Estrange, when he would come, to take me away with him as an apprentice illusionist. I knew that a busy man like him could do with an assistant who would organise

his tours, and see to advance bookings, and look after his accoutrements. My plans were not altogether impracticable: I had a small bicycle of my own; and from my mentor I would learn his craft so that when he would retire I would become a professional illusionist myself. Throughout the year I had put all my pocket money into a cocoa tin so that when my apprenticeship would begin I would have a measure of financial independence. I told no one of my scheme.

And that March, as I wheeled M. L'Estrange's bicycle from the school to the house, I remember watching the others clowning around me, and thinking how young and silly they were. Little did they know the wonderful future that was before me.

Father and M. L'Estrange sauntered in about half-an-hour later. As father's good humour unaccountably dwindled, the illusionist's increased. He bowed theatrically to mother, and addressed her as Madame, and I believe he would have raised her hand to his lips had she not pulled it away, and said in her flattest Tyrone accent, 'I suppose you're famished as usual, Mister, are you?'

'I'll not say no to a morsel, Madame,' said the illusionist with a roguish smile. 'I'll not say no.'

And for a man with such white hands and such a lean, patient face he had a huge appetite. Indeed so hungrily did he eat that father did all the talking, and M. L'Estrange only grunted 'I see' or 'Yes' or 'Imagine' between mouthfuls. When the meal was over father produced a bottle of whiskey, pulled two chairs up to the range, and the illusionist and himself sat talking and drinking at the fireside, as they did every year, until night came down on Beannafreaghan, and the whiskey was done.

That winter had been particularly severe. There was still snow on the hill-tops and the fields were rigid with black frost when M.

L'Estrange came. We hadn't heard a bird in five months. Had I not had the evidence of the illusionist sitting in our kitchen and chatting to my father I would not have believed that spring was at hand. Their talk followed the usual pattern. At first they spoke of the satisfaction to be got from teaching school in a small rural community, 'striking a spark that could cause a conflagration,' as the illusionist called it, and from travelling around the countryside, 'opening the ready hearts of children to laughter,' as father called it. They agreed that each vocation had its unique rewards. Then they talked about the changes they had witnessed over the years: only really dedicated teachers now taught in decaying, shrinking schools; and only really altruistic troupers still entertained their pupils. Then they went away back to the past, and from there on it wasn't really a conversation at all, but two monologues spoken simultaneously, each man remembering and speaking his memories aloud. And eventually, when the bottle was empty, father became sarcastic.

Mother refused to be drawn into their talk. M. L'Estrange would try to engage her, but she shook him off quickly: 'You're nothing but a pair of bletherskites!' Throughout the whole afternoon and evening she never stopped working, baking bread, washing clothes in the zinc bath, boiling nettles for the hens, scalding the milking tins, chopping vegetables for dinner the next day, all the time bustling about the kitchen so that she was constantly coming between me and the two men, and making so much noise with her buckets and basins that I missed a lot of what was being said. Not that I minded missing father's reminiscences—I had heard them so often that I knew them backways—but now that I was on the brink of a new life every word that M. L'Estrange had to say about his early career was of the utmost interest. But worse than the din she made, she tried to make conversation with me—'Have you no exercise to do?' 'Any fun at school today?' 'Why don't you go out for a run on your bicycle?' 'Are you not taking the dog out for a walk?'—and when I answered her in sharp monosyllables she invented jobs for me to do: feed the calf; bring in sticks; get water from the well; close the meadowgate. The result was that I heard only part of the monologues and witnessed only the last half of the row when M. L'Estrange called father a soured old failure and father called M. L'Estrange a down-at-heel fake and warned him never to set foot in Beannafreaghan again.

'The summer I qualified,' father was saying into his glass as I spread the sticks for the morning fire along the front of the range, 'I came first place in the whole of Ireland. And there wasn't a manager in the thirty-two counties who wouldn't have given his right arm for me. His right arm, Sir.'

'France is the country,' said M. L'Estrange, turning his rings idly. 'That's where they had appreciation. A hundred thousand francs for an hour's performance. La belle France.'

'Dublin—Cork—Galway—crying out for me. An old P.P. drove up the whole way from Kerry, three hundred and fifty miles, to ask me personally to take over a school in Killarney. "We would be honoured to have you, Mr Boyle," he said.'

'Ah, the drawing-rooms of London in the early Twenties! Lords and ladies and all the quality of the land. Lloyd George once shook my hand and said it was a pleasure to see me perform.'

'But would I go? Oh, no! Beannafreaghan, I said. That's the place for me. Beannafreaghan. Because Beannafreaghan needed a teacher that had something more to give, just that little bit more than the other fellow.'

'A pleasure to see me perform. The year 1920. In Londonderry House, London, capital of the world.'

'I'm telling you, if I hadn't taken up the challenge that summer, bloody Beannafreaghan Primary School would have been closed down, and all the bloody children would have grown up illiterate.'

'Top of the bill in Leeds and Manchester and Glasgow and Brighton.'

'Bloody illiterates and too bloody good for them.'

'Mr L'Estrange, Prince of the Occult.'

'Fifteen years ago the Very Reverend John Shiels, P.P., came out to me here, and stood in this very kitchen and asked me—bloody-well begged me—to take over the new school in the town. Wasn't another man in the whole of County Tyrone competent to tackle it.'

'I drove my own car, and stayed in the best hotels, and picked and chose the engagements I wanted. There was respect for illusionists in those days, respect and admiration.'

'And what, said I straight out to him, and what would happen to Beannafreaghan?'

'I saw me ordering swank dinners for the whole cast and tipping the waiters with pound notes.'

'That never occurred to him. Oh, no! But it occurred to me. They may be country children, I said to him, and they may not have the most modern school building, but by God they deserve the best teacher in the country, top of my class the summer I qualified, and they're bloody-well going to have the best teacher in the country! I'm not going to desert them, I said to him.'

'My Lords, Ladies, and Gentlemen, things are not what they appear. The quickness of the hand deceives the eye. I was entrusted with the secret of this next act by the Sultan of Mysore—,' 'And I didn't desert them. I'm bloody-well still here, amn't I? In spite of all the offers I got. Hundreds of them. Only fifteen years ago in this very kitchen—'

'In his white marble palace in the hills where the sun shines all day—'

'I'm still here! The proof of the pudding is in the eating!'

'It's all in the mind. The powers of the mind are beyond our comprehension.'

At that stage mother ordered me out to the byre with her to milk the cow. I held the hurricane lamp while she milked. She could do the job in five minutes when she wished, but that night she seemed to take hours at it. 'Hurry up! Hurry up!' I kept saying because I was afraid M. L'Estrange would have gone before we got back to the house.

'What do you want to be listening to the ravings of two drunk men for?' she said. 'I don't know what takes that trickster here anyway, upsetting everybody.' And she rested her forehead against the red cow's side and pulled the teats as if she never wanted the milking to end.

While we were out, the row began. In the still, frosty night we heard their angry voices as we turned the gable of the byre. Their talk always ended with father taunting the illusionist. But never until that night had M. L'Estrange answered him back; he just lifted his hat from behind the kitchen door and went off without a word into the darkness. But that year, when my whole future depended on him, he had to lose his temper.

'My God!' said mother. 'They'll kill each other.' And the pair of us ran up to the house.

M. L'Estrange was on the street, and father was standing in the doorway, and they were shouting at each other. Father held on to the doorposts for support, and the illusionist swayed back and forward and pointed an accusing finger at him. They were both ugly with hate.

'Go home to your hovel, wherever it is!' father roared. 'Bloody tramp!'

'Beannafreaghan is the place for you!' M.

L'Estrange called back. 'The back end of nowhere!'

'And where did you pick up the name L'Estrange, eh? I know who you are, Monsieur Illusionist L'Estrange: your real name's Barney O'Reilly, and you were whelped and bred in a thatched cottage in County Galway!'

'They wouldn't give you a job in the town if there wasn't another teacher in the whole country!'

'You were never in London or Paris in your life! And your wee cheap tricks wouldn't fool a blind jennet!'

'You're stuck here till the day you die!'

'Mister Barney O'Reilly—fake!'

'A soured old failure!'

'Never put a foot in Beannafreaghan again or we'll set the dogs on you!'

'Don't you worry, Boyle. You'll never see me again.'

Mother sprang between them. She pushed father into the hallway and then wheeled on the illusionist.

'Get out of this place!' she spat at him with a fierceness I never saw in her before. 'Get away out of here and never darken the door again, you—you—you sham, you fake, you!'

Then she saw me standing with the hurricane lamp in my hand.

'Get inside at once!' she snapped. 'You should have been asleep hours ago.'

I did not dare disobey her, so mad was she. As I passed her on my way into the house she shoved me roughly in the back and bolted the door behind me.

Father was standing uncertainly in the middle of the kitchen floor. He tried to look defiantly at her.

'I told him a thing or two that he needed to—' he began.

'Get off to your bed,' said mother sharply. 'And shame on you making a scene like that before the child.'

'I told him a few home truths. I let him know what I thought of—'

'Shut up! Hasn't there been enough said for one night? Go and get some sleep, or you won't be fit to go to work tomorrow.'

As he lurched towards the door he tried to wink at me, but his two eyes closed.

'He forgot his beautiful hat!' he said, sniggering, lifting the shabby topper down from behind the door.

'Run after him with it,' said mother to me. 'I don't want him coming back to look for it. Run, child, run.'

That should have been my opportunity. Confused and frightened as I was with the shouting and the hate and the sickening sight of father and M. L'Estrange abusing each other, a part of my mind was still lucid, still urged me: Now, now, now. I saw the cocoa tin on the mantlepiece; I knew my bicycle, polished, oiled, pumped, was in the turf shed; I thought of the Dublin boarding school. But suddenly the dream that I had nursed all winter lost its urgency, required an effort and determination I couldn't muster. If by some miracle mother were to say, 'Go off with M. L'Estrange, son. Travel the world with him,' or if M. L'Estrange were to come back and say in his persuasive voice, 'Your son and I have planned to make a grand tour of Ireland and England and the whole of Europe,' then I would have floated off with him, and together we would have drifted happily from theatre to theatre, from country to country. But now I stood trembling, numbed, petrified with irresolution.

'Will you hurry up! He won't have got the length of the school yet,' said mother.

I unbolted the door and ran out into the hushed night.

I found M. L'Estrange on his hands and knees on the road below the byre. He was crawling towards his bicycle which lay spinning five yards beyond him. He smiled drunkenly up at me.

'It would appear, my friend, that my trusty steed and I parted company.'

The moonlight gave his face the pallor of a corpse. His long, thin fingers were spread out before him like the witch's in Hansel and Gretel.

'You forgot your hat.'

'Would you be kind enough to lift my bicycle for me? Once I get up on it nothing can stop me. The problem is—' He hiccoughed and mumbled, 'Excuse me'—'The problem is to get mounted, if you understand what I mean.'

I left the hat within his reach and went to lift the bicycle.

Before I got it I found the giant tooth lying on the road. Beside it was the square of black cloth. Further on I found four sheets of cardboard, and the mask, and a packet of balloons. I picked them up and carried them to the bicycle. It was then that I saw that the box on the carrier was open and empty. The rabbit! The rabbit had escaped! I was about to shout, to cry out to M. L'Estrange that his rabbit was gone when I saw it crouching beside the front wheel. Silently, cautiously I tiptoed over to it. But there was no need for silence or caution: it never moved. I gathered it gently in my arms and looked into its face. Its dull, weary eyes, mother's eyes, stared back at me, beyond me. Had its heart not tapped against my finger-tips I might have thought it was dead. I put it in the box on top of the black cloth and closed the lid.

M. L'Estrange was at my side.

'All set?' he said, 'Once more into the breach, dear friends, once more.'

He was wearing the top hat now, and it sat jauntily on the side of his head.

'As I say,' he went on, 'once I get mounted nothing can stop me, nothing in the wide world.' He put an arm on my shoulder to steady himself. 'As for you, my good friend, accept this little token from M. L'Estrange, Prince of the Occult.'

He slipped a coin into my hand. Then he gripped the handlebars, held the bicycle away from him, and said in his resonant voice that carried over the still, dead countryside, 'Au revoir!'

Then he moved off. He looked back at me to see was I watching him (I think he was going to attempt to get up on the bicycle). But when he saw me looking after him he waved to me and went on walking. A bend in the road hid him from me.

In the light of the kitchen I saw that he had given me a penny. I dropped it into the cocoa tin. Father was in bed, and mother was spooning my night porridge into a bowl.

'He's away, is he?' she asked.

I said he was.

'Sit down and take your supper,' she said. 'You're famished with the cold.'

'He gave me half-a-crown!' I blurted it out because I thought I was going to cry.

'Aye?' she said, giving me a shrewd look.

'And he said that he'll come to see me in the boarding school in Dublin.' I couldn't stop myself now. 'And he said that when I'm a big man he'll take me away with him and teach me all his magic and we'll see the seven seas and visit great palaces and carry red-and-gold parrots on our shoulders and drive about in big cars and stay in grand hotels and—and—and—'

Then the tears came, pouring out of me, and mother's arms went around me, and I buried my face in her breast, and sobbed my heart out.

'And—and he was so drunk he fell off his bicycle and he could hardly walk. And only for me he would have lost his rabbit and his giant tooth and—'

'There, there, there,' said mother, rocking me against her and stroking the back of my head. 'It's all over now. It's all over. All over.

It'll be forgotten in the morning. And before we know where we are, spring will be here, and you'll be away in Tracey's lorry to the bog to cut turf, and the birds will come back and begin nesting—'

'I told you a lie—it was a penny he gave me!'

'—and we'll bring the skep of bees up to the mountain for the heather,' she went on as if she hadn't heard me. 'And we'll whitewash the byre until it sparkles—remember the fun we had last year?—and before we know it will be summer, and we'll take the rug down to the meadow, and lie in the shade of the chestnut tree, and listen to the cow eating the clover, and we'll take a packet of biscuits with us and a can of buttermilk, and we'll have a competition to see who can drink it the quickest—remember last year?—and on the hottest day of summer—oh, it'll be so hot it will kill us to laugh!—we'll empty the well and climb down into it in our bare feet, and scrub it out, and yo-ho to each other down there—remember? remember?—and we'll laugh until we're weak, and oh my God, oh the great fun we'll have—oh dear God it'll be powerful—when the good weather comes.'

I stopped crying and smiled into her breast because every word she said was true. But it wasn't because I remembered that it was true that I believed her, but because she believed it herself, and because her certainty convinced me.

## EXPLORING THE STORY

*1. Think about the boy in the story: Is he happy in school? What is his view on M. L'Estrange? Does he get on well with his mother and father? What are his plans for the future? Does he learn anything from the incident? Do you think he would make a good actor? Discuss these questions in your groups. Remember you need evidence from the story to support your views.*

## R E P O R T   B A C K

*2. If you had to write a short play based on the story how would you describe the character of the father? Is he a quick-thinking man; moody; generous; happy? Read carefully the parts of the story featuring the father and make notes about how you see him.*

*3. Re-read the description of M. L'Estrange in paragraph 4. What does it suggest about the man and his way of life? Is there evidence elsewhere in the story to support your views.*

*4. How would you play the part of the mother? Read it again for details.*

*5. DIALOGUE: You will notice that the style of dialogue varies to suit each particular scene. Father's speech of appreciation, in the schoolroom, is very formal: he thanked M. L'Estrange for 'including humble Beannafreaghan in his overcrowded itinerary.' But his drunken outbursts are very different: 'You were never in London or Paris in your life! And your wee cheap tricks wouldn't fool a blind jennet!'*

*In pairs improvise a dialogue a) between the boy and a school friend next day; b) between the mother and father, on the following morning (first look at the way the mother usually speaks); c) between the inspector and the teacher.*

*Script the one you consider best and perform it for the class.*

**6.** *Write a letter which might have been sent by M. L'Estrange to the Principal, after the visit.*

**7.** *In what way might it be correct to say that all the characters in this story are illusionists?*

**8.** *Re-read the paragraph where the author describes the tricks. Notice how he makes the descriptions alive with colour words and similes: 'out came a heavy wooden molar, the size of a turnip' ... 'a rabbit who had dull, weary eyes like mother's' ... 'to our horror collapsed the box with a great thump of his fists' ... 'with a tired smile he' ...*

*Did you ever have an unusual visitor to your classroom? Write about it, in a colourful way. Or write about a visit to a circus or a magic show you viewed on TV.*

**9.** *Did you ever have a burning ambition to be something? How do you feel about the boy in the story. Discuss.*

**10.** *Study all the difficult words in this story and have a SPELLING AND MEANING COMPETITION, i.e. your teacher will call out 20 words from the story, you write down each one correctly and explain the meaning. One mark for spelling and one for meaning.*

**11.** *Now that you have mastered the vocabulary, read the story one last time and rate it out of ten, on the following:*

| | |
|---|---|
| Interesting | |
| Good Characters | |
| Dramatic Quality | |
| Descriptions | |

# 'The Confessional'

## *Sean O'Faolain*

In the wide nave the wintry evening light was faint as gloom and in the shadows of the aisle it was like early night. There was no sound in the chapel but the wind blowing up from the river valley, or an occasional tiny noise when a brass socket creaked under the great heat of a dying flame. To the three small boys crouched together on a bench in the farther aisle, holding each other's hands, listening timidly to the crying wind, staring wide-eyed at the candles, it seemed odd that in such a storm the bright flames never moved.

Suddenly the eldest of the three, a red-headed little ruffian, whispered loudly; but the other two, staring at the distant face of the statue, silenced him with a great hiss like a breaking wave. In another moment the lad in the centre, crouching down in fear and gripping the hand on each side of him, whispered so quietly that they barely heard, 'She's moving.'

For a second or two they did not even breathe. Then all three expelled a deep sigh of disappointment.

It was Monday afternoon, and every Monday, as they had each heard tell over and over again in their homes, Father Hanafin spoke with the Blessed Virgin in the grotto. Some said she came late at night; some said in the early morning before the chapel was opened; some said it was at the time when the sun goes down; but until now nobody had dared to watch. To be sure, Father Hanafin was not in the chapel now, but for all that the three little spies had come filled with high hope. The eldest spoke their bitter disappointment aloud.

'It's all my eye,' he said angrily. The other two felt that what he said was true, but they pretended to be deeply shocked.

'That's an awful thing you said, Foxer,' whispered the boy in the middle.

'Go away, you, Philpot!' said Foxer.

'Got! I think it's a cause for confession, Foxer!' whispered Philpot again.

'It's a mortal sin, Foxer!' said the third, leaning over to say it.

'Don't you try to cod me, Cooney, or I'll burst yer jaw!' cried Foxer angrily.

Philpot hushed them sternly and swiftly, but the spell was broken. They all leaned back in the bench.

Beside them was Father Hanafin's confession box, its worn purple curtains partly drawn back, his worn purple stole hanging on a crook on the wall inside, and as Foxer gazed into the box with curiosity the Adversary tempted him in his heart.

'Come on, Cooney!' he invited at last. 'Come on, and I'll hear yer confession.'

'Got! Come on.' said Cooney, rising.

'That's a sin,' said Philpot, though secretly eager to sit in the priest's chair.

'You're an awful ould Aunt Mary!' jeered Foxer, whereupon all Philpot's scruples vanished and the three scrambled for the confessor's seat.

But Foxer was there before either of them, and at once he swished the curtain together as he had seen Father Hanafin do, and put the long stole about his neck. It was so nice in there in the dark that he forgot his two penitents waiting beyond the closed grilles on either side, and he was putting imaginary snuff into his nostrils and flicking imaginary specks of snuff from his chest when Cooney's angry face appeared between the curtains.

'Are yeh going to hear me confession, Foxer, or are yeh not?' he cried in rage, eager for his turn to be priest.

'Go back, my child,' said Foxer crossly, and he swished the curtains together again. Then, as if in spite, he leaned over to the opposite grille and slowly and solemnly he drew the slide and peered into the frightened eyes of Philpot.

'Tell me how long since your last confession, my child,' he said gravely.

'Twenty years,' whispered Philpot in awe.

'What have you done since then?' intoned Foxer sadly.

'I stole sweets, Father. And I forgot my prayers. And I cursed, Father.'

'You cursed!' thundered Foxer. 'What curse did you say?'

'I said that our master was an ould sod, Father,' murmured Philpot timidly.

'So he is, my child. Is there anything else?'

'No, Father.'

'For your penance say two hundred and forty-nine Rosaries, and four hundred and seventy Our Fathers, and three hundred and thirty-two Hail Marys. And now be a good, obedient boy. And pray for me, won't you? Gawd bless you, my child.'

And with that Foxer drew the slide slowly before the small astonished face.

As he turned to the other side his hand fell on a little box—it was Father Hanafin's consolation during the long hours spent in that stuffy confessional listening to the sins and sorrows of his parishioners. Foxer's awkward fingers lifted the cover and the sweet scent rose powerfully through the darkness as he coaxed the loose snuff down from the cover. Then drawing the slide on Cooney, he gravely inhaled a pinch and leaned his ear to the cool iron of the grille.

Outside a footstep sounded on the marble floor, and peering out Foxer saw the priest walk slowly up the farther aisle, turn and walk slowly down again, his breviary held high to the slanting radiance of the Virgin's altar.

'It's Father Hanafin,' whispered Foxer to Cooney; and to Philpot. 'Keep quiet or we're all ruined.'

Up and down the solemn footsteps went, and high above their heads in the windows of the clerestory and along the lath and plaster of the roof the wind moaned and fingered the loose slates, and now and again they heard the priest murmur aloud the deep, open vowels of his prayer, Gaudeamus Domine, or Domine, Domine meo, in a long breathing sigh.

'He's talking to the Virgin,' breathed Cooney to Foxer.

'He's talking to the Virgin,' breathed Foxer in turn to Philpot. 'Amen,' sighed the priest, and went on his knees before the candles that shone steadily and were reflected brilliantly in the burnished brass.

The three spies had begun to peep from their hiding place when the snuff fell on Foxer's lap and the grains began to titillate his nose. In agony he held his mouth for a full minute and then burst into a furious sneeze. In astonishment the priest gazed about him and once again Foxer held his breath and once again he sneezed. At the third sneeze the priest gazed straight at the box.

'Come out!' he said in a loud voice. 'Come out of that box!'

And as the three guilty forms crept from the three portals he commanded 'Come here!'

Awkwardly they stumbled forward through the seats, trying to hide behind one another until they stood before him.

'What were you doing in there?' he asked Foxer.

'I was hearing their confession, Father,' trembled Foxer, and half raised his arm as if to ward off a blow.

For a moment the priest glared at him and he

302

asked, 'And what penance did you give?'

'I—I gave three hundred and thirty-two Hail Marys, Father, and I think four hundred Our Fathers, Father, and two hundred and forty-nine Rosaries, Father.'

'Well!' pronounced the priest in a solemn voice. 'Go home and let each one of ye say that penance three times over before nine o'clock tomorrow morning.'

Stumbling over one another's heels the three crept down the dark aisle and crushed out through the green baize door and into the falling night that was torn by the storm. The street lamps were lit and under one of these they halted and looked at each other, angry and crestfallen.

'Nine hundred and ninety Hail Marys!' wailed Philpot, and Cooney squared up to Foxer with clenched fists.

'Yerrah!' said Foxer. 'It's all a cod!'

And he raced suddenly away to his supper, followed by the shouts and feet of the other two.

## E X E R C I S E

*1. Tell or write about a dramatic event which happened to you.*
*or*
*2. Mime - in pairs or small groups mime a dramatic incident and have the rest of the class guess what it is.*
*3. Write new words into your Word Copy.*

Read this story by yourself, at one go, underlining words you do not understand. Then go back to it and find out the meanings of any underlined words. Write them into your Word Copy.

# 'At the River-Gates'

*Philippa Pearce*

Lots of sisters I had (said the old man), good girls, too; and one elder brother. Just the one. We were at either end of the family: the eldest, my brother John—we always called him Beany, for some reason; then the girls, four of them; then me. I was Tiddler, and the reason for that was plain.

Our father was a flour miller, and we lived just beside the mill. It was a water-mill, built right over the river, with the mill-wheel underneath. To understand what happened that wild night, all those years ago, you have to understand a bit about the working of the mill-stream. About a hundred yards before the river reached the mill, it divided: the upper river flowed on to power the mill, as I've said; the lower river, leaving the upper river through sluice-gates, flowed to one side of the mill and past it; and then the upper and lower rivers joined up again well below the mill. The sluice-gates could be opened or shut by the miller to let more or less water through from the upper to the lower river. You can see the use of that: the miller controlled the flow of water to power his mill; he could also draw off any floodwaters that came down.

Being a miller's son, I can never remember not understanding that. I was a little tiddler, still at school, when my brother, Beany, began helping my father in the mill. He was as good as a man, my father said. He was strong, and he learnt the feel of the grain, and he was clever with the mill machinery, and he got on with the other men in the mill—there were only ten of them, counting two carters. He understood the gates, of course, and how to get just the right head of water for the mill. And he liked it all: he liked the work he did, and the life; he liked the mill, and the river, and the long river-bank. One day he'd be the miller after my father, everyone said.

I was too young to feel jealousy about that; but I would never have felt jealous of Beany, because Beany was the best brother you could have had. I loved and admired him more than anyone I knew or could imagine knowing. He was very good to me. He used to take me with him when you might have thought a little boy would have been in the way. He took me with him when he went fishing, and he taught me to fish. I learnt patience, then, from Beany. There were plenty of roach and dace in the river; and sometimes we caught trout or pike; and once we caught an eel, and I was first of all terrified and then screaming with excitement at the way it whipped about on the bank, but Beany held it and killed it, and my mother made it into eel-pie. He knew about the fish in the river, and the little creatures, too. He showed me fresh-water shrimps, and leeches— 'Look, Tiddler, they make themselves into croquet-hoops when they want to go any-where!' and he showed me the little underwa-ter cottages of caddis-worms. He knew where to get good watercress for Sunday tea—you

could eat watercress from our river, in those days.

We had an old boat on the river, and Beany would take it upstream to inspect the banks for my father. The banks had to be kept sound: if there was a breach, it would let the water escape and reduce the water-power for the mill. Beany took Jess, our dog, with him in the boat, and he often took me. Beany was the only person I've ever known who could point out a kingfisher's nest in the river-bank. He knew about birds. He once showed me a flycatcher's nest in the brickwork below the sluice-gates, just above where the water dashed and roared at its highest. Once, when we were in the boat, he pointed ahead to an otter in the water. I held on to Jess's collar then.

It was Beany who taught me to swim. One summer it was hotter than anyone remembered, and Beany was going from the mill up to the gates to shut in more water. Jess was following him, and as he went he gave me a wink, so I followed too, although I didn't know why. As usual, he opened the gates with the great iron spanner, almost as long in the handle as he was tall. Then he went down to the pool in the lower river, as if to see the water-level there. But as he went he was unbuttoning his flour-whitened waistcoat; by the time he reached the pool he was naked, and he dived straight in. He came up with his hair plastered over his eyes, and he called to me: 'Come on, Tiddler! Just time for a swimming lesson! Jess sat on the bank and watched us.

Jess was really my father's dog, but she attached herself to Beany. She loved Beany. Everyone loved Beany, and he was good to everyone. Especially, as I've said, to me. Just sometimes he'd say, 'I'm off on my own now, Tiddler,' and then I knew better than to ask to go with him. He'd go sauntering up the river-bank by himself, except for Jess at his heels. I don't think he did anything very particular

when he went off on his own. Just the river and the river-bank were happiness enough for him.

He was still not old enough to have got himself a girl, which might have changed things a bit; but he wasn't too young to go to the War. The War broke out in 1914, when I was still a boy, and Beany went.

It was sad without Beany; but it was worse than that. I was too young to understand then; but, looking back, I realize what was wrong. There was fear in the house. My parents became gloomy and somehow secret. So many young men were being killed at the Front. Other families in the village had had word of a son's death. The news came in a telegram. I overheard my parents talking of those deaths, those telegrams, although not in front of the girls or me. I saw my mother once, in the middle of the morning, kneeling by Beany's bed, praying.

So every time Beany came home on leave, alive, we were lucky.

But when Beany came, he was different. He loved us as much, but he was different. He didn't play with me as he used to do; he would sometimes stare at me as though he didn't see me. When I shouted 'Beany!' and rushed at him, he would start as if he'd woken up. Then he'd smile, and be good to me, almost as he used to be. But, more often than he used to, he'd be off all by himself up the river-bank, with Jess at his heels. My mother, who longed to have him within her sight for every minute of his leave, used to watch him go, and sigh. Once I heard her say to my father that the river-bank did Beany good, as if he were sickening for some strange disease. Once one of the girls was asking Beany about the Front and the trenches, and he was telling her this and that, and we were all interested, and suddenly he stopped and said, 'No. It's hell.' And walked away alone, up the green, quiet river-bank. I suppose if one place was hell, then the other was heaven to him.

After Beany's leaves were over, the mill-house was gloomy again; and my father had to work harder, without Beany's help in the mill. Nowadays he had to work the gates all by himself, a thing that Beany had been taking over from him. If the gates needed working at night, my father and Beany had always gone there together. My mother hated it nowadays when my father had to go to the gates alone at night: she was afraid he'd slip and fall in the water, and, although he could swim, accidents could happen to a man alone in the dark. But, of course, my father wouldn't let her come with him, or any of my sisters, and I was still considered much too young. That irked me.

Well, one season had been very dry and the river level had dropped. The gates were kept shut to get up a head of water for the mill. Then clouds began to build up heavily on the horizon, and my father said he was sure it was going to rain; but it didn't. All day storms rumbled in the distance. In the evening the rain began. It rained steadily: my father had already been once to the gates to open the flashes. He was back at home, drying off in front of the fire. The rain still drove against the windows. My mother said, 'It can't come down worse than this.' She and my sisters were still up with my father. Even I wasn't in bed, although I was supposed to have been. No one could have slept for the noise of the rain.

Suddenly the storm grew worse—much worse. It seemed to explode over our heads. We heard a pane of glass in the skylight over the stairs shatter with the force of it, and my sisters ran with buckets to catch the water pouring through. Oddly, my mother didn't go to see the damage: she stayed with my father, watching him like a lynx. He was fidgeting up and down, paying no attention to the skylight either, and suddenly he said he'd have to go up to the gates again and open everything to carry all possible floodwater into the lower river. This was what my mother had been dreading. She made a great outcry, but she knew it was no use. My father put on his tarpaulin jacket again and took his oil lamp and a thick stick—I don't know why, nor did he, I think. Jess always hated being out in the rain, but she followed him. My mother watched him from the back door, lamenting, and urging him to be careful. A few steps from the doorway and you couldn't see him any longer for the driving rain.

My mother's lingering at the back door gave me my chance. I got my boots on and an oilskin cape I had (I wasn't a fool, even if I was little) and I whipped out of the front door and worked my way round in the shelter of the house to the back and then took the path my father had taken to the river, and made a dash for it, and caught up with my father and Jess, just as they were turning up the way towards the gates. I held on to Jess's tail for quite a bit before my father noticed me. He was terribly angry, of course, but he didn't want to turn back with me, and he didn't like to send me back alone, and perhaps in his heart of hearts he was glad of a little human company on such a night. So we all three struggled up to the gates together. Just by the gates my father found me some shelter between a tree-trunk and a stack of drift-wood. There I crouched, with Jess to keep me company.

I was too small to help my father with the gates, but there was one thing I could do. He told me to hold his lamp so that the light shone on the gates and what he was doing. The illumination was very poor, partly because of the driving rain, but at least it was better than nothing, and anyway my father knew those gates by heart. Perhaps he gave me the job of holding the light so that I had something to occupy my mind and keep me from being afraid.

There was plenty to be afraid of on that night of storm.

Directing what light I could on to my father also directed and concentrated my attention on him. I could see his laborious motions as he heaved the great spanner into place. Then he began to try to rack up with it, but the wind and the rain were so strong that I could see he was having the greatest difficulty. Once I saw him stagger sideways nearly into the blackness of the river. Then I wanted to run out from my shelter and try to help him, but he had strictly forbidden me to do any such thing, and I knew he was right.

Young as I was, I knew—it came to me as I watched him—that he couldn't manage the gates alone in that storm. I suppose he was a man already just past the prime of his strength: the wind and the rain were beating him; the river would beat him.

I shone the light as steadily as I could, and gripped Jess by the collar, and I think I prayed.

I was so frightened then that, afterwards, when I wasn't frightened, I could never be sure of what I had seen, or what I thought I had seen, or what I imagined I had seen. Through the confusion of the storm I saw my father struggling and staggering, and, as I peered and peered, my vision seemed to blur and to double, so that I began sometimes to see one man, sometimes two. My father seemed to have a shadow-self besides himself, who steadied him, heaved with him, worked with him, and at last together they had opened the sluice-gates and let the flood through.

When it was done, my father came back to where Jess and I were, and leant against the tree. He was gasping for breath and exhausted, and had a look on his face that I cannot describe. From his expression I knew that he had felt the shadow with him, just as I had seen it.

And Jess was agitated too, straining against my hold, whining.

I looked past my father, and I could still see something by the sluice-gates: a shadow that had separated itself from my father, and lingered there. I don't know how I could have seen it in the darkness. I don't know. My father slowly turned and looked in the direction that he saw me looking. The shadow began to move away from the gates, away from us; it began to go up the long river-bank beyond the gates, into the darkness there. It seemed to me that the rain and the wind stilled a little as it went.

Jess wriggled from my grasp and was across the gates and up the river-bank, following the vanished shadow. I had made no move, uttered no word, but my father said to me, 'Let them go!' I looked up at him, and his face was streaming with tears as well as with rain.

He took my hand as we fought our way back to the house. The whole house was lit up, to light us home, and my mother stood at the open back door, waiting. She gave a cry of horror when she saw me with my father; and then she saw his face, and her own went quite white. He stumbled into her arms, and he sobbed and sobbed. I didn't know until that night that grown men could cry. My mother led my father indoors, and I don't know what talk they had together. My sisters looked after me, dried me, scolded me, put me to bed.

The next day the telegram came to say that Beany had been killed in action in Flanders.

It was some time after that that Jess came home. She was wet through, and my mother thought she was ill, for she sat shivering by the fire, and for two days would neither eat nor drink. My father said: 'Let her be.'

I'm an old man: it all happened so many years ago, but I've never forgotten my brother Beany. He was so good to us all.

# EXPLORING THE STORY

*1. What was the function of the sluice gates?*

*2. 'Beany was the best brother you could have had.' Why do you think he says that?*

*3. Describe the atmosphere at home after Beany has gone to the war?*

*4. Write out the telegram as you think it may have been worded.*

*5. In your groups make a list of all the words and phrases you might use if you had to describe a storm. REPORT BACK. Note down the unusual ones.*

*6. Write the description.*

*7. This is a very dramatic story which builds up slowly to a climax. Where would you locate the climax? Do you know of any story you could reshape so that it has a very dramatic ending like this one? It can be a ghost story or any other. Plan one and then tell it to the class.*

*8. If you enjoyed this story you will find other tales of the supernatural in the collection, 'The Shadow Gate' by Philippa Pearce, published by Macmillan M books. Her most famous book is 'Tom's Midnight Garden'.*

## FOLLOW ON

*1. Read these three poems. Can you work out the message intended by the writer in each poem? Discuss them in your groups.*

### THE REAR-GUARD

Groping along the tunnel, step by step,
He winked his prying torch with patching glare
From side to side, and sniffed the unwholesome air.
Tins, boxes, bottles, shapes too vague to know,
A mirror smashed, the mattress from a bed;
And he, exploring fifty feet below
The rosy gloom of battle overhead.
Tripping, he grabbed the wall; saw someone lie
Humped at his feet, half-hidden by a rug,
And stopped to give the sleeper's arm a tug.
'I'm looking for headquarters.' No reply.
'God blast your neck!' (For days he'd had no sleep.)
'Get up and guide me through this stinking place.'
Savage, he kicked a soft, unanswering heap,
And flashed his beam across the livid face
Terribly glaring up, whose eyes yet wore
Agony dying hard ten days before;
And fists of fingers clutched a blackening wound.
Alone he staggered on until he found

Dawn's ghost that filtered down a shafted stair
To the dazed, muttering creatures underground
Who hear the boom of shells in muffled sound.
At last, with sweat of horror in his hair,
He climbed through darkness to the twilight air,
Unloading hell behind him step by step.

*Siegfried Sassoon*


## KILL THE CHILDREN

On Hallowe'en in Ship Street,
quite close to Benny's bar,
the children lit a bonfire
and the adults parked a car.

Sick minds sing sentimental songs
and speak in dreary prose
and make ingenious home-made bombs—
and this was one of those.

Some say it was the UVF
and some the IRA
blew up that pub on principle
and killed the kids at play.

They didn't mean the children,
it only was the blast;
we call it KILL THE CHILDREN DAY
in bitter old Belfast.

*James Simmons*

## WAR GAMES

In a Star Wars T-shirt,
Armed with an Airfix bomber,
The young avenger
Crawls across the carpet
To blast the wastepaper basket
Into oblivion.

Later,
Curled on the sofa,
He watches unflinching
An edited version
Of War of the Day
Only half-listening
As the newsreader
Lists the latest statistics.

Cushioned by distance,
How can he comprehend
The real score?

*John Foster*

*2. Have a class debate on some aspect of: 'WAR' or 'VIOLENCE IN SOCIETY' or 'THE EFFECTS OF TELEVISION' or 'THE SUPERNATURAL'.*
*3. Design an Army Recruiting Poster.*
*4. Listen to stories:*
*You may enjoy listening to some of Eamon Kelly's stories or one from 'The Abbey Reads' series of tapes (see Collections, at the end of this section).*

Read this story, underline the words you do not understand and come back to them later.

# 'The Story-Teller'

*Saki (H.H. Munro)*

It was a hot afternoon, and the railway carriage was correspondingly sultry and the next stop was at Templecombe, nearly an hour ahead. The occupants of the carriage were a small girl, and a smaller girl, and a small boy. An aunt belonging to the children occupied one corner seat, and the further corner seat on the opposite side was occupied by a bachelor who was a stranger to their party, but the small girls and the small boy emphatically occupied the compartment. Both the aunt and the children were conversational in a limited, persistent way, reminding one of the attentions of a housefly that refused to be discouraged. Most of the aunt's remarks seemed to begin with 'Don',' and nearly all of the children's remarks began with 'Why?' The bachelor said nothing out loud.

'Don't, Cyril, don't,' exclaimed the aunt, as the small boy began smacking the cushions of the seat, producing a cloud of dust at each blow.

'Come and look out of the window,' she added.

The child moved reluctantly to the window. 'Why are those sheep being driven out of the field?' he asked.

'I expect they are being driven to another field where there is more grass,' said the aunt weakly.

'But there is lots of grass in that field,' protested the boy; 'there's nothing else but grass there. Aunt, there's lots of grass in that field.'

'Perhaps the grass in the other field is better,' suggested the aunt fatuously.

'Why is it better?' came the swift, inevitable question.

'Oh, look at those cows! exclaimed the aunt. Nearly every field along the line had contained cows or bullocks, but she spoke as though she were drawing attention to a rarity.

'Why is the grass in the other field better?' persisted Cyril.

The frown on the bachelor's face was deepening to a scowl. He was a hard, unsympathetic man, the aunt decided in her mind. She was utterly unable to come to any satisfactory decision about the grass in the other field.

The smaller girl created a diversion by beginning to recite 'On the Road to Mandalay.' She only knew the first line, but she put her limited knowledge to the fullest possible use. She repeated the line over and over again in a dreamy but resolute and very audible voice; it seemed to the bachelor as though some one had had a bet with her that she could not repeat the line aloud two thousand times without stopping. Whoever it was who had made the wager was likely to lose his bet.

'Come over here and listen to a story,' said the aunt, when the bachelor had looked twice at her and once at the communication cord.

The children moved listlessly towards the aunt's end of the carriage. Evidently her reputation as a story-teller did not rank high in their estimation.

In a low, confidential voice, interrupted at frequent intervals by loud, petulant questions from her listeners, she began an unenterprising, and deplorably uninteresting story about a little girl who was good, and made friends with everyone on account of her goodness, and was finally saved from a mad bull by a number of rescuers who admired her moral character.

'Wouldn't they have saved her if she hadn't been good?' demanded the bigger of the small girls. It was exactly the question that the bachelor had wanted to ask.

'Well, yes,' admitted the aunt lamely, 'but I don't think they would have run quite so fast to her help if they had not liked her so much.'

'It's the stupidest story I've ever heard,' said the bigger of the small girls, with immense conviction.

'I didn't listen after the first bit, it was so stupid,' said Cyril.

The smaller girl made no actual comment on the story, but she had long ago recommenced a murmured repetition of her favourite line.

'You don't seem to be a success as a storyteller,' said the bachelor suddenly from his corner.

The aunt bristled in instant defence at this unexpected attack.

'It's a very difficult thing to tell stories that children can both understand and appreciate,' she said stiffly.

'I don't agree with you,' said the bachelor.

'Perhaps you would like to tell them a story,' was the aunt's retort.

'Tell us a story,' demanded the bigger of the small girls.

'Once upon a time,' began the bachelor, 'there was a little girl called Bertha, who was extraordinarily good.'

The children's momentarily aroused interest began at once to flicker; all stories seemed dreadfully alike, no matter who told them.

'She did all that she was told, she was always truthful, she kept her clothes clean, ate milk puddings as though they were jam tarts, learned her lessons perfectly, and was polite in her manners.'

'Was she pretty?' asked the bigger of the small girls.

'Not as pretty as any of you,' said the bachelor, 'but she was horribly good.'

There was a wave of reaction in favour of the story; the word horrible in connection with goodness was a novelty that commended itself. It seemed to introduce a ring of truth that was absent from the aunt's tales of infant life.

'She was so good,' continued the bachelor, 'that she won several medals for goodness, which she always wore, pinned on to her dress. There was a medal for obedience, another medal for punctuality, and a third for good behaviour. They were large metal medals and they clicked against one another as she walked. No other child in the town where she lived had as many as three medals, so everybody knew that she must be an extra good child.'

'Horribly good,' quoted Cyril.

'Everybody talked about her goodness, and the Prince of the country got to hear about it, and he said that as she was so very good she might be allowed once a week to walk in his park, which was just outside the town. It was a beautiful park, and no children were ever allowed in it, so it was a great honour for Bertha to be allowed to go there.'

'Were there any sheep in the park?' demanded Cyril.

'No,' said the bachelor, 'there were no sheep.'

'Why weren't there any sheep?' came the inevitable question arising out of that answer.

The aunt permitted herself a smile, which might almost have been described as a grin.

'There were no sheep in the park,' said the bachelor, 'because the Prince's mother had once had a dream that her son would either be killed by a sheep or else by a clock falling on him. For that reason the Prince never kept a sheep in his park or a clock in his palace.'

The aunt suppressed a gasp of admiration.

'Was the Prince killed by a sheep or by a clock?' asked Cyril.

'He is still alive, so we can't tell whether the dream will come true,' said the bachelor unconcernedly; 'anyway, there were no sheep in the park, but there were lots of little pigs running all over the place.'

'What colour were they?'

'Black with white faces, white with black spots, black all over, grey with white patches, and some were white all over.'

The story-teller paused to let a full idea of the park's treasures sink into the children's imaginations; then he resumed:

'Bertha was rather sorry to find that there were no flowers in the park. She had promised her aunts, with tears in her eyes, that she would not pick any of the kind Prince's flowers, and she had meant to keep her promise, so of course, it made her feel silly to find that there were no flowers to pick.'

'Why weren't there any flowers?'

'Because the pigs had eaten them all,' said the bachelor promptly. 'The gardeners had told the Prince that you couldn't have pigs and flowers, so he decided to have pigs and no flowers.'

There was a murmur of approval at the excellence of the Prince's decision; so many people would have decided the other way.

'There were lots of other delightful things in the park. There were ponds with gold and blue and green fish in them, and trees with beautiful parrots that said clever things at a moment's notice, and humming birds that hummed all the popular tunes of the day. Bertha walked up and down and enjoyed herself immensely, and thought to herself: "If I were not so extraordinarily good I should not have been allowed to come into this beautiful park and enjoy all that there is to be seen in it," and her three medals clinked against one another as she walked and helped to remind her how very good she really was. Just then an enormous wolf came prowling into the park to see if it could catch a fat

little pig for its supper.'

'What colour was it?' asked the children, amid an immediate quickening of interest.

'Mud-colour all over, with a black tongue and pale grey eyes that gleamed with unspeakable ferocity. The first thing that it saw in the park was Bertha; her pinafore was so spotlessly white and clean that it could be seen from a great distance. Bertha saw the wolf and saw that it was stealing towards her, and she began to wish that she had never been allowed to come into the park. She ran as hard as she could, and the wolf came after her with huge leaps and bounds. She managed to reach a shrubbery of myrtle bushes and she hid herself in one of the thickest of the bushes. The wolf came sniffing among the branches, its black tongue lolling out of its mouth and its pale grey eyes glaring with rage. Bertha was terribly frightened, and thought to herself: "If I had not been so extraordinarily good I should have been safe in the town at this moment." However, the scent of the myrtle was so strong that the wolf could not sniff out where Bertha was hiding, and the bushes were so thick that he might have hunted about in them for a long time without catching sight of her, so he thought he might as well go off and catch a little pig instead. Bertha was trembling very much at having the wolf prowling and sniffing so near her, and as she trembled a medal for obedience clinked against the medals for good conduct and punctuality. The wolf was just moving away when he heard the sound of the medals clinking and stopped to listen; they clinked again in a bush quite near him. He dashed into the bush, his pale grey eyes gleaming with ferocity and triumph and dragged Bertha out and devoured her to the last morsel. All that was left of her were her shoes, bits of clothing, and the three medals for goodness.'

'Were any of the little pigs killed?'

'No, they all escaped.'

'The story began badly,' said the smaller of the small girls, 'but it had a beautiful ending.'

'It is the most beautiful story that I ever heard,' said the bigger of the small girls, with immense decision.

'It is the only beautiful story I have ever heard,' said Cyril.

A dissentient opinion came from the aunt.

'A most improper story to tell to young children! You have undermined the effect of years of careful teaching.'

'At any rate,' said the bachelor, collecting his belongings preparatory to leaving the carriage, 'I kept them quiet for ten minutes, which was more than you were able to do.'

'Unhappy woman!' he observed to himself as he walked down the platform of Templecombe station; 'for the next six months or so those children will assail her in public with demands for an improper story!'

## DISCUSSION

**1.** Rate the story, out of 10. In your group, explain the reasons for your rating.

**2.** The following 10 words are taken from the first part of the story. Can you match them with the explanations underneath? If not, use your dictionary.

sultry; persistent; bachelor; fatuously; inevitable; listlessly; resolute; audible; petulant; retort

| impatient, irritable | |
|---|---|
| answer back | |
| can be heard | |
| sweltering, hot | |
| unmarried man | |
| foolishly | |
| continue firmly, obstinate | |
| determined | |
| without energy | |
| unavoidable, sure to happen | |

3. Make similar charts for other words from the story and test each other.

4. If you were directing a film of this story what instructions would you give to each of the actors as to how they should play the character?

For example: Would the aunt be silly; aggressive; gentle; or what? Base your views on the evidence of the story. In your group discuss each character.

313

## REFLECT

By now you will have noticed that a good short story:

* is usually BASED ON A SINGLE INCIDENT.

(Don't try to conduct the entire Second World War in three pages!)

* is DRAMATIC and often builds up to a single point of great tension.

* has INTERESTING CHARACTERS.

(You need to spend some time thinking about your characters.) Describe them for the reader.

* has brief but memorable DESCRIPTIONS so that the reader can easily visualise the scene.

Now write your own short stories.

Have a class competition.


Here is a story which won first place in the Junior section of 1987 Prudential Awards/Irish Schools' Creative Writing Competition. It was written by Elaine Stapleton, then aged 13.

# 'Somewhere Through the TV Screen'

*Elaine Stapleton, Age 13*

'Hi! I'm home.' No reply. Same as usual. Sometimes, I don't really know why I bother. This house couldn't sound happy even if it tried. I flung my schoolbag into a dark corner. Maybe I'd do me lessons after tea if I felt like it. I opened the fridge—a few bits of mouldy cheese, half a packet of Bird's Eye oven chips and a carton of sour milk. I switched on the telly and curled up on the couch, tucking my legs beneath me. Telly was my fantasy. The place I could escape to. My Narnia— except it was through a screen not a wardrobe I disappeared. I fought against Colonel Decker with the A-Team, flew through the air with Superman and died a thousand deaths with Alexis and Colby Co. I loved TV. It was a break from the constant barging and fighting of 'The 2'. By 'The 2' I mean me Ma and me Da. Suddenly the door banged. Oh no, it was them.

'What are we going to do?'

'Well, I don't know. It wasn't my fault.'

'Money doesn't just get up and walk out, y'know.'

'I did it for ye all. Since our Michael lost his job and joined the IRA there's hardly been any money.'

'Don't talk rubbish, I'm not all that thick y'know. You just went out and spent it in the pub, drinking 'til closing time, every night.' I shuddered at the screaming pitch of my mother's voice.

'What's wrong?' I asked.

'It's your Da that's wrong,' she answered. 'He's just gone and lost his job. Stealing money for booze. He's bloody well lost his job! How're we goin' to live, tell me? On my wage? 60 a week from working in an ironmonger's? How am I goin' to support six kids and an idle, good-for-nought drunk on 60 a week? Tell me!'

There remained for some time a strained silence. Then the floor creaked, the door opened, 'twas me little brother, Sean. His face was tear-streaked. His eyes looked pleadingly at me. Me Da was the first to speak. 'What's that little brat doin' down here? Did you not lock him in his room?'

'I did,' me Ma answered, 'I don't know how he got out. How did you get out, Sean?' He didn't say a word. 'Tell me, you little brat. Tell me!' She spoke angrily and raised her hand as if to strike me.

'Ma, Ma, please. He's only three years old!' I ran and scooped him up in my arms.

'Take him back to his room, Blathnaid.' I raced up the stairs, Sean in my arms, tears streaming down his sad little face. 'There now, Seanin. Don't cry. Blathnaid is here now. Everything will be OK. All right. Please don't cry, Seanin.'

I left him three hours later. He was asleep, exhausted after becoming hysterical. I too felt drained of energy. After all I was not yet fifteen years old.

'All right. That's it. I'm going,' my father announced after 'Today Tonight'.

'Where?' my mother's frantic voice called.

'Out!'

'The boozer no doubt.'

'Ah, Da, please. No. We can't afford it now. Daaaaaa!' My attempt failed. As he banged the door a dog began to bark. I turned dismally and slowly ascended the stairs. Kicking each step violently a picture of me Da in me mind.

'Blathnaid, have you done the dishes?'

'I'll do them in the morning, Ma,' I called down the long dark corridor. I undressed quickly not bothering to brush my teeth. The dog began to bark. I heard me next-door neighbour, Mrs O'Reilly, shove down her window and roar, 'Shut up, ya bleedin' dog!' I smiled to myself, an image forming in my mind of Mrs O'Reilly in her cold cream and curlers! I jumped into bed, the rusty old springs creaked terribly.

'Blathnaid McDonagh! Just you creak those springs once more and you'll get it from me. D'you want the house to come down round me ears?' 'Twas me Ma. Who else? I drifted off into a heavy, dreamless sleep.

'If the TV is going to have to be sold I'm not staying here,' I said aloud to the darkness. Who'd miss me anyway.

# SHORT STORY COLLECTIONS

You may enjoy dipping into some of these.
- 'Exploring English I'—published by Browne & Nolan/Gill and Macmillan.
- 'The Lucky Bag'—published by Lucky Tree/O'Brien Press.
- George Layton—'The Fib and Other Stories', published by Collins Lions.
- Bill Naughton—'The Goalkeeper's Revenge and Other Stories', Puffin.
- Philippa Pearce—'The Shadow Cage and Other Tales of the Supernatural', published by Macmillan M Books.
- Roald Dahl—'The Wonderful Story of Henry Sugar and Others', Penguin.
- Macmillan Basic English Series, Story 1, 2 and 3.
- Rosemary Sutcliff—'The High Deeds of Finn Mac Cool', Puffin.
- 'Heroic Tales from the Ulster Cycle', published by O'Brien Press.
- 'Island Stories, Tales and Legends from the West', O'Brien Press.
- 'The Faber Book of Greek Legends', edited by Kathleen Lines, Faber and Faber.
- 'The Faber Book of North American Legends', edited by Virginia Haviland, Faber and Faber.

# LISTEN TO STORIES

- You will find 'The Rockfish', 'The Windows of Wonder', 'His First Flight', 'The Potato Gatherers' and others, read by members of the Abbey Theatre Company in 'The Abbey Reads' series of tapes.
- You might enjoy listening to some of Eamon Kelly's stories: 'Stories from Ireland'; 'The Irish Story Teller'; and 'Live from Ireland'. These collections are available on tape from Lunar Records.

# APPENDIX C
# D R A M A

---

DRAMA FROM  PHOTOGRAPHS

DRAMA SCRIPTS

# Thoughts / monologue

# Conversation for Pairs

# Group Conversation or improvisation

# The Break

*by Aidan C. Matthews*

[Note: This play was originally written for radio so there are directions for sound effects. You can have great fun taping sound effects but if that is too cumbersome, the play can be performed without them.]

**Narrator:** Billy Mac lived in a little terrace of red-brick buildings near to the Dublin Zoo. In fact, he still lives there, though he hasn't been the same fellow since the famous episode I'm going to tell you about. The only thing I can't tell you is his surname because he doesn't want any publicity. After all, what he tried to do is against the law, and we don't want him taken off in a Black Maria to some filthy dirty dungeon. Now you may think there are no such places anywhere near Dublin, but I can assure you there are, and some of them are only a stone's throw from schools and churches. However, what happened was this. Billy loved the Zoo; he was crazy about it. At nights he'd lie awake and listen to the pelicans shrieking and the tigers snoring. Sometimes, over the soft roar of the late night traffic passing in the wet streets beneath his window, he could even make out the big grumbling of the hippo as it rolled over in its sludgy den. That was a noise he loved. But sure what am I describing them for? Can't you listen to them for yourselves?

**Sound Effects (SFX):** NOISE OF FLAMINGOS CALLING, MONKEYS CHATTERING, LIONS ROARING, ELEPHANTS TRUMPETING: A WHOLE MENAGERIE OF JUNGLE SOUNDS.

**Narrator:** To make a long story short—and that, by the way, is the whole aim of literature—Billy listened so closely and carefully to those noises that *(AWED TONE)* at last he began to understand them. That was where all the trouble started, because as soon as you begin understanding other people, life becomes much more complex. It's much easier to misunderstand people; but Billy had to find out the hard way.

**SFX:** FADE OUT, AND FADE IN ZOO NOISES.

**Billy:** Oh! You're such a handsome, hardy lion. So shaggy and sad-eyed. And what a beautiful cage you have all to yourself. It's as big as a penthouse.

| | |
|---|---|
| **Lion:** | Would you ever shove off, you little twerp?  You're disturbing my siesta. |
| **Billy:** | I was only trying to be pleasant, to make conversation.  You're very cranky. |
| **Lion:** | *(ROARING)* Scram.  Clear off.  Vamoose. |
| **Billy:** | There's so much anger in you; so much aggression.  But it's good for you to express it. |
| **Lion:** | Last night I had to suffer those bloody drunks in their monkey suits making a mockery of the Zoo Ball and throwing peanuts and bottle-tops into my own bedroom.  Today I have to endure a prissy little pipsqueak.  Is there no peace and quiet in this world, I ask you? |
| **Billy:** | But that's why I come here, Mr. Lion.  Because it's so peaceful.  I love the stink of the lion-house and the smell of the elephant bread. |
| **Lion:** | Peaceful!  *(ROARS)* This isn't a monastery; it's a concentration camp.  I'd give you peace, I would.  If I could work the lock on this door, I'd strip you in one swallow from your eyeballs to your ankles.  You think I'm happy here?  I'm doing a life-sentence, a life sentence, d'ya here me?  And I still don't know where I went wrong.  My days are a misery, my nights are all memory. *(WRETCHEDLY)* I dream that I'm back at the waterhole, lying in the long grass, waiting for the antelope and watching the distance shiver in the heat haze.  Then, just as they stretch their lovely lean necks over the water and sip from its surface, I — |
| **Billy:** | Yes?  Yes?  What? |
| **Lion:** | I wake up back in Dublin with my fur full of straw.  It's not fair, it's not fair ... |
| **SFX:** | FADE OUT, FADE IN NARRATOR'S VOICE. |
| **Narrator:** | Billy upped and fled to the monkey house.  He couldn't bear seeing an animal suffer.  It was worse than watching a human cry. |
| **SFX:** | FADE OUT, FADE IN SOUND OF MONKEY HOUSE. |

| | |
|---|---|
| **Billy:** | Oh, Miss Monkey, Miss Monkey, I feel so sorry for your pal in the lion-house. I think he's on the point of a nervous breakdown. His outlook is very gloomy. |
| **Monkey:** | I couldn't care less about any old lion. My first cousin was never the same after being eaten by one of them. Besides, I'm on my day off. So just leave me in peace. I'm trying to find a flea that's been plaguing me. |
| **Billy:** | Let me help you. I want to be your friend. |
| **Monkey:** | Ugh! I couldn't bear the thought of being touched by a human. It gives me the creeps. Horrible little pink fingers. |
| **Billy:** | But I love the zoo. I love the stink of the lion cage and the smell of the elephant bread. |
| **Monkey:** | Well, you can't monkey around with me. In the old days, when I was free ... *(SCREAMS)* free, free! ... my brother would have pelted you with coconuts just for talking to me. |
| **Narrator:** | And with that she just turned her bottom on him and walked off in a monkey huff. Billy was beside himself, which is a curious way to be, but he pulled himself together and galloped off as hard as his heels would carry him, to where the elephant was. |
| **SFX:** | FADE UP SOUND OF ELEPHANT HOOTING. |
| **Billy:** | Oh, Mr. Elephant, I'm so confused. I love the zoo. I love the stink of the lion house and the smell of the elephant bread, but the lion only growled at me and showed me his fillings, and the monkey only grumbled and showed her bottom. Why? What have I done? |
| **Elephant :** | I can't talk right now. I'm too depressed. |
| **Billy:** | But you must fight it. You must force yourself to be ecstatic. |
| **Elephant :** | *(IRRITABLY)* How would you like to have to perform for toddlers twice a day? And have them hanging out of your tusks? Hum? My teeth are going soft from elephant bread. I want to chew maple leaves and cherry blossom. You've no notion how tasty African foliage is. It makes my trunk twitch just to think of it. |

| | |
|---|---|
| **Billy:** | I'm sorry for your trouble. |
| **Elephant :** | *(TEARFULLY)* Look at me. Dressed up like a performing animal. When Europe was icebound, I grazed in Asia; when Alexander drank from the Ganges, I was in his train. And that wasn't yesterday nor the day before. *(ELEPHANT HOOTS)* |
| **SFX:** | FADE OUT, FADE IN NARRATOR. |
| **Narrator:** | Well, Billy flew home, crying his eyes out. His tears were the size of glass marbles. I tell you no word of a lie. He had never imagined how much animals and other people suffer; which is, in fact, the basic problem with our species: we just don't imagine. Anyhow, the first thing Billy did was, he let the canary out of its cage in the conservatory (which is what his mother liked to call the bit of a pantry out the back), and he waved to it as it flew straight up and away like a shuttlecock. He knew his mother would, well, have a canary once she heard what he'd done, but he didn't care. He felt better, and so for that matter did the bird as well, at least until a magpie tore his head off thirty minutes later. But by that time Billy was in bed, hatching the weirdest schemes. |
| **SFX:** | SOUND OF ELEPHANT TRUMPETING. |
| **Narrator:** | Three day later it was reported to the Assistant Keeper that the duplicate set of keys to the major complex was ... missing. |
| **SFX:** | SOUND OF LION ROARING. |
| **Narrator:** | Three days after that, it was discovered that the wire stockade behind the polar bears' enclosure had been *(WHISPER)* severed by a wirecutters. |
| **SFX:** | SOUND OF MONKEYS CHATTERING FIENDISHLY. |
| | Something was up! |
| **SFX:** | FEET APPROACHING SOFTLY. THEY STOP, CONTINUE. A DOOR CREAKS OPEN. FEET AGAIN. ANOTHER DOOR. |
| | Stop it! Stop! We could be here all night. The truth is, folks, that Billy had to pass through sixteen sets of double doors before finally, fearlessly *(SOUND OF NOSE SMELLING THE AIR)* he knew where he was. Imagine the smell of a crowded classroom in January, and multiply it by ten. He was back in the lion house! |

| | |
|---|---|
| **Billy:** | Mr. Lion. Mr. Lion, sir. |
| **Lion:** | It's the twerp. What are you doing, twerp? |
| **Billy:** | *(WHISPER)* I've come to set you free. |
| **Lion:** | Are you mad, twerp? |
| **Billy:** | Shhh! I can help you make your escape to Africa. |
| **Lion:** | To Africa! Home to Agatha! |
| **Billy:** | Who's Agatha? |
| **Lion:** | My wife. At least, my favourite wife. |
| **Billy:** | Try to whisper. We might be heard. Here's the key. |
| **Lion:** | Now hold on, twerp. |
| **Billy:** | What is it? |
| **Lion:** | Well, it isn't that I'm not grateful. I am. I ... am indeed. Very. But ... |
| **Billy:** | Hurry! Hurry! |
| **Lion:** | You don't understand. I'm too old for this sort of stunt. Besides, I couldn't ..... leave my friends. They depend on me. No, I couldn't just walk out on them. Their morale would suffer. Sorry, old man. You might have more luck with the monkeys. Flighty fellows, what? |
| **SFX:** | FADE OUT, AND FADE IN NARRATOR'S VOICE. |
| **Narrator:** | Billy was led by his nose straight to the monkey house. When he got there, feeling his way along the bars of the cages ... |
| **Billy:** | Psss! Psss! Miss Monkey. |
| **Monkey:** | Psss! yourself. What are *you* doing here? |
| **Billy:** | I've come to free you. |

333

| | |
|---|---|
| **Monkey:** | Free me from what? |
| **Billy:** | From cruel captivity. |
| **Monkey:** | Mind your manners. How dare you! 'Cruel captivity' indeed. Why on earth would I want to leave all this? |
| **Billy:** | Shhh! We haven't much time. |
| **Monkey:** | I have all the time in the world, thank you very much; and I propose to spend it here. Where else is the grub so good? Where else would I get free central heating? Social welfare? Medical expenses? Annual leave? Besides, the public adores me. I have obligations to my fans. So scram! |
| **SFX:** | FADE IN NARRATOR'S VOICE. |
| **Narrator:** | And Billy did. He made a beeline for the elephant house, but it was the same story there. |
| **Elephant:** | You're just a troublemaker. That's the long and the short of it. There should be a law against people like you. You should be stamped out. In fact, I'd stamp on you myself if I had the energy, but I don't. So hump off and leave me alone with my depression. I was enjoying it until you came along. |
| **Monkey:** | I was enjoying it until you came along. |
| **Lion:** | I was enjoying it until you came along. |

CACOPHONY OF ANIMAL NOISES GROWING TO A CRES-
CENDO OVER SEVERAL SECONDS. THEN SUDDEN
SILENCE.
END.

# MATTHEW, COME HOME

*by Berlie Doherty*

### THE CHARACTERS
Matthew, aged 13
The Man In Grey
Katie, Matthew's sister, aged 18
Mum
Sarah, Matthew's sister, aged 12
Dad
Simon, Matthew's friend, aged 13

| | |
|---|---|
| **Matthew:** | (*Matthew is riding home from school on his bike.*) I hate this crossing. I'm going to have to learn how to do it, though. I can't get off my bike and walk over every time. This time I'll do it ... No, not yet. There's a lorry coming. Now. Quick! Now ... there's another .. oh quick, quick. (*Sound of brakes squealing, bike falling. Then silence.*) |
| **Man in Grey:** | Ah! It's happened at last, has it? I knew this crossing would be worth watching. I've been waiting for this. Let's see, who've I got here? A boy. A boy in a bit of a state. Come on, now. Up you get. |
| **Matthew:** | My head. Oh, my head! |
| **Man in Grey:** | Oh, yes, it's a mess, boy. A mess of blood and bones. Don't you worry, you're in good hands with me. The very best hands. I'll get you home. |
| **Matthew:** | It hurts! |
| **Man in Grey:** | Of course it hurts. You mustn't expect this to be easy. Come on now. |

- - - - - - - - - - - - - - - - - - - - - - - - - - - - - - - - - - - - -

| | |
|---|---|
| | (*Later. A grey room.*) |
| **Man in Grey:** | Now, boy, let me take a look at you. Oh yes. Just right. Neither here nor there! Just the way I like them! Come on now, I should think you could open your eyes now. |

| | |
|---|---|
| **Matthew:** | Where am I? |
| **Man in Grey:** | Ah, don't ask me that.  You're not lying under a lorry, which is where I saw you a few hours ago.  No, you're not there. |
| **Matthew**: | Then where am I? |
| **Man in Grey:** | It doesn't matter where you are.  You're safe.  That's what matters.  Safe with me.  For now. |
| **Matthew**: | I want to go home. |
| **Man in Grey:** | Of course you do.  They always do.  They always want to go home.  Well, I'll do what I can for you.  You haven't got much time, though.  The only way to do it is to mix up time, that's as much as I can say, really.  Can you manage that? |
| **Matthew**: | I don't know what you mean. |
| **Man in Grey:** | Don't you?  Not much I can do, then.  *(Pause)*  Well now, I've got work to do.  I can't spend any more time with you.  But look, you'll still feel pain for a bit.  When it comes, concentrate on the pain.  Don't try to get away from it.  But don't let it win. |
| **Matthew**: | Are you a doctor? |
| **Man in Grey:** | A doctor?  That's a strange idea.  That's the last thing I'd call myself.  More like a receptionist, really.  I take people through the door.  That one ... the black one.  That's the usual one.  But sometimes through that one, the red one.  Which one would you like to go through? |
| **Matthew**: | I don't know.  I just want to go home. |
| **Man in Grey:** | I know, so you keep saying.  Well, I'll let you try the red one then.  I'll have a go at a time-mix for you, but I don't always get it right.  Now hurry up.  I've got work to do.  There's been a pile-up on the motorway, I can hear the tyres squealing.  I've a very good ear for things like that.  Off you go.  I'd better hurry. |
| **Matthew**: | I don't know how to get home from here.  I don't know if I can get there ... |

**Man in Grey:** Good gracious, of course you can get there, if you really want to. Just through that door. Up you get.

**Matthew:** I think I'm going to faint.

**Man in Grey:** I suppose I'd better help you, then. There you go. Through the door.

■ ■ ■ ■ ■ ■ ■ ■ ■ ■ ■ ■ ■ ■ ■ ■ ■ ■ ■ ■ ■ ■ ■ ■ ■ ■ ■ ■ ■ ■ ■ ■ ■

**Matthew:** Through here? But it's ... I don't understand. I'm home.
*(Mum is in the kitchen. Sarah is in the living-room, doing her homework, Katie comes downstairs to the door.)*

**Mum:** There's a terrible draught. Has the front door come open, Katie?

**Katie:** I'll have a look. Yes, it has. That's funny.

**Matthew:** Hello, Katie.

**Mum:** I thought it might be Matthew coming back.

**Matthew:** It is, Mum I'm here.

**Mum:** He's late, isn't he? It must be nearly five by now.

**Matthew:** Mum! I'm here.

**Katie:** He might be at Simon's.

**Mum:** Of course. I'd forgotten. He often calls at Simon's on a Friday.

**Matthew:** Stop messing about, Mum. I've been hurt ..

**Katie:** It's dark already.

**Mum:** So it is. I really don't like him to be out in the dark.

**Matthew:** Mum. Mum. Look at me. Katie!

**Mum:** And I wanted us to have tea early tonight, too. I've a good mind to ring Simon's and tell him to send him home.

**Katie:** I've got to nip up to the bike shop before it closes. D'you want me to pop in for him?

**Mum:** Would you, Katie? I'll give him a ring, and then I'll get on with tea. Where's Sarah?

**Sarah:** I'm in here, Mum. Doing my homework.

**Matthew:** Sarah! Sarah, look at me.

**Sarah:** Mum. I'm cold.

**Matthew:** It's the draught from that door. It blew open just now.

**Sarah:** It's freezing.

**Matthew:** Sarah. Please look at me.

**Sarah:** I've gone and left my French dictionary at Mandy's. Now what do I do?

**Matthew:** My head hurts so much! I'm so tired. Concentrate on the pain, he said. I can't get outside this pain ... it hurts ... it hurts ...

■ ■ ■ ■ ■ ■ ■ ■ ■ ■ ■ ■ ■ ■ ■ ■ ■ ■ ■ ■ ■ ■ ■ ■ ■ ■ ■ ■ ■ ■ ■ ■ ■ ■ ■ ■

**Man in Grey:** Hello there! Back again!

**Matthew:** You! What's happening? How did I get here again?

**Man in Grey:** You didn't do very well, did you? I must say I thought you'd be quicker than this. I can't let you stay much longer, you know. There's a queue outside.

**Matthew:** I don't want to stay here. I want to go home.

**Man in Grey:** Very well, very well. You know where the door is. Off you go. And please hurry.

**Matthew:** A red door ... from a room I've never seen before ... and into ... our hall. Mum in the kitchen getting tea ready. Dad back home, making some coffee. Sarah doing her homework by the fire. Mum! Mum!

■ ■ ■ ■ ■ ■ ■ ■ ■ ■ ■ ■ ■ ■ ■ ■ ■ ■ ■ ■ ■ ■ ■ ■ ■ ■ ■ ■ ■ ■ ■ ■ ■

| | |
|---|---|
| **Mum:** | I really can't understand why he's so late, John. Katie's going to pop in to Simon's on the way back from the shops to see if he's there, but there was no answer when I rang up just now. Where's he got to? If he's not at Simon's, then I can't think where he'll be. |
| **Matthew:** | But I'm here. You must be able to see me. |
| **Dad:** | Of course he'll be there. But he'll get a good telling-off when he does come in ... staying out till teatime. |
| **Matthew:** | I'd rather have a good telling-off than this, any day. I'm HERE. |
| **Dad:** | Are you sure there's nothing on at school, Sarah? |
| **Sarah:** | There's never anything on at school these days. Except lessons. |
| **Mum:** | I don't understand it. I wish Katie had waited for you to come home now, John. She'd have been quicker in the car. |
| **Sarah:** | Stop fussing, Mum. You never fuss about me like this. |
| **Dad:** | That's what you think. You're a born worrier, Joan. |
| **Mum:** | Anyway, after tomorrow he'll have no excuse for coming in late. |
| **Sarah:** | It's gone cold again, Mum. |
| **Mum:** | Yes, it has. I thought I heard the door just now, but it must have been down the road. Oh, there it is now. Matthew? |
| **Matthew:** | I'm here. |
| **Katie:** | It's me. There's no one in at Simon's Mum. And I only just got to the shop in time. I'll run up and hide these in my room. Is he back? |
| **Matthew:** | Yes. |
| **Mum:** | No. Oh, John. I'm getting worried. |
| **Dad:** | Let's have tea. If he hasn't come in when I've had my tea I'll drive down to the school. Come and set the table, Sarah. |

| | |
|---|---|
| **Sarah:** | Can I just finish this? |
| **Dad:** | All right. I'll leave you in peace for a few minutes. You can wash up instead. |
| **Matthew**: | Sarah. |
| **Sarah:** | Freezing in here. |
| **Matthew**: | Sarah, I don't know what you're playing at, but stop it. Stop it. It's horrible. |
| **Sarah:** | Colder than our classroom even. Wish Matthew would come back. He'd do my homework for me. |
| **Matthew**: | Please, Sarah. Look at me. |
| **Sarah:** | I just can't work when it's as cold as this. Can't think. *Noir, noire, noirs*. Before or after the noun? The black water ... |
| **Matthew**: | Give me your pen. |
| **Sarah:** | Hey! What's happening? |
| **Matthew**: | Now read this, read it. 'Matthew is here. I'm here.' |
| **Sarah:** | Mum! Dad! |
| **Dad:** | What's up, Sarah? |
| **Sarah:** | I can't believe it. Look at this. My pen started moving on its own. Look! Look what it's written. |
| **Mum:** | You've got *noir* in the wrong place. |
| **Sarah:** | Look what it says. 'Matthew is here. I'm here.' Mum, look at it. |
| **Dad:** | Don't be silly. Of course it doesn't say that. It says 'the fish swim in the black water' in very bad French. |
| **Sarah:** | But look at it! Matthew wrote it. It's his handwriting ... |
| **Mum:** | Stop it, Sarah. |

| | |
|---|---|
| **Dad:** | This isn't funny, Sarah. You're upsetting your mother. |
| **Sarah:** | But that's what it says. It is! 'Matthew is ..' |
| **Dad:** | Sarah! I'm really surprised at you. Get on with your work and let me get on with setting the table. And Joan can get on with worrying. You know what she's like—but there's no need to make matters worse. |
| **Sarah:** | But Dad! |
| **Matthew:** | Oh no. The pain's coming back. Just when I seem to be reaching Sarah, at least ... I feel as if I'm slipping away again. I must stay awake this time. I mustn't let the pain win. Help me, someone. Please, please help me. |
| **Man in Grey:** | I'll help you. |
| **Matthew:** | You! |

. . . . . . . . . . . . . . . . . . . . . . . . . . . . . . . . . . . . . . . . . . . . . . . . . . . . . . . . . . . .

| | |
|---|---|
| **Man in Grey:** | Yes. I'm afraid you're back here with me again. You don't seem to be doing very well, do you? Perhaps you don't really want to go home ... |
| **Matthew:** | I do! I'm trying to get home. Why can't I get there? Why can't they see me? It's as if I don't exist any more! |
| **Man in Grey:** | I'm afraid you're in the grey world of inbetween. You might make it ... you might not. Who can say? But you've very little time left. I really shouldn't have given you this long. |
| **Matthew:** | Please can I try again? |
| **Man in Grey:** | You know the way. Through the door. Are you sure you want the red one again? It would be much easier all round if you went through the black one. I should never have mentioned the red one to you really. You're obviously not strong enough. |
| **Matthew:** | I am! I want to go home! Please let it work this time. I'll go slowly, don't rush it, take my time. Open the door very gently. Our carpet. Our stairs. Mum coming out of the kitchen. And Simon! Simon's here! |

| | |
|---|---|
| **Mum:** | Hello, Simon, love. I thought it was Katie coming in. |
| **Simon:** | I'm sorry, Mrs Peace. The front door was open so I came straight in. |
| **Mum:** | Who keeps leaving it open like that? We must have ghosts! |
| **Dad:** | Has Matthew gone upstairs? |
| **Simon:** | Matthew? I haven't come with Matthew, Mr Peace. I haven't seen him today. I didn't go to school—we've been at my Grandma's because she was ill. I've come to ask Matthew if there was any homework. |
| **Mum:** | John! Now what? |
| **Dad:** | I don't know, love. I felt sure he'd be with Simon. |
| **Sarah:** | Mum. Something's happened to Matthew. |
| **Dad:** | Stop it, Sarah. Simon, let me give you a lift home, and then I'll drive on to school and see if he's still there. |
| **Simon:** | Thanks, Mr Peace. I hope he's all right. |
| **Matthew**: | Simon! Surely you can see me! |
| **Simon:** | Perhaps he's at Mandy's. |
| **Sarah:** | Mandy's! |
| **Simon:** | Well ... he does sometimes walk her home. |
| **Sarah:** | I never knew that. Wait till I see her tomorrow! |
| **Mum:** | Is Mandy on the phone, Sarah? |
| **Sarah:** | No. She lives in Moss Street. Number 4. Shall I go round there? I know he's not there, though. |

| | |
|---|---|
| **Mum:** | No. I can't stand this any longer. I'll have to go myself. And if he isn't there ... I'll ring the police. |
| **Dad:** | Don't get panicky, love. |
| **Sarah:** | He won't be there, Dad. He isn't at Mandy's, and he isn't at school. I know he isn't. |
| **Dad:** | Don't start that again, Sarah. |
| **Simon:** | Can I help you look for him, Mr Peace? |
| **Dad:** | Let's get going. If he turns up, Sarah, don't let him go out again. *(Door bangs. Mum, Dad and Simon have gone.)* |
| **Matthew:** | Sarah. |
| **Sarah:** | It's happening again. As soon as they go, I can feel you here. You are here, aren't you? |
| **Matthew:** | Yes. I'm here. Right by you. I'm here. |
| **Sarah:** | I can't hear your voice, but my head's telling me what you're saying. I can't see you, but I know you're there. It's so cold here, now. Matthew, come back. |
| **Matthew:** | I'm trying. |
| **Sarah:** | Your voice is like a whisper in my head. But it's you, I know. Tell me what's happening. |
| **Matthew:** | I don't know. Whatever it is, I'm frightened. I'm frightened of slipping away again and never coming back, never, never. I'm frightened of the black door. |
| **Sarah:** | What black door? Why can't I see you? What happened to you? |
| **Matthew:** | I was on my way home from school. I must have crashed into a car and come off my bike ... |
| **Sarah:** | You did what? |
| **Matthew:** | I came off my bike: I smashed my head ... |

| | |
|---|---|
| **Sarah:** | You haven't got a bike. |
| **Matthew:** | My bike. The bike I got for my birthday last week. |
| **Sarah:** | Your birthday is tomorrow. |
| **Matthew:** | But I got a bike. A blue bike. You gave me a saddle bag. Katie got me some lights ... |
| **Sarah:** | Your bike is in the garage. It's still got cardboard and wrappings round it. Katie's been up to the bike-shop to get the lights now. I've got your saddle-bag hidden under my bed ... |
| **Matthew:** | But I was riding it, Sarah! I was at that crossing up near Simon's. I crashed into something. My head was all blood and bones, the man said ... |
| **Sarah:** | What man? |
| **Matthew:** | The grey man. I thought he was a doctor, but he said that was the last thing he'd call himself. He said I mustn't let the pain win, but every time it comes I seem to drift away and then I'm in his grey room on the other side of our door ... a big, cold, grey room with a black door on one wall and a red door on the other. I can't escape, Sarah. I can get through the red door into here but I can't come back home. Nobody can see me. |
| **Sarah:** | But I know you're here! Surely if I can hear you, there must be a way of bringing you back. |
| **Matthew:** | I can't help myself. When the pain comes I drift away again. It's coming again now. I can't help it, Sarah. I don't know if I can come back through the door again. I can't do it on my own. Help me, Sarah. It's something to do with time, he said. Mixing up time ... |
| **Sarah:** | I want to help you, Matthew. Mixing up time? But time's already mixed up ... you're in a different time from me. My time is today, and your birthday is tomorrow. But why aren't you home? And your time is next week ... you've already had your birthday ... you've had your bike ... and a terrible thing has happened to you. How can I stop the terrible thing from happening? Unless ... unless I stop tomorrow! |

I know!  I know!  It might work!
*(She runs out.)*

----

**Man in Grey:**  She knows what to do.  Pity she's left it so late.

**Matthew:**  You again.  Please let me go.

**Man in Grey:**  I could let you go one way, and that would be for eternity.  I could let you go another way, and that would be home again, if you were strong enough to get there.  I don't think you are.  You've no time left, Matthew.

**Matthew:**  Can't I just go back once more?  Just to say goodbye?

**Man in Grey:**  One last time.  There's nothing more I can do for you.  Time's slipping back, boy.  Go on.  Go on.

**Matthew:**  I'm coming home from school.  I'm running up the road.  I'm pushing open the door.  Please!  Please!

----

**Mum:**  Hello, Matthew!  Good, I'm glad you're back early.  I've got to go out tonight.

**Katie:**  I'm going up to the shops, Mum.  I want to get the you-know-what for tomorrow.

**Mum:**  Wait till your dad comes in, Katie.  He might let you take the car. This'll be him now.  Heavens.  What was that?

**Katie:**  Sounds as if he's run over a load of tin cans.

**Dad:**  *(Outside):*  Joan!

**Mum:**  Go and see what he wants, Matthew.  Oh, wait ... you'd better not go in the garage ...

**Dad:**  Joan!  Some stupid fool has left the bike in the middle of the garage floor, and I've just reversed the car over it.  It was lying on the floor ... right in the middle.  It's ruined!

**Matthew**:     My bike!

**Dad:**     I'm sorry, Matthew. I didn't know you were there. That was your birthday surprise for tomorrow. You might as well come and look at it ... but you'll never ride it now, I'm afraid. It's just a mess of metal and rubber.

**Katie:**     Saved me a journey, anyway. I was just going to get you some lights for it.

**Sarah:**     Oh, Matthew. Your lovely bike. I'm sorry.

**Matthew**:     Thanks, Sarah.

**Sarah:**     What d'you mean, thanks! I don't know anything about it, anyway. I've been trying to do my French homework. Want to help me?

**Man in Grey:**     Matthew!

**Matthew**:     No! What do you want?

**Man in Grey:**     I just want to say - goodbye!

**Matthew**:     It's cold out here. Let's go in, shall we? I'm starving!

# EVACUEES

*by Marianne Cook*

### THE CHARACTERS
Memory Voice
Peter Bateman, aged 11
Teacher
Woman
Colonel Holmes, ex-army officer
Jim Saunders, farmer
Mrs. Saunders
John Saunders, aged 11
Bob Saunders, aged 12
Brenda Saunders, aged 13
Sally Saunders, aged 9
Rick
Goofy
Mrs Bateman, Peter's mum
Sailor

**Note:** the words spoken by the Memory Voice are the actual reminiscences of Mel Calman the cartoonist, recorded with his permission.

*1.  A platform at Paddington Station.  A class of children aged about 11 or 12, are waiting on the crowded platform with their teacher.  It is a railway terminus in London, in October 1939, and the children of the capital are whistling or humming while they wait.  The background whistling or humming fades away, until just one child, from the group on the platform, is whistling.  The children are passing the time the best they can, chattering, in twos and threes.  One boy stands alone, trying to hold back his tears.*

| | |
|---|---|
| **Memory:** | I have this image of a small boy with a label tied round his neck. The boy has no features and is crying.  He is carrying a cardboard box, which contains his gas mask. |
| **Teacher:** | *(Bustling up to Peter, the boy standing alone)* Peter ... are you crying? |
| **Peter:** | *(Sniffing hard)* No, Miss. |
| **Teacher:** | I should think not too, a big boy like you.  I've got enough to do without worrying about cry-babies. |

| | |
|---|---|
| **Peter:** | When will the train come, Miss? |
| **Teacher:** | Any minute now. I just asked the porter. |
| **Peter:** | Where are we going? |
| **Teacher:** | You'll have to wait and see. |
| **Peter:** | *(Anxiously)* Miss ... |
| **Teacher:** | Yes, Peter? |
| **Peter:** | The Germans are going to drop bombs on London aren't they? |
| **Teacher:** | That's why you're going to the country. |
| **Peter:** | I will come back again, won't I? |
| **Teacher:** | *(Her patience has almost run out)* Of course you will. |
| **Peter:** | *(Quickly - this has been worrying him for some time)* But what if they drop a bomb on my house and it's not there any more? How will I know where to go? And what about my mum and dad? They're not going to the country. What will happen to them if a bomb drops on our house? |
| **Teacher:** | You must try not to worry. |
| **Peter:** | But they might be killed, Miss. |
| **Teacher:** | You know you're always worrying about things, and most of the time they never happen. |
| **Peter:** | And Miss, how are Mum and Dad going to know where I've gone? |
| **Teacher:** | *(Relieved to be on less difficult ground)* I've already told you that. You'll be given a postcard with a stamp on it. Tomorrow you can write to your parents and send them your address. |
| | *(The sound of a train approaching)* |
| **Children:** | *(Jumping up and milling about)* The train's coming! It's here! Come on! *(Cheering)* |

348

| | |
|---|---|
| **Peter:** | You are coming with us, aren't you Miss? |
| **Teacher:** | Yes, Peter. *(She begins to try and organise the children)* Keep still, all of you. Don't crowd forward. Wait till the train stops. Don't push. There's room for everyone. Stand still! |

*(The train is heard drawing to standstill)*

| | |
|---|---|
| **Peter:** | Miss ... |
| **Teacher:** | What is it now, Peter? |
| **Peter:** | *(Feeling better now the train has actually arrived)* Can we eat our sandwiches as soon as we get on the train? |
| **Teacher:** | *(Herding the children on to the train)* Come on, quickly. Get yourselves on to the train. Don't leave your suitcase! |

*(The platform empties)*

**2.** *A Church Hall. The children have arrived at their destination. Tea and squash and biscuits are being served to them from trestle tables. Ladies in WVS uniforms are rushing around with lists, trying to sort them out. Village people wait to be allocated their quota of 'vacees'.*

| | |
|---|---|
| **Woman:** | *(Behind one of the refreshment tables)* Cup of tea or orange squash? |
| **Peter:** | What? |
| **Woman:** | *(More slowly)* What do you want to drink? A cup of tea or orange squash? |
| **Peter:** | Squash, please. |
| **Woman:** | *(Pouring him some squash)* You'll have to wake up, son. You'll find yourself left behind when all the others have gone to their new homes. *(Gives him the squash)* And you don't want to spend the night in the Church Hall, do you? |
| **Peter:** | No. |
| **Woman:** | No, you don't. I can tell you that for nothing. It's a grim old place. Haunted ... I shouldn't wonder. |

| Peter: | Please, Mrs ... where is this? |
|---|---|

| Woman: | St Bartholomew's Church Hall. |
|---|---|

| Peter: | No, I mean, where in the country? Where in England? |
|---|---|

| Woman: | Gracious love us, child! Somerset of course! Wherever did you think? Around twelve miles from Bristol. Honest, I think you must have left your wits behind you in London. Next! *(Peter moves away from the table as the queue shuffles forward)* |
|---|---|

*3. Another part of the hall, a bit later. Peter sits, nursing his empty glass, staring into space.*

| Memory: | I remember that labels with our names on were pinned to our clothes before we left London. I think I felt that I had no identity, and was a parcel being posted to the country. The labels frightened me as much as the idea of leaving my parents. A child of 11, if lost, can tell people his name. A label assumes that he does not know his name, or worse, that he has no name, and is given one at random from a list of names. |
|---|---|

*(Colonel Holmes comes up to Peter, list in hand. He is too old for active service, but would feel more at home on the front line)*

| Colonel Holmes: | Well, well, and what have we got here, eh? *(Pause)* Name! |
|---|---|

| Peter: | *(Mumbles)* Peter Bateman, sir. |
|---|---|

| Colonel Holmes: | Speak up. Is this your name? *(He bends down and holds Peter's label so he can read it)* |
|---|---|

| Peter: | *(Quick and loud in his ear)* Peter Bateman! |
|---|---|

| Colonel Holmes: | *(Drawing back)* So it is! And how old are you, Peter? Do you know? |
|---|---|

| Peter: | *(Disgusted)* Of course I do. I'm 11 years, two months, and ... *(Counting)* ... 27 days. |
|---|---|

| Colonel Holmes: | Good. And have you any brothers or sisters? |
|---|---|

| Peter: | No. |
|---|---|

| | |
|---|---|
| **Colonel Holmes:** | All alone eh? Good. *(He looks down his list)* Here we are ... Strong healthy lad, are you? Lots of muscle? Lots of stamina? |
| **Peter:** | I don't know. |
| **Colonel Holmes:** | Like animals? |
| **Peter:** | I suppose so. |
| **Colonel Holmes:** | Yes ... all boys like animals, don't they? |
| **Peter:** | I had some white mice once. |
| **Colonel Holmes:** | What I had in mind was rather larger than white mice! How would you like to live on a farm, eh? *(He turns away from Peter and calls out)* Saunders ... Jim Saunders ... Is Jim Saunders in the hall? *(Jim Saunders leaves the group of villagers he has been chatting with and hurries over to the Colonel)* |
| **Jim Saunders:** | Here, Colonel Holmes, sir. |
| **Colonel Holmes:** | *(Looking at his list)* You've only got room for one. Is that right? |
| **Jim Saunders:** | Quite right. I've got four of my own already. |
| **Colonel Holmes:** | There you are, Peter. Four brothers and sisters for you. A ready-made family. Jolly, eh? |
| **Peter:** | *(Not too sure about this)* Yes ... |
| **Colonel Holmes:** | *(To Jim)* Don't work him too hard, will you? These town lads, they're not bred like country boys. Treat him gently. |
| **Jim Saunders:** | *(Puzzled)* I'll treat him like one of mine, Colonel. I can't say fairer than that. *(To Peter)* Come on ... Peter, is it? Let's get you home. You must be dog-tired. *(Jim and Peter go off together)* |

**4.** *A bedroom in the Saunders' farmhouse, 3 a.m. A distant church clock strikes three. Peter is sleeping in John Saunders' bed. John sleeps in a camp bed squeezed beside it. Peter wakes from a bad dream and cannot at once remember where he is.*

| | |
|---|---|
| **Peter:** | *(Calling out)* Mum ... |
| **John:** | *(Not at all pleased at being woken)* What? |
| **Peter:** | Mum ...? |
| **John:** | I'm not your mum. |
| **Peter:** | Oh ... sorry. I didn't know where I was for a minute. Sorry. *(John turns over to go back to sleep)* Please ... who are you? |
| **John:** | John. Mum told you when you arrived. I'm John and this is my room. |
| **Peter:** | Oh, yes. |
| **John:** | And that's my bed. |
| **Peter:** | Your bed? But what are you ... |
| **John:** | *(Interrupts him, peeved)* I'm sleeping on a rotten old camp bed. If you can call it sleeping. |
| **Peter:** | I'm sorry, really I am. You have your bed back. I don't mind a camp bed. Honest. |
| **John:** | I don't want your sheets after you've been lying in them. That's not decent. |
| **Peter:** | We could change them round. |
| **John:** | Go to sleep. It's the middle of the night. |
| **Peter:** | In the morning then. I don't want to be ... |
| **John:** | *(Pulling the covers over his head)* Shut up and go to sleep! |
| **Peter:** | Okay. *(He whispers)* Sorry ... |

**5.** *The Saunders' kitchen at breakfast time. Mrs Saunders sits at the table with Bob, Sally and Brenda.*

**Mrs Saunders:** He's got a name.

**Brenda:** Peter Whatsit ...

**Mrs Saunders:** Bateman. You mind your manners.

*(Peter and John come into the kitchen)*

**Mrs Saunders:** Peter ... You sit here ... *(Peter sits where she has pointed. John sits and begins to help himself to toast, etc.)* Cup of tea?

**Peter:** Yes, please.

**Mrs Saunders:** *(Pouring the tea)* Help yourself. There's toast and butter, and home-made marmalade. *(She gives Peter and John cups of tea)* Sally, pass Peter the marmalade.

**Bob:** I haven't finished with it yet.

**Mrs Saunders:** You've had quite enough already.

**John:** It's my turn next.

**Mrs Saunders:** Do as you're told.

**Peter:** It's all right. I don't want any, thanks all the same, Mrs Saunders.

**Sally:** Don't he talk funny!

**Mrs Saunders:** *(Glares at Sally)* Sally!

**Sally:** *(Mutters)* Well, he does.

**Mrs Saunders:** *(Kindly to Peter)* You can call me 'Auntie' if you want. *(The other children giggle)* That'll do! Now, it's Saturday today. No school. You can show Peter over the place. I don't expect he's ever been on a farm before. *(Groans from the children)*

**Peter:** No, I haven't, Mrs Saunders ... Auntie.

**Mrs Saunders:** I didn't think you would have. But come on, eat up. You've hardly started.

| | |
|---|---|
| **Peter:** | I'm not very hungry. |
| **Mrs Saunders:** | You must keep up your strength. |
| **Peter:** | Really ... |
| **Mrs Saunders:** | Oh well, the country air will soon give you an appetite. |
| **Peter:** | Can I get down please? I've got to write a postcard home. I want to catch the post. |
| **Mrs Saunders:** | Yes, you must do that. You must let your mum and dad know where you are. Bob will show you where the post box is. |
| **Bob:** | I've got to feed my rabbits. |
| **Mrs Saunders:** | And Sally's got to go down the shop for me. |
| **Sally:** | It's not my turn. Anyhow, I can't. I've got a puncture. |
| **Mrs Saunders:** | You'll have to borrow Brenda's bike, then. |
| **Brenda:** | Let her mend her puncture ... or walk. She's not having my bike. |
| **Mrs Saunders:** | Don't be so selfish. I've never known such children for always arguing and complaining. John ... |
| **John:** | I'm not going with him. I've had to put up with him all blooming night, keeping me awake. |
| **Peter:** | I'll find the box for myself, Mrs Saunders. Don't worry. |
| **Mrs Saunders:** | I'm not having you get lost your first day. Brenda will show you. (*Brenda starts to protest but Mrs Saunders silences her*) And that'll be the end of it! (*Brenda scowls*) Now, you go and write your postcard, or it'll be too late. (*Peter goes off. The family clear breakfast off*) |

**6.** *By the post box. Brenda shows Peter to the post box.*

| | |
|---|---|
| **Brenda:** | (*Resentfully*) What did you write to your mum and dad, then? |
| **Peter:** | That's my business. |

| | |
|---|---|
| **Brenda:** | (*Tries to take the card from Peter*) Let's see. |
| **Peter:** | Get off! |
| **Brenda:** | That's only a postcard. Postcards aren't private. |
| **Peter:** | (*Drops the card in the box*) Well, you can't see. It's too late now. |
| **Brenda:** | No, it's not. I'll ask my uncle. He'll tell me. He's postman. |
| **Peter:** | They'll give him the sack if he reads other people's letters. |
| **Brenda:** | Who will? |
| **Peter:** | The Post Office. |
| **Brenda:** | How will they know? Anyhow, it's not a letter. It's a postcard. |
| **Peter:** | Same thing. |
| **Brenda:** | It's not. |
| **Peter:** | It is. |
| **Brenda:** | It's not! |
| **Peter:** | (*Who has just about had enough*) Oh, shut up! (*They stand awkwardly for a moment*) |
| **Brenda:** | Do you want to see the farm then? |
| **Peter:** | (*Aggressively*) No! Leave me alone. |
| **Brenda:** | Mum said I had to show you the farm. |
| **Peter:** | (*Near to tears*) Shove off! |
| **Brenda:** | I'm not getting into trouble with Mum on your account. She'd lay into me no end if I was to go and leave you. |
| **Peter:** | I won't tell her .. really. Can't I just have a wander round by myself for a bit? |

| | |
|---|---|
| **Brenda:** | There's no fun in being by yourself. |
| **Peter:** | Please ... |
| **Brenda:** | Suit yourself, then!  But if you tell Mum ... I'll get Bob to push you down the well, head first.  Understand?  *(Peter nods)*  And don't for heaven's sake go and lose your gas mask.  Okay? |
| **Peter:** | I won't. I'm not daft. |
| **Brenda:** | *(On her way)* That's a matter of opinion!<br>*(She goes off.  Peter goes off in the opposite direction.)* |

**7.** *The school playground.  Rick, Goofy and John are planning something.  They stand beside the entrance to the boys' lavatory waiting for Peter.*

| | |
|---|---|
| **Children:** | *(Some distance away, half chanting, half singing)*<br>Whistle while you work,<br>Hitler is a twerp,<br>He's gone barmy, so's his army,<br>Whistle while you work. |
| **Memory:** | I remember we had to take our gas masks everywhere.  *(The children's chanting continues softly, as he reads)*  The gas mask felt like a second face, a mask that would replace my own face as soon as I left London.  It looked inhuman with its celluloid eye shield and metal snout.  I remember that it smelt of rubber and that I could not breathe properly inside it.  The shield misted over with condensation and it felt warm and suffocating inside this second face.  *(The chanting dies away)* |
| **Rick:** | Ready? |
| **John:** | *(Unhappy about what is going on)* What are we going to do? |
| **Rick:** | Goofy? |
| **Goofy:** | Don't call me that. |
| **Rick:** | Did you remember to bring the string? |
| **Goofy:** | Course I did. |
| **John:** | What are we going ... |

| | |
|---|---|
| **Rick:** | *(Sees Peter still some way off)* He's coming! |
| **John:** | But what ... |
| **Rick:** | Nothing! Shh! |
| **John:** | My mum'll kill me if anything happens to him. |
| **Rick:** | Nothing's going to happen to him. |
| **Goofy:** | Well, nothing much. |
| **Rick:** | Quiet.  Act casual. |
| | *(Peter approaches.  Goofy whistles nervously.)* |
| **Rick:** | Hey you, Vacee. |
| **Peter:** | Me? |
| **Rick:** | Where are you going? |
| **Peter:** | Just to the lav. |
| **John:** | Let him go, Rick. |
| **Rick:** | You shut up. |
| **Peter:** | John ... *(Rick and Goofy bar the door)* |
| **John:** | Please Rick ... |
| **Peter:** | Let me get past. |
| **Goofy:** | Say 'Excuse me'. |
| **Peter:** | 'Scuse me. |
| **Rick:** | How about it then?  Shall we excuse him? |
| **Goofy:** | Excuse him for what?  What's he done?  *(Rick and Goofy think this is a tremendous joke)* |
| **Peter:** | I ain't done nothin.  Let me get past. |

| | |
|---|---|
| **Rick:** | I'm not stopping you. |
| **Peter:** | You're standing in the way. |
| **Rick:** | In the way? We've got as much right to stand here as you have. More. It's our school. |
| **Goofy:** | Yeah. |
| **Rick:** | Vacees! Think they own the place! *(Peter tries to push past)* Don't push! Didn't they teach you up in London? It's rude to push. |
| **Peter:** | You keep getting at me. You got no reason. I never done you no harm. I couldn't help being sent here. |
| **John:** | *(Weakly)* That's true, Rick. |
| **Rick:** | We don't have to have a reason. You're a vacee. |
| **Goofy:** | Ugly things, vacees. All soft, like maggots. And white. |
| **Rick:** | Don't get no sun up in London. |
| **Goofy:** | Soft, squashy, white maggots. |
| **Rick:** | Got your gas mask, maggot? |
| **Peter:** | *(His hand closes protectively on the cardboard box holding his gas mask)* Yes ... |
| **Rick:** | Give it here. |
| **John:** | I don't think we should ... *(Goofy grabs Peter's gas mask and gives it to Rick)* |
| **Rick:** | Hold him still. |
| **Goofy:** | Pleasure. *(Goofy holds Peter, who struggles in vain to escape).* |
| **Rick:** | Hands behind his back. *(Goofy gets Peter's hands behind his back. Rick forces the gas mask on him)* John ... you tie him up. |
| **John:** | But Rick ... |

**Rick:** Get on with it!

**Goofy:** The string's in my pocket.
*(John ties Peter's hands ... not very tightly)*

**Rick:** That's better.
*(Rick and Goofy let go of Peter. They look at him.)*

**Peter:** *(His voice muffled from inside his gas mask)* Untie me. Take it off ...

**Rick:** *(Looking at the mask)* A distinct improvement, I'd say.

**Peter:** *(Shouts)* Take it off!

**Goofy:** If he keeps shouting like that, he'll steam it up.

**John:** We're not supposed to play with gas masks.

**Rick:** I'm not playing, I'm doing him a favour. Improving his appearance.

**Goofy:** *(As Peter goes to kick Rick on the shin)* Watch out! *(The kick lands)*

**Rick:** Ow! Kick me, would you, maggot?
*(The bell marking the end of break begins to ring)*
Nobody kicks me and gets away with it.

**Goofy:** They're lining up. Come on!

**John:** We can't leave him.

**Rick:** Why not?

**John:** Not with his hands tied.

**Rick:** Why not?

**Goofy:** Someone might see.

**Rick:** So what?

**Goofy:** I don't want any more trouble.

| | |
|---|---|
| **Rick:** | He won't say it was us, will he?  Not if he knows what's good for him.  Come on ...<br>*(Rick and Goofy begin to go)* |
| **Peter:** | John ... |
| **Rick:** | *(Calls as he disappears off stage)* Come on.  John! |
| **John:** | *(Whispers to Peter)* It's okay.  It's not tied properly.  You can slip out. |
| **Rick:** | *(Calls from off stage)*  John! |
| **John:** | Coming! *(He runs off)*<br>*(Peter struggles against the string as the lights change)* |

**8.** *A crowded train corridor.  Mrs Bateman is perched on a large suitcase beside a young sailor.*

| | |
|---|---|
| **Sailor:** | *(Offers Mrs Bateman a cigarette)* Cigarette? |
| **Mrs Bateman:** | No thank you.  I don't. |
| **Sailor:** | *(Lighting one for himself)*  You don't mind? |
| **Mrs Bateman:** | No.  It's nice of you to let me sit on your case. |
| **Sailor:** | There's not really room to stand.  You going far? |
| **Mrs Bateman:** | Bristol. |
| **Sailor:** | Family down that way? |
| **Mrs Bateman:** | My son.  He was evacuated. |
| **Sailor:** | Going to visit him? |
| **Mrs Bateman:** | I'm  going to fetch him home again. |
| **Sailor:** | To London? |
| **Mrs Bateman:** | They led us right up the garden path saying we should send our kids away.  There's no danger.  It'll all be over by Christmas.  I heard it on the wireless. |

| | |
|---|---|
| **Sailor:** | What does your husband say? |
| **Mrs Bateman:** | He doesn't know. He's joined up and been posted heaven knows where. I'm all on my own now. |
| **Sailor:** | What's his name? Your boy, I mean. |
| **Mrs Bateman:** | Peter. |
| **Sailor:** | Nice name. |
| **Mrs Bateman:** | I had a letter. He hates it down there. |
| **Sailor:** | Give him time to settle in. It takes time. |
| **Mrs Bateman:** | I've made up my mind. I'm fetching him home. |
| **Sailor:** | It won't be over by Christmas ... not by a long way. *(Mrs Bateman shrugs)* Take it from me, it's going to get worse before it gets better ... |
| **Mrs Bateman:** | You don't know. |
| **Sailor:** | If he was mine, I'd leave him where he is, I promise you I would. |
| **Mrs Bateman:** | Well, he's not yours, is he? He's mine, and I want him home with me, where he belongs, and that's all there is to it. *(She moves away from the sailor. The conversation is finished.)* |

**9.** *The Saunders' kitchen. Peter is making paper chains for Christmas. Mrs Bateman comes on with a cup of tea.*

| | |
|---|---|
| **Peter:** | Auntie said we could decorate our room, John and me. |
| **Mrs Bateman:** | You get on all right with John, do you? |
| **Peter:** | He's not bad. |
| **Mrs Bateman:** | Only you said when you wrote ... |
| **Peter:** | John's not so bad. |
| **Mrs Bateman:** | Do they bully you, at school? |

| | |
|---|---|
| **Peter:** | I manage.  Don't fuss, Mum. |
| **Mrs Bateman:** | I don't know what the teachers think they're doing.  They shouldn't allow it. |
| **Peter:** | You're not to go moaning to the school.  *(Pause)* |
| **Mrs Bateman:** | Your room's exactly as you left it. |
| **Peter:** | You'd better take down the models.  I don't want them smashed if there's a hit. |
| **Mrs Bateman:** | Don't even say that. |
| **Peter:** | Put them somewhere safe.  In a box or something. |
| **Mrs Bateman:** | There's not been any raids.  It's as quiet as the grave. |
| **Peter:** | Just in case.  I expect there will be. |
| **Mrs Bateman:** | Do you get homesick? |
| **Peter:** | No.  *(He sees Mum is taken aback)* Well, a bit. |
| **Mrs Bateman:** | *(Opening her handbag)* I bought you some chocolate. |
| **Peter:** | *(Takes the chocolate she offers)* Thanks.  Have you got a shelter yet? |
| **Mrs Bateman:** | Don't need one. |
| **Peter:** | You might.  You will get one, won't you? |
| **Mrs Bateman:** | I suppose so ... Are you frightened, about the bombs?  *(Peter remains silent)* You mustn't be ... You mustn't worry about me.  I'll be all right.  Peter ...?  Look at me.  *(Peter looks up)* Everything's going to be all right ... *(Neither of them is convinced)* ... Now! *(She bustles)* Aren't you going to offer your old mum a piece of that chocolate?  And how about showing me where you're going to hang those paper chains?  *(They move off)* |
| **Memory:** | Even nowadays, whenever I travel anywhere and have to say |

goodbye to my own children, I identify with that boy. I remember the label and the gas mask and feel anxiety gripping my bowels. I write my name on the luggage labels and hope I do not return to find my home bombed to ruins and my identity lost somewhere underneath the rubble.

## REFLECTION

*Successful drama depends on a lot of factors, but there are a few obvious things you need to get right.*

*A. A GOOD PLOT. This will usually have a dramatic issue, some conflict between characters leading to a climax. Conflict can be expressed in actions and words or just as internal tension which the characters let the audience feel.*
*- Discuss this in relation to any of the dramas you have performed.*

*B. INTERESTING CHARACTERS. These need to be fairly realistic, if it is that kind of drama. If they are too simple they will not be convincing.*
*- Discuss this in relation to the dramas you have performed.*

*C..GOOD DIALOGUE attracts your attention and holds it. It needs to suit the character speaking. If you can think up some memorable lines or phrases, all the better. Humorous dialogue is very difficult to write.*
*All dialogue must have a purpose - tell us something about the speaker or plot, create atmosphere, add to the suspense etc. So cut unnecessary dialogue.*

*D. ACTORS AND ACTRESSES, or at least people willing to get into the world of make-believe and take the audience with them, are obviously important.*

*FOLLOW-UP EXERCISES.*
*(i) Write a short script of an evening scene with your family at home, or any scene you like.*
*(ii) Prepare a 3-minute speech, to be delivered in front of the class, on some aspect of 'The needs of young people in today's society'.*
*(iii) Compose a 'newspaper report' on some issue of interest in your locality.*
*(iv) Working in small groups plan and perform an improvised scene on some issue of your choice such as: a dare; bullying; petty jealousy in school; after a nuclear war; castaways on a desert island; meeting a Yeti etc. Don't forget that you can situate your drama outside school altogether, in railway stations, prisons, haunted houses, supermarkets, imaginary villages or towns, maternity hospitals, old people's home, Roman villas or Celtic forts, American pioneer settlements or future space stations.*
*(v) Write a report or a poem about your drama class. Hopefully it will have worked as well as this one!*

**Drama Lesson**

'Let's see some super shapes you Blue Group,'
Mr Lavender shouts down the hall.
'And forests don't forget your trembly leaves
And stand up straight and tall.'

But Phillip Chubb is in our group
And he wants to be Robin Hood
And Ann Boot is sulking because she's not with
her friend
And I don't see why I should be wood.

The lights are switched on in the classrooms,
Outside the sky's nearly black,
And the dining-hall smells of gravy and fat
And Chubb has boils down his back.

Sir tells him straight that he's got to be a tree
But he won't wave his arms around.
'How can I wave my branches, Sir,
Friar Tuck has chopped them all down.'

Then I come cantering through Sherwood
To set Maid Marion free
And I really believe I'm Robin Hood
And the Sheriff's my enemy.

At my back my trusty longbow
My broadsword clanks at my side,
My outlaws gallop behind me
As into adventure we ride.

'Untie that maid you villain,' I shout
With all the strength I have,
But the tree has got bored and is picking his nose
And Maid Marion has gone to the lav.

After rehearsals, Sir calls us together
And each group performs their play,
But just as it comes to our turn
The bell goes for the end of the day.

As I trudge my way home through the city streets
The cars and the houses retreat
And a thunder of hooves beats in my mind
And I gallop through acres of wheat.

The castle gleams white in the distance,
The banners flap, golden and red,
And distant trumpets weave silver dreams
In the landscape of my head.

*Gareth Owen.*

# INDEX

# ACKNOWLEDGMENTS

**For permission to reproduce copyright material grateful acknowledgment is made to the following:**

Peters, Fraser and Dunlop Group Ltd for 'Sarah Byng' from Cautionary Tales by Hilaire Belloc;
David Higham & Associates Ltd for 'The Hunchback in the Park' from Under Milk Wood by Dylan Thomas;
George Sassoon for 'The Rear Guard' by Siegfried Sassoon;
Faber and Faber Ltd for an extract from The Iron Man by Ted Hughes;
Ian Serraillier for his poems 'The Diver' from Happily Ever After and 'The Icefall' from Everest Climbed;
Rogers Coleridge & White for 'The Polar Bear' by Edward Lucie-Smith;
Gregory Harrison for his poem 'Distracted, the Mother said to her Boy' from A Fourth Poetry Book;
John Foster for his poem 'War Games' from A Fourth Poetry Book and 'There are four chairs around the table' from A Fifth Poetry Book;
Oxford University Press for an extract from The Trouble with Donovan Croft by Bernard Ashley;
O'Brien Press for extracts from Stories of the Seanchaí by Seán O'Sullivan and Your Dinner's Poured Out by Paddy Crosbie (including the table of contents and index) and for 'The Illusionists' from The Diviner by Brian Friel;
Macmillan for 'Two Children' by Fay Goldie from story 2 (ed. John L. Foster) and for Evacuees by Marianne Cook from the series Upheavals - Drama Workshop Plays published by arrangement with B.B.C. Radio;
Peters, Fraser & Dunlop for 'First Haiku of Spring' by Roger McGough from The Kingfisher Book of Comic Verse;
Severn House Publishers Ltd for 'Oh I wish I'd looked after me teeth' and 'The Slimming Poem' by Pam Ayres;
George Houston Bass for 'I Too' by Langston Hughes;
Collins Publishers for 'Empty House', 'Dear Examiner' and 'Drama Lesson' from Salford Road and Other Poems by Gareth Owen;
Doubleday & Co. Inc. for 'The Tomcat' from Poetry of Marquis by Don Marquis;
Faber and Faber Limited for an extract from Paper - How it is Made by Lesley Perrins; for 'Leaves', 'The Warrior of Winter' and 'Work and Play' from Season Songs by Ted Hughes; for 'Boy at the Window' from Poems 1943 - 1956 by Richard Wibur; for 'The Early Purges' from Death of a Naturalist and 'The Railway Children' from Station Island by Seamus Heaney;
Harper and Row Ltd for 'Mushrooms' from The Colossus by Sylvia Plath and 'Travelling Through The Dark' from Travelling Through The Dark by William Stafford;
Mercier Press for 'Autumn's End' by John B. Keane;
Brenden Kennelly for his poem 'The Sea';
Mrs A. M. Walsh for 'The New Boy' by John Walsh from Poets in Hand (Puffin Books);

The James Reeve Estate and Laura Cecil for 'Spells', 'The Wind' 'Slowly' and 'The Sea' from The Wandering Moon and Other Poems by James Reeves;
William Henemann Ltd for 'Midnight' by Baljit Kang, first published in Young Writers;
Brandon Book Publishers for an extract and the poem 'A Memory' from To School through the Fields by Alice Taylor;
Hutchinson Ltd for an extract from The Brendan Voyage by Tim Severin;
Methuen & Co. Ltd for an extract from The Secret Diary of Adrian Mole by Sue Townsend; for 'The Cobra' and 'The Cow' from Free Wheeling and 'The Pig' and 'Song of the Open Road' from Happy Days by Ogden Nash and for 'Hymn of the Scientific Farmers' by Clive Sansom;
Andre Deutsch Ltd for 'Dear Maureen' from Wouldn't You Like to Know by Michael Rosen;
Doubleday & Co. Inc., for 'The Fun They Had' by Isaac Asimov from Earth is Room Enough;
Gallery Press for 'The Illusionists' from Selected Stories by Brian Friel;
The author; for the following poems from Nine O'Clock Bell chosen by Raymond Wilson (Penguin): 'School' by Jane, Paul and Christine; 'Oh bring back higher standards' by Peter Dixon; 'Timothy Winters' by Charles Causley; 'School with Holidays' by Stanley Cook;
A. P. Watt for 'The Confessional' by Sean O'Faolain from A Purse of Coppers;
James Simmons for his poem 'Kill the Children';
Attic Press for the extract on Grace O'Malley from More Missing Pieces - The story of Irish Women;
Penguin Books Ltd for 'The Sniper' by Liam O'Flaherty and 'Birth of the Foal' by Ferenc Juhasz (translated by David Wevill);
Peter Fallon for 'Beech Tree' from Ploughman and Other Poems and 'The Tinker's Wife' by Patrick Kavanagh;
Aiden C. Matthews for his play The Break;
RTE and John Quinn for 'A Lethal Striker' by Maeve Binchy (extract from RTE interview) from A Portrait of the Artist as a Young Girl edited by John Quinn;
Berlie Doherty for her play Matthew Come Home;
Books and Toys Ltd for word puzzles from The Giant Book: Wordsearch Compendium;
Bord Failte for extracts from Westmeath County Guide;
Oxford University Press for page 563 of the Oxford Senior Dictionary and an entry from the Oxford Dictionary of Current English;
Jonathan Cape Ltd for 'Out Out' from The Poetry of Robert Frost edited by Edward Connery Lathem and for 'Poem about an apostrophe' from In the Glassroom by Roger McGough;
Murray Pollinger for an extract from Boy by Roald Dahl (Jonathan Cape/Penguin Books);
Souvenir Press Ltd for an extract from Nan: The Life of an Irish Travelling Woman by Sharon Gmelch;
George Weidenfeld and Nicholson Ltd for an extract from

Under the Eye of the Clock  by Christopher Nolan;
Hamish Hamilton for 'The Poppycrunch Kid' from Letters of Fire by Adele Geras;
Dobson Books Ltd for 'The Walrus' by Michael Flanders from All Creatures Great and Small  ;
John Montague for 'Time Out' from his Selected Poems and A Chosen Light  ;
Elaine Stapleton for her story Somewhere through the TV screen (first prize in Irish Schools Creative Writing Competition sponsored by Prudential Insurance);
Wolfhound Press for 'A Crow Fligh' by Liam O'Flaherty from The Pedlar's Revenge and other Stories  ;
W.H.Smith for crossword puzzles from Investigating English through Newspapers and Magazines  by Dor Shiach;
A. & C. Black fo 'The Cremation of Sam Magee' from The Songs of Sourdough  by Robert Service;
Macmillan Co. of Australia for 'Send three and fourpence, we are going to a dance' by Jan Mark and for an extract 'Words' from Media Workshop  by Richard McRoberts;
Penguin books Ltd for 'At the River Gates' by Philippa Pearce from The Shadow Cage and Other Tales of the Supernatural;
John Rice for his poem 'A Chemistry Student from Gillingham';
Wes Magee for his poem 'Christmas Haiku';
Eric Finney for his poems 'Sarky Devil' and 'Poem about writing a Poem';
Longman for 'The Mile' from The Fib and other Stories  by George Layton;
Prunella Power for her poem 'First Day at Boarding School';
The Society of Authors for an extract from A Portrait of the Artist as a Young Man by James Joyce;
Grafton Books for eight limericks from The Lure of the Limerick by W.S. Baring-Gould;
Faber and Faber Ltd. for 'Preludes' from Collected Poems 1909-1962 by T.S. Elliot.
News Group Newspapers for material from The 4th Penguin Book of Sun Crosswords  ;
Verney Naylor for the article Gardening: Feathered Visitors  first featured in the Irish Times ;
Wayland Publishers for an extract from Shakespeare by Christopher Martin;
Blond Education for 'I had a Hippopotamus' by Patrick Barrington.

**The publishers have made every effort to trace copyright holders but if they have inadvertently overlooked any, they will be pleased to make the necessary arrangements at the first opportunity.**

For permission to reproduce photographs grateful acknowledgment is made to the following:
The Irish Cancer Society for the following photographs from One Day for Life in Ireland  (Tranworld Publishers, 1988):
'Forgotton Reality of Dublin' (Mark Galbraith) p.37, (top)
'Shoulder of Lamb' (Joseph Murphy, age 13) p.37,
'Always "Paws" before Crossing' (John O'Reilly/Phyllis O'Shea) p.39,
'A Character' (Peter McGorman) p.42,
'A Child at Peace' (Catherine Brady) p.69 (top),
'Early Start'  (Jonathan Redmond, age 14) p.71,
'Travelling Family' (Dermot Dolan) p.216,
'Casual Trading Area' (Paddy Prior) P.319, (right),
'In the Money' (Tom Connolly) p.320,
'Pups for Sale' (David Dillon) p.322, (top),
'Time for A Chinwag' (Pat McKenna) p.322, (bottom),
'Nearly Time to Part' (Michael Johnson) p.323,
'Waiting for Buyers' (Patsy Conway) p.325,
'Heading for the Hills' (Jess Walsh) p.327, (top);
Tom Lawlor for:
'Fireworks Display' p.72,Maureen Potter p.318,'Girl with Lipstick' p.321, 'Blackrock Park' p.324, 'Monks on the Green' p.327, (bottom),
St. Kilian's Community School, Bray, p.6;
Liam Burke for 'The Burren' p.38;
RTE for stills from the sets of 'Fair City' and 'Glenroe' p.49 and p.51 and studio shot p.171;
Michael Scott for the still from Torchlight and Laser Beams  , based on the writings of Christopher Nolan adapted for the stage by Christopher Nolan and Michael Scott, directed by Michael Scott, photo: Amelia Stein, Original Dublin Theatre Festival Production with Conor Mullen as Joseph Meehan, Eve Watkinson as The Lamp Woman and Geraldine Plunkett as Nora Meehan, p.53;
Klaus Roedler for 'Dog with Bandage' p.68;
Veikko Wallstrom for 'Girl with Haircut' p.69, (bottom);
Slide File / Liam Blake for 'Hubbard Bridge' p.70;
National Gallery of Ireland p.79;
The Cork Examiner for the following photographs from Picture that Again  (ed. Stephen Coughlan 1986):
'Trawler on the Rocks' p.83;
'War Years Scene' p.326;
'Ascent' p.328;
Photo Nathan Benn/Brendan Archive p.88;
Bord Failte P.91, p.212, p.213;
Zefa p.129;
Aidan Dowling for 'Park Scene' p.135;
Irish Press, Irish Independent, Cork Examiner, The Star, Irish Times, p.141;
Irish Time for photos on p.154 and p.155;
John Frost p.166;
Club Orange/Hunter Advertising p.177 and p.179;
Clarks Shoes/The Media Bureau p.184;
Medised /Greenhill Parry Advertising p.185;
Raleigh/Irish International Advertising & Marketing p.186;
Bord Gais p.187;
Agfa Gevaert/Bell Advertising p.188;
Iarnrod Eireann p.199;
Martin Langer for 'Dog Repairs Car' p.204;
A. Bradlow /Reflex p.221;
Slide file p.233;
British Library (Woodcuts)p.242;

Syndication International p.247;
AKG Berlin p.248;
Bruce Coleman/F. Greenway p.273;
Sally and Richard Greenhill p.283;
Reflex Picture Agency p.286;
Rainer Grosskopf for 'The Sad Clown' p.319 (left).

For permission to reproduce covers of books, grateful
acknowledgment is made to the following:
Penguin Books for the following, all published under the
Puffin imprint:
  The Diddakoi by Rumer Godden,
  The T.V. Kid by Betsy Byars,
  The Silver Sword  by Ian Serraillier,
  The Machine Gunners by Robert Westall
  (and on extract from the inside cover introduction)
   Freaky Friday by Mary Rodgers,
  The Midnight Fox by Betsy Byars,
  Under Goliath by Peter Carter,
  Boy by Roald Dahl,
  I like this Story chosen by Kaye Webb,
  Going Solo by Road Dahl,
  Biddy by Nigel Hinton,
  The Earthsea Trilogy by Ursula Le Guin,
  (and an extract from chapter 1 of 'A Wizard of Sea Earth'),
  Over Sea, Under Stone by Susan Cooper,
  and Roald Dahl by Chris Pawling.
Collins for:
The Lion the Witch and the Wardrobe by C. S. Lewis
(Lions), Journey to Jo'Burg by Beverley Naidoo (Young
Lions);
Wolfhound Press for:
Bob Geldof by Charlotte Gray and
Run with the Wind by Tom McGaughren;
Mandarin Books for:
Why the Whales Came by Micahel Morpurgo;
Methuen Childrens Books for:
The Haunting by Margaret Mahy;
Poolbeg Press for:
Spike and the Professor by Tony Hickey (Cover design by
Robert Ballagh);
Macmillan for:
The Great Gilly Hopkins by Katherine Peterson
(and an extract from the back cover blurb of the M books
edition);
The Children's Press for:
Silas Rat by Dermot O'Donovan;
O'Brien Press for:
Bike Hunt by Hugh Galt
(and an extract from the inside cover blurb);
Unwin Hyman for:
The Hobbit by J.R.R. Tolkien
(and an extract from the introduction).